Emotions in the Field

Emotions in the Field

The Psychology and Anthropology
of Fieldwork Experience

Edited by James Davies and Dimitrina Spencer

Stanford University Press
Stanford, California

Stanford University Press
Stanford, California

Printed in the United States of America on acid-free, archival-quality paper

Library of Congress Cataloging-in-Publication Data

Emotions in the field : the psychology and anthropology of fieldwork experience / edited by James Davies and Dimitrina Spencer.
     p. cm.
  Includes bibliographical references and index.
   ISBN 978-0-8047-6939-6 (cloth : alk. paper) -- ISBN 978-0-8047-6940-2 (pbk. : alk. paper)
  1. Ethnology--Fieldwork--Psychological aspects. 2. Emotions--Anthropological aspects.
I. Davies, James (James Peter) II. Spencer, Dimitrina. GN346.E46 2010
  305.8'00723--dc22
                                        2009046034

Typeset by Bruce Lundquist in 10/14 Minion

Contents

Acknowledgments   vii

Contributors   ix

Introduction: Emotions in the Field   1
James Davies

Part I   Psychology of Field Experience

1   From Anxiety to Method in Anthropological Fieldwork:
    An Appraisal of George Devereux's Enduring Ideas   35
    Michael Jackson

2   "At the Heart of the Discipline":
    Critical Reflections on Fieldwork   55
    Vincent Crapanzano

3   Disorientation, Dissonance, and Altered Perception
    in the Field   79
    James Davies

4   Using Emotion as a Form of Knowledge
    in a Psychiatric Fieldwork Setting   98
    Francine Lorimer

Part II   Political Emotions in the Field

5   Hating Israel in the Field:
On Ethnography and Political Emotions   129
Ghassan Hage

6   Tian'anmen in Yunnan:
Emotions in the Field during a Political Crisis   155
Elisabeth Hsu

7   Emotional Engagements:
Acknowledgement, Advocacy, and Direct Action   171
Lindsay Smith and Arthur Kleinman

Part III   Non-cognitive Field Experiences

8   Emotional Topographies:
The Sense of Place in the Far North   191
Kirsten Hastrup

9   What Counts as Data?   212
Tanya Luhrmann

10   Ascetic Practice and Participant Observation, or,
the Gift of Doubt in Field Experience   239
Joanna Cook

Index   267

Acknowledgments

TO REALIZE THE COMPLETION OF THIS VOLUME, we relied upon the generous support of so many individuals. To all of you we owe enormous gratitude. We thank, firstly, Professor David Parkin, whose kindness, diplomacy, and intellectual acumen were a constant resource. Other important people include Professor Marcus Banks, Professor David Gellner, Professor Del Loewenthal, Professor Roland Littlewood, and Dr. Louise Braddock. We thank all those involved in the early meetings at Oxford University and the seminars held at Harvard University. A special thanks to Michael Jackson for bringing some excellent scholars on board, and for his tireless intellectual guidance and advice. We thank Nick James from the Society of Indexers for his good work on the index. We are also grateful to Peter Agree and Jennifer Hammer for their suggestions and guidance. And finally we thank Jennifer Helé, who was instrumental in helping the project along during the first stages of review and editorial work.

We also thank the British Academy, the Institute for Social and Cultural Anthropology (University of Oxford), the Centre for Therapeutic Education (Roehampton University), and the Oxford Anthropology Society for their financial support and institutional backing.

Contributors

Joanna Cook is George Kingsley Roth Research Fellow in Southeast Asian Studies at Christ's College, University of Cambridge. Her Ph.D. research explored *vipassanā* meditation in Thailand as a monastic practice. Her current research focuses on the use of Buddhist meditation techniques in medical and healthcare practices in Thailand. Her forthcoming monograph is titled *Meditation in Modern Buddhism: Renunciation and Change in Thai Monastic Life.*

Vincent Crapanzano is Distinguished Professor of Comparative Literature and Anthropology at the Graduate Centre of the City University of New York. His publications include *The Hamadsha: A Study in Ethnopsychiatry* (1981), *Tuhami: A Portrait of a Moroccan* (1985), *Waiting: The Whites of South Africa* (1986), *Hermes' Dilemma and Hamlet's Desire: On the Epistemology of Interpretation* (1992), and *Imaginative Horizons: An Essay in Literary Philosophical Anthropology* (2003). At present, he is finishing a book on the Hakris.

James Davies, coeditor of this volume, is a member of St. Cross College at the University of Oxford, where he obtained his doctorate in social anthropology. He is also a qualified and practicing psychotherapist working in the NHS at Oxford and a senior lecturer in anthropology and psychotherapy in the School of Human and Life Sciences at Roehampton University, London. He has undertaken fieldwork in Nepal, where he studied Tibetan monastic communities. He is the author of *The Making of Psychotherapists: An Anthropological Analysis* (2009).

Ghassan Hage is a Fellow of the Australian Humanities Association and the University of Melbourne's Future Generation Professor of Anthropology and

Social Theory. He joined the University of Melbourne in 2008 after fifteen years of teaching and researching at the University of Sydney. As a Future Generation Professor, he works at fostering interdisciplinary research across the university. He has researched and published widely in the comparative anthropology of nationalism, multiculturalism, racism, and migration. For many years, and until Bourdieu's death, he was an associate researcher in the latter's research center at the Ecole des Hautes Etudes en Sciences Sociales.

Kirsten Hastrup is Professor of Anthropology at the University of Copenhagen. She has conducted both historical research and long-term fieldwork in Iceland and, more recently, in Greenland. She has published extensively from both fields and on more general methodological and epistemological issues in anthropology.

Elisabeth Hsu is a Reader in Social Anthropology at the Institute of Social and Cultural Anthropology, University of Oxford, and a Fellow of Green Templeton College. She has studied and worked in China since 1978. Her research interests lie within the fields of medical anthropology and ethnobotany, language and historical textual studies. Among her research concerns are Chinese medicine, body and personhood, pulse diagnosis, touch, pain, feelings, emotions, and sensory experience. Her current field research is on Chinese medicine in East Africa.

Michael Jackson is Distinguished Visiting Professor of World Religions at Harvard Divinity School. He has done extensive ethnographic fieldwork in Sierra Leone and Aboriginal Australia, and is the author of numerous books of anthropology, including the prizewinning *Paths toward a Clearing: Radical Empiricism and Ethnographic Inquiry* (1989) and *At Home in the World* (2000). He has also published three novels and six books of poetry (*Latitudes of Exile: Poems 1965–1975* [1976] was awarded the Commonwealth Poetry Prize, and *Wall* [1981] won the New Zealand Book Award for Poetry). His most recent books include *The Palm at the End of the Mind: Relatedness, Religiosity, and the Real* (2009) and the forthcoming *Life within Limits: Wellbeing in a World of Want*.

Arthur Kleinman is Esther and Sidney Rabb Professor of Anthropology at Harvard University, Professor of Medical Anthropology and Professor of Psychiatry at Harvard Medical School, as well as Victor and William Fung Director of Harvard University's Asia Center. He is both a psychiatrist and an anthropologist and has conducted research in Chinese society since 1968. Kleinman is the author of 6 books, editor or coeditor of 28 volumes and special issues of journals, and the author of more than 200 research and review articles and chapters. His chief publications include *Patients and Healers in the Context of Culture* (1981), *The Illness Narratives: Suffering, Healing, and the Human Condition* (1989), *Rethinking Psychiatry: From Cultural Category to Personal Experience* (1970), and *What Really Matters: Living a Moral Life amidst Uncertainty and Danger* (2007).

Francine Lorimer has done anthropological fieldwork among the Warlpiri of Central Australia and the Kuku-Yalanji of Southeast Cape York, as well as in a psychiatric hospital in Copenhagen, Denmark. She has taught anthropology at the University of Copenhagen and at Harvard University. Her interests lie in exploring how anthropology, psychiatry, and psychology can be combined to deepen their different perspectives. She is currently completing training as an analytical psychologist at the C.G. Jung Institute–Boston and as a clinical psychologist at the Massachusetts School of Professional Psychology.

Tanya Luhrmann is Professor of Anthropology at Stanford University. She trained at the University of Cambridge (Ph.D., 1986) and taught for many years at the University of California, San Diego. Prior to moving to Stanford, she was Max Palevsky Professor and a Director of the Clinical Ethnography Project at the University of Chicago. She has published three books: *Persuasions of the Witch's Craft: Ritual Magic in Contemporary England* (1989), *The Good Parsi: The Fate of a Colonial Elite in a Postcolonial Society* (1996), and *Of Two Minds: An Anthropologist Looks at American Psychiatry* (2000).

Lindsay A. Smith is a Postdoctoral Fellow in the Program on Science in Human Culture at Northwestern University. Her research focuses on the political and cultural impact of new forensic technologies in post-conflict settings. She is currently working on a book to be titled *Subversive Genes,* which explores the co-production of forensic DNA and transitional justice in contemporary Argentina.

Dimitrina Spencer, coeditor of this volume, obtained her doctorate at the Institute for Social and Cultural Anthropology and Linacre College, University of Oxford. She works at the Department of Education, University of Oxford, teaching anthropology and conducting research on young people and technology in the United Kingdom. She has conducted fieldwork in Bulgaria, Greece, Turkey, Nigeria, Macedonia, and the United Kingdom on religion, migration and social networks, well-being, European Islam, and postsocialist transition. In addition, she has been working as a relational psychotherapist in training since 2006.

Introduction

Emotions in the Field*

James Davies

THE AIM OF THIS BOOK is to help retrieve emotion from the methodological margins of fieldwork. Our task is to investigate how certain emotions evoked during fieldwork can be used to inform how we understand the situations, people, communities, and interactions comprising the lifeworlds we enter. By emphasising the relevance of emotion in anthropological research, we take up a theme that the "reflexive turn" of 1980s and early 1990s anthropology considerably overlooked. While this school explored how the ethnographer's position in the field influences the data he or she acquires (and the varying ways our identity, gender, ethnicity, and personal history affect how we understand, interact with, and write about our field sites), it left comparatively under-investigated the researcher's *states of being* during fieldwork and how these states may either enable or inhibit the understanding that fieldwork aims to generate. This relative neglect has naturally left many pages unwritten in our methodological canon. And so it is the aim of this volume to give voice to the growing chorus of researchers (within these pages and beyond) who are working to redress the imbalance. Our objective is to show how certain emotions, reactions, and experiences that are consistently evoked in fieldworkers, when treated with the same intellectual vigour as our empirical work demands, can more assist than impede our understanding of the lifeworlds in which we set ourselves down. Counting these subjective phenomena as data to be translated through careful reflection

* I would like to thank Michael Jackson for his careful reading of this introduction and his advice. I must also thank Vincent Crapanzano, Elisabeth Hsu, Arthur Kleinman, David Parkin, Karem Roitman, and Dimitrina Spencer for their additional help and support.

into anthropological insight is the central and unifying aim of this volume, the contributors to which, by building upon existing work on intersubjective and experiential fieldwork, explore new ways to achieve these translations.

Two Beliefs We Contest

To situate this volume amidst existing research, let me first survey historically how researchers' emotions have been understood in social science methodology. To preface this task, I will start by identifying two beliefs that have significantly influenced the history of modern field methods—beliefs that we contest insofar as they reject the idea that emotion can have epistemological worth. The first and most recent stems from a school of postmodernism advanced in the 1970–80s. Its intention was to demonstrate the inherently imperialistic and oppressive nature of fieldwork. It held that by submitting "others" to the anthropological gaze, ethnographers often replicated in mitigated form the exploitative dynamics of the colonial era. This critique presupposed that researchers were riddled with many barely perceptible self-interests and/or assumptions which distorted and biased their observations, leading them to construct more than to reveal their object in ways that rendered their object oppressed. As objectivity was therefore seen as an illusion, any claim researchers made to assured knowing was naïve or, at worst, politically self-serving. While many important insights emerged from this critique, and at times many sobering and useful lessons, one central argument that it implied is inevitably contested by the chapters of this volume: that subjectivity undermines the process of knowledge construction and never enables it—this is to say, *subjectivity has only a corrosive effect upon the process of research.*

The second idea that we dispute stems from what we call "traditional empiricism." This tradition drew firm lines between the researching subject and the researched object, and also defined across the social sciences what attributes of the researcher could usefully contribute to the activity of knowledge construction—namely, rationality and the capacity for detachment.[1] This approach meant that anything believed to undermine those attributes, such as encroaching feelings or affects, had to be methodologically removed or subdued. The marginalisation of emotion was consistent with the belief that subjectivity in both quantitative and qualitative research is something to be controlled and restrained, as it invariably introduces irregularities that cloud and bias research. For traditional empiricism the idea that emotion could actually be used to generate understanding was therefore simply a non-starter. Indeed, much sociocultural research influenced by this tradition, and keen to avoid its unsparing censure, not only under-investigated our emotions in the field but at times actively under-reported or concealed them—the irony being that the neglect of these data offended empiricism more deeply. True empiricism does not ignore the facts but is obliged to accept them, embrace them, and advance theoretical formulations upon them.

Both "postmodern" and "traditional empirical" beliefs, no matter how divergent the traditions from which they spring, share common ground on one critical point—they agree that the personal equation, wherever it may arise, is the *saboteur par excellence* of all generalising aspirations. While postmodernism by viewing subjectivity as belligerently omnipresent developed this into a radical repudiation of all universalising aims, traditional empiricism, taking the opposite route, developed ever more stringent methodological controls to create spaces in which so-called pure investigation could proceed, free from subjective distortion. The response of each made unavoidable for both one restrictive but all-pervasive corollary: subjectivity itself offers no royal road to insight, discernment, or any species of knowing.

It is clear, then, that any project placing emotion onto an epistemologically relevant plane implies a critique of both streams of thought: firstly, by showing how the concealed and neglected aspects of the researcher's emotional experience can actually present opportunities for understanding; and secondly, by developing a new and re-humanised methodological framework which exposes the weaknesses of the old. Why we in this volume and many colleagues outside it have arrived at such a position demands some deeper historical elaboration. This I shall now advance with respect to the social sciences more broadly and to anthropology in particular. After offering this historical account, I shall then describe the exact contribution that each chapter makes before finally outlining the precise methodological position that this volume advocates: one that we call, after William James, *radical empiricism*—namely, a position that refuses the epistemological cut between subject and object, that endows transitive and intransitive experiences with equal status, and that investigates phenomena which the inductive methods of traditional empiricism were never designed to treat.

A History of Emotions in the Field

The basic rule of method in the early natural sciences was that scientists should remain detached from their object of enquiry, and through systematic observation of available data seek hidden uniformities which could be translated into quantitative terms. The physicist, chemist, and biologist all followed a similar procedure, each observing the facts of his respective domain with varying degrees of control over the context of investigation. Methods were developed to remove distortions caused by either the research environment or the researcher (Bruyn 1966:27). Such methods, especially with respect to the researcher, were considered to restrain those incursions of subjectivity whose unbridled expression was thought to otherwise corrupt research.

When in the early twentieth century this particular approach was applied to the study of social and human life, certain problems arose in method and theory. For one, the dichotomies upon which traditional empiricism rested (i.e., observer/observed, subjectivity/objectivity, subject/object), if supporting certain quantitative methods in early sociology, anthropology, and experimental psychology, seemed only to impede research into those areas of life that resisted being quantified. It was therefore argued that since so many human phenomena could not be explored quantitatively, if we restricted our investigations to only those facts which could be measured and counted, we would be forced to omit so much from our studies of social and human life that our sciences would become somewhat sterile (Storr 1960).

As the limits of quantification and objectification were more widely acknowledged in social science research, and as scepticism spread about whether detachment could reach what is most essentially human in society, these particular methods were less indiscriminately applied in other social science domains. This development brought the advance of alternative methods that had their foundations in the phenomenological and interpretivist thinking of the late nineteenth and early twentieth centuries. Philosophers such as Gottfried Herder, Martin Heidegger, and Wilhelm Dilthey invoked the ideas of *Einfühlung* (feeling into the world), *Gestimmtheit* (attuning to the world), and *tonalité* (adjusting to the pitch of the world), respectively, giving legitimacy to the participatory methods of which Frederic LePlay's *Les Ouvriers Européens* (1855) provides an early example. These thinkers urged that participation and detachment were methodological postures that could each reach distinct species of fact, and that therefore *both* belonged in social research. The same view was also implied in Max Weber's insistence that the observer and the observed were after all constituted of the same human essence, an idea grounding the concept of *Verstehen*, or knowing through empathic attunement.

In these ideas many early anthropologists found encouragement. For although fieldwork had been undertaken in anthropology since the late 1890s

(Franz Boas led his North Pacific expedition in 1897, and A. C. Haddon, W. H. R. Rivers, and C. G. Seligman led the Cambridge expedition to the Torres Straits in 1898), there was still a reluctance to accept participant observation as a distinct method until the early 1920s. It was Bronislaw Malinowski at that time who proclaimed a philosophy of fieldwork in his *Argonauts of the Western Pacific*. He distinguished between "native statements" and the "inferences" research-ers drew from insights gathered through participation. The fieldworker would document data with "camera, note book and pencil" after "joining in himself in what is going on" (Malinowski 1960 [1922]:21). Being "in touch" with the natives, Malinowski was certain, clearly marked the "preliminary condition of being able to carry on successful fieldwork" (1960:8).

If at this point participation gained legitimacy in anthropology, it was less accepted that participation could evoke in fieldworkers powerful subjective re-actions and emotions which implicated the method itself. Methods were still seen to have more to do with minds than with emotions or feelings or with what Plato called *thymos* (the heart). And to the extent that this belief was ac-cepted, reflection was inhibited upon whether the personal consequences of participation could be of any scientific value. Consider, for example, the advice received by Edward Evans-Pritchard when studying at the London School of Economics in the 1920s. Seeking guidance from experienced fieldworkers about what to expect, both emotionally and practically, during his fieldwork in Cen-tral Africa, he recounts humorously the advice he received:

> I first sought advice from Westermarck. All I got from him was "don't converse with an informant for more than twenty minutes because if you are not bored by that time he will be." Very good advice, even if somewhat inadequate. I sought instruction from Haddon, a man fore-most in field-research. He told me that it was really all quite simple; one should always behave as a gentleman. Also very good advice. My teacher Seligman told me to take "ten grains of quinine every night and to keep off women." The famous Egyptologist, Sir Flinders Petrie just told me not to bother about drinking dirty water as one soon became immune to it. Finally I asked Malinowski and was told just to remember not to be a bloody fool. (Evans-Pritchard 1973:1)

While Evans-Pritchard no doubt enjoyed raising smiles with this quote, there was also a more serious point to be made. At the time of his apprenticeship little was being said about the experiential consequences of participatory re-search. If participation was accepted, its personal effects for the researcher (and ultimately the work) were not. This particular predilection for emotion to be borne but never broached remained widespread throughout the first half of the twentieth century, for during this period anthropology was fully aware that the "personal equation" tested its scientific place in the academy. As Dumont has told us, the founders of modern anthropology such as Franz Boas, Alfred Kroeber, Alfred R. Radcliffe-Brown, and Evans-Pritchard were highly conscientious about how they represented themselves as researchers— for "it was the status of anthropology as science which was at stake with them" (Dumont 1978:7). Anthropology was not alone with these concerns, as the misgivings of psychoanalysis and analytical history at that time indicate. Psychoanalysis, for instance, revealed its anxiety by regarding as inadmissible the powerful subjective reactions evoked in analysts by the analytical relationship. Thus the analyst's "countertransference" (i.e., his or her emotional reaction to the patient) was until the 1950s largely perceived as a nuisance or as something to be eliminated. Freud would not acknowledge a subjective influence that he felt would render his aspiring science unscientific in the eyes of his peers. Analytical history, too, had its earnest denials—grand historical works by Arnold Toynbee, Oswald Spengler, and earlier by Karl Marx all relied on the belief that exact historical method sufficiently removed the personal equation, and thus if one proceeded correctly, further reflexivity was not required. This belief was compounded by the myth endemic to the socio/human sciences of the day: that conceding subjectivity was conceding status, and possibly privilege and position.

The late publication of Malinowski's fieldwork diary symbolised this disquiet within anthropology, for although it was written in the 1920s, it did not finally emerge until the safer ground of the 1960s. The diary contained all the emotions and experiences which Malinowski excluded from his formal methodological writings. Indeed, it was not until the 1950s that the experiences and emotions that participant observation evoked were reported at all. And yet even when such reports did emerge, as with Malinowski's diary, they were still safely shorn from mainstream anthropology and relegated to personalised fieldwork accounts. For example, in 1954 Laura Bohannan published her novel/account of fieldwork *Return to Laughter*, behind the pseudonym Elenore Smith Bowen. Presumably this nom de plume accorded security enough to flout a taboo which many honoured. Others were emboldened and followed suit. Gerald Berreman's experiences in India found articulation in *Behind Many Masks* (1962); K. E. Read documented his vexations in *The High Valley* (1965);

Hortense Powdermaker's experiences in the southwest Pacific and Madagascar found outlet in her *Stranger and Friend* (1966); and Claude Lévi-Strauss' *Tristes Tropiques* (1963) disclosed his troubled ruminations in Amazonia. Although these confessional accounts brought awareness of fieldwork's emotional underside, the experiences they documented were largely lyrical reflections that were detached from any systematic enquiry into their implications for method or theory-making. In short, these works, as Paul Rabinow accurately noted, "all ... [clung] to the key assumption that the field experience itself is basically separable from the mainstream of theory in anthropology" (Rabinow 1977:5)—a thought earlier stated by Joseph Casagrande in *In the Company of Men* (1960)[2] and later echoed by Morris Freilich in *Marginal Natives* (1970).[3]

During the 1970s attitudes changed somewhat, as the experiential became slightly more formulaic. Solon Kimball and James Watson's *Crossing Cultural Boundaries* (1972) and Peggy Golde's *Women in the Field* (1970) opened the decade with insightful compendiums on the human face of fieldwork. Golde's edited work touched upon certain vagaries of culture shock, guilt, and the need for identity protection, while Kimball and Watson's volume comprised papers telling "off-the-record" stories of anthropologists at work in the field and beyond.[4] Also at this time a few interesting articles on the psychology of the fieldwork experience were published, though their impact was minimal. Scholars such as Morris Freilich (1970), Barbara Anderson (1971), Dennison Nash and Ronald Wintrob (1972), Deirdre Mentiel (1973), and Carole Hill (1974) dealt closely with the researcher's identity in the field—its shifting position explaining for them certain personal field crises that anthropologists may undergo.

In many respects the early 1970s marked a kind of unfulfilled high point of psychological reflection on fieldwork—the apogee of which was George Devereux's (1967) penetrating discussion of the relationship between anxiety and method usage. As Michael Jackson discusses in chapter 1 of this volume, Devereux stood alone in broaching the interplay of method and emotion: methods were not tools for gathering knowledge, he would flatly assert, but rather psychological devices used to confirm our biased perceptions and the stability of our outlook. Certain applications of method could act as a "defence mechanism" bolstering steadiness in disorienting conditions and ordering phenomena down preconceived conceptual channels. As method usage could thus subordinate unfamiliar cultures to the familiar epistemic visions in which these methods were rooted, we would often bring to the cultural facts the theories we claimed to derive from them.

When reading Devereux's work we are forced to consider how it undermined a core assumption precious to the traditional empiricist—namely, that if methods affected the researcher's subjectivity, they did so only in a very specific and controlled way: by creating in the researcher a detached and uninvolved relationship towards the object studied. The traditionalists believed that their methods rather tempered than enervated sentiment, rather quelled than aroused subjective response. This idea that methods could subjugate or even efface personality was one most easily received in the natural sciences. For here the personal reactions that methods provoked rarely appeared exaggerated or conspicuous, especially because the long tenure of scientific training made experimental activities so routine to scientists that performing them rarely upset their states of mind. Moreover, if one's research activity provoked any marked emotion at all, there were always other sciences that could explain it away. Laboratory workers' depression could be located in factors unlinked to their scientific activity, just as the biologists' *maladie du siècle* could be traced to anything but the psychological posture that their training and practice compelled them to adopt.

Thus, while the traditional empiricists asserted that methods essentially restrained sentiment, they were less ready to admit that these very same methods could *evoke emotions of a different order*. For had they recognised that the application of certain methods could generate new emotions, then the view that methods effaced feelings and personality would at once have become untenable. Thus traditional empiricists were careful to assert that it was only the link between method and mind that mattered. For them, methods created new states of mind (clear, rational, unencumbered by affect) and never new states of emotion. This was echoed in idioms depicting method usage as an essentially "technical" and "intellectual" affair: users "took up," "applied," or "discarded" these "tools" as one would solid items from shelves. And if these detachable apparatuses implicated persons at all, they did so only cognitively: to fail methodologically was primarily an *intellectual* failing—one traceable to mishandled procedure, misunderstood or misapplied design. The principle *cognitio fit per assimilationem cogniti et cognoscentis* (knowledge comes about through the assimilation of the thing known and the knower) was left everywhere unconsidered.

The irony here is that the traditional belief that method usage implicates only the intellect draws upon the old "faculty psychology" idea (i.e., that individuals can be partitioned into discrete components of "intellect," "emotion," "memory," etc.), rejected by many of these same traditionalists.[5] Many traditional empiricists did not reflect that to link method to a discrete "intellect" is no less problematic than to relate it to pure "emotion." "Intellect" and "emotion" are not analytical distinctions reflecting actualities of the "soul," but are rational categories imposed upon the total context of experience. Thus, when these categories are reified in the domain of methodology they come to support a kind of intellectualist myth: that methods function independently of the *total* personalities wielding them. This myth ignores, as William James long ago stated, that passion, taste, emotion, and practice cooperate in science as much as in any other practical affair (James 1995:40). Thus exercising method can be nothing other than a total psychological happening, for not only do we adapt personally to what methods dictate, but particular methods are most fully realised in those personalities best able to apply them. In this sense the popular yarn that the "obsessional" is always a more effective laboratory scientist than the "narcissist" (who would rather parade the results) strums more than only a humorous chord. It underlines an insight emphasising the importance of personal suitability and/or the process of its construction through professional training or socialisation.

Late 1970s/Early 1980s

Admitting the link between emotion and method gained a little more credence in the late 1970s, even though these admissions somewhat veered away from the psychological links being made in the early 1970s. By the late 1970s a number of discursive works appeared, such as Paul Rabinow's *Reflections of Fieldwork in Morocco* (1977), Jeanne Favret-Saada's *Les mots, la mot, les sorts* (1977), Jean-Paul Dumont's *The Headman and I* (1978), and Vincent Crapanzano's *Tuhami: Portrait of a Moroccan* (1980). While still reflexive, and in some measure psychological, these works explored fieldwork as an "intersubjective practice"; in other words, here ethnographic knowledge was seen to surface out of interaction and dialogue between subjects. Reflecting upon the emotional effects of intersubjectivity, however, was subsidiary to revealing and philosophising upon the contours of a dialogic approach. Describing and understanding the role of emotion was thus secondary to challenging a model of objectivity that denied the value of dialogue and intersubjectivity.

The impact of these works was doubtless served by the critical politicisation of objectivity that was burgeoning in the same period—a critique grounded in the existentialism of Nikolai Berdyaev and Jean-Paul Sartre, and developed in the Frankfurt School by Jürgen Habermas and Theodor Adorno. These thinkers rendered objectivity doubled-edged. While to the researcher objectivity brought status and results, it could also oppress its subjects, supporting a growing dehumanisation and "rationalisation of man." It achieved this by subordinating divergent knowledges, technologies, and perceptions to its all-consuming, totalising vision: the mythopoetic, non-rational and inspirational elements of individual and social life were being increasingly demystified by rational inspection. The implications for anthropology of such scientific colonisation were traced by Dell Hymes and Eric Wolff and others in the late 1960s and early 1970s. In their view, anthropology must cease objectifying its subjects, become political, and show its subjects how they could overcome the conditions of their own oppression. Anthropologists could do this by teaching their subjects to objectify the causes of their oppressed state for the purpose of understanding and removing them. This petition initiated much of the Marxist anthropology of the 1970s as well as the reflexive turn of the 1980s, where objectivity, as the *Writing Culture* school (1984) claimed, was at heart a textual construct.

Revealing the duplicities of objectivity, if not wholly legitimating research into subjectivity, did generate more interest in it in the 1980s. For example, the decade was flanked by two works showing how emotion in the field is not mere gratuitous interference but could constitute an entrée into knowing. Rentano Rosaldo (1980) argued that emotion could be used as a prism through which the perplexities of difference could be discerned. He reflected upon how his wife's sudden death in the field sensitised him to the source of headhunting among the Illongot. He understood their "grief that could kill" only after suffering the deep woe of his own personal loss. Unlike detachment, where one learns culture from afar, Rosaldo believed that through exploring this unsought-for and tragic affinity, he had winched up culture to apprehend human unity underneath, just as a tapestry's interconnections are revealed only if the embroidery is turned and viewed from its underside. In a similar vein, and at the end of the decade, Tanya Luhrmann's (1989) work on contemporary witchcraft illustrated how the interestedness of the anthropologist often meant learning from the inside (*inter-esse* means, after all, "to be in") and afforded experiential recognition of a binding sentiment integral to the life of the community. In both accounts emotion was not believed to be antithetical to thought or reason, but was seen as a source of insight that could later be disengaged and communicated through anthropological reflection.[6]

Late 1980s/Late 1990s

The assertion that some of the most profound and intimate modes of apprehension could be generated through the emotional domain was complemented
by a stream of work emerging from the 1980s. Authors such as Cesara (1982),
Stoller (1987), Wengle (1988), Jackson (1989), Heald (1989), Obeysekere (1990),
Wikan (1992), and later Hastrup (1995) and Crapanzano (1998) stressed the
collaborative nature of fieldwork, a mutuality that changed both parties. John
Wengle developed the psychological ideas of the 1970s showing that understanding was forged via processes of primary and secondary identification.
Kirsten Hastrup, asserting that culture is learned through a process of "gradual
familiarisation in practice" and that this familiarisation has its subjective con-
comitants, expressly linked praxis and affectivity and thus implicated subjectivity. Gananath Obeysekere in particular redefined the concept of detachment: "It
is not a reversal to *methodological objectivism*," but rather is, and to invoke T. S.
Eliot, "a recollection in tranquillity"—it is "the capacity to stand outside the
experience and to mould the experienced into pregiven stanzic forms" (Obeysekere 1990:227–228). The collapsing of the subject/object, observer/observed
distinctions that these works implied was explicitly articulated in Michael Jackson's *Paths towards a Clearing* (1989). He contrasted traditional empiricism
with *radical empiricism*, which rather investigated the *interplay* of the dichoto-
mous domains. Knowledge is born of this space *between*, teased from the fabric
of its interactions and intersubjectivity. Insofar as objectivity bars entrance to
this space, it is defensively used to protect ourselves from "the unsystematic,
unstructured nature of our *experiences* within that reality" (Jackson 1989:3).[7]

At this point it is important to note that this stimulating stream of thought
which stemmed from the 1980s was by no means the main tributary of writings
on field research. In fact, we might even say that such periodic and scattered research on field emotions constituted a number of smaller subaltern streams in
anthropology, which, when flowing into the mainstream,[8] were overwhelmed
by the greater methodological tide whose source was in the 1970s. This dominant tide was largely advanced by sociologists who attempted to systematise
fieldwork into a series of more positivistic research procedures and strategies.
The trend gained pace in the 1990s and early 2000s by offering work that, if it
discussed emotions at all, did so only from a traditional standpoint—e.g., it offered advice about how emotions could be "managed" and "tamed" in ways that
would free fieldworkers to undertake more unclouded research. This dominant
treatment of emotions in field research is one unfortunate symptom of what

we shall call "codification"—that is, the process by which participant observation has been increasingly formalised over recent decades into a series of neat research strategies and procedures more or less positivist in orientation. While it is sensible to recognise that such codification has had an important role to play, by being rooted in traditional empiricism it has been one of the essential factors animating resistance to the study of how emotion and intersubjectivity can be of empirical worth. Accounts by sociologists such as Jorgensen (1989), Shaffir and Stebbins (1991), Lee (1995), Kleinman and Copp (1993), Quinn Patton (2002), Adler and Adler (2000), Lichterman (2002), and Klandermans and Staggenborg (2002) when considering emotion at all, largely did so with the intention of offering guidelines about how researchers could navigate and control difficult field experiences that were commonly reported. The same may be argued for work by De Vaus (2001), Handwerker (2001), Spradley (1997), Hammersley and Atkinson (1995), and more recently in anthropological fieldwork volumes and texts by de Laine (2000), DeWalt and DeWalt (2002), Walsh (2004), and Bernard (2006)—all of which are very useful pieces in themselves but not works that open new doors to the pertinence of affectivity and emotion.[9]

While codification evermore dominates official fieldwork manuals written not only for ethnologists but for psychologists, cultural theorists, sociologists, and educators as well, many anthropologists have remained privately if not always publicly committed to taking seriously the value of fieldwork's intersubjective and experiential dimensions. Many of these anthropologists share an affinity with feminist theorists who have fought to retrieve emotion and subjectivity from marginal spaces. The abandonment of emotion into zones of pathology, radical and racial otherness and into the feminine, the outlawed, the exotic, the mad, or the bad is part of a wider traditional empirical movement in which the emotional, as Catherine Lutz has criticised, is "considered as an unfortunate block to rational thought" (1990:104).[10] If emotion is linked with irrationality, and the irrational with a kind of distorted vision, then emotion is simply grit in the eye of rational inspection. The syllogism misleads (as all syllogistic fallacies do) when empirical work produces data which contradict the syllogism's first premises. And such data now increases, if still only on the margins.

For instance, Lynne Hume and Jane Mulcock's (2004) recent volume shows with impressive clarity how ethnographic discomfort and awkwardness can be sources of insight and revelation; Antonius Robben (2006) has revealed the dangers of "ethnographic seduction" in his interactions with powerful generals—seduction which can disarm critical detachment; Jean-Guy Goulet and Bruce Miller (2007) show how "extraordinary" field experiences (visions, dreams, illuminations) can be epistemologically informative; Linda Green's (1999) work illustrates how her own fear offered a way of understanding that of Mayan widows in Guatemala; and Michael Taussig's (1992) metaphor of a "nervous system" accounts for how ethnographers connect emotionally, viscerally, and intellectually with their fields. In addition, Ruth Behar (1996) and, more recently, Gina Ulysse (2002) have offered experience-based fieldwork narratives which attempt to give greater credence to the emotions and experiences that inform understanding.

While these works keep reflection on the emotional alive in a few corners of our expansive discipline, their numbers are not sufficient to stem the dominant tide which has seen systematic work into the researcher's consciousness significantly and precipitously slow since the early 1990s. To what extent this trend reflects a growing need in mainstream anthropology to present the face of participant observation in terms attractive to the current funding market is at present a moot point. But as the growing audit and regulatory culture increasingly privileges and monetarily rewards the kind of "trade-research" that C. W. Mills (2000 [1959]) feared would ultimately dominate all social science,[11] the imperative grows to continue the critical commentary on traditional empiricism's tendency to underplay the scientific, personal, and political consequences of the affective dimensions of fieldwork.[12] Any radicalisation of empiricism must take to task the traditional myth that methods purify subjectivity. It should rather ask how far methods *mould* subjectivity, not into patterns that efface all emotion (for this indeed is impossible) but into patterns that produce emotions of a different order, and also into attitudes too often prone to privilege only cognitive learning and cognitively driven procedures in social research.

As an important aside, as different academic fields aspire to reveal dissimilar dimensions of reality by means of their distinct methods, it hardly needs reiterating that when one discipline falls unduly servile to the admired methods of another, or else bends itself to fit a popular epistemological trend, it may not only compromise its own internal methodological development but also darken the critical and informative light that its maturation could have shed on neighbouring research procedures. Because "reality" tends to unfold in response to the particular set of methods by which it is studied, our formal understandings of the "real" are always somewhat bound by the limits of the methods we employ. The danger, of course, is that those aspects of reality which sit beyond the reach of the specified method, by being seen as methodologically inaccessible, are somehow depreciated in their empirical existence. This is true with regard to what is researched and with regard to what aspects of the researcher are deemed methodologically useful. In this sense, methods constrain both what can be discovered and what spheres of subjectivity are viewed as empirically useful in the act of discovery. One way to loosen such a double closure is to bring within our investigative scope new dimensions of human and social reality by devising new modes of learning (cognitive and non-cognitive) by which they may be apprehended.

The Individual Chapters

In this spirit of opening rather than closing enquiry, let me turn to the chapters of this current volume—chapters that seek to build upon the existing strengths and insights of scholars whose work on emotions and method has not always been appreciated in mainstream sociocultural anthropology. Each individual contributor attempts from his or her unique standpoint to advance thinking on the use of emotion in varying domains of fieldwork. By necessity, the resulting inventory is far from exhaustive, and avowedly more exploratory than didactic. The volume on composite presents differing solutions to the problems arising when the traditional cords constraining the use of emotion are cut. It focuses on how certain disavowed and disassociated experiences can be shown to have heuristic, epistemological, and practical currency—experiences which, from the standpoint of traditional empiricism, have been viewed as impeding rather than assisting social research.

Many readers will doubtless be able to think of experiences and theoretical points that are under-emphasised in the coming pages. They may point to our exclusion of a more sustained consideration of how subjectivity, the field, and emotion are defined[13] and may call attention to how we could have further elaborated on how different anthropological traditions (national, thematic) have variously responded to the problem of subjectivity. Some might have hoped for a larger inventory of the subjective experiences viewed as corrosive to the research project, and there may be questions as to what extent encouraging the researcher's introspection may introduce into anthropology some of the common dilemmas that have historically inundated academic psychology. That there are many excluded standpoints we accept, but not without hope that these absences will encourage others to devote their energies to explicating themes that the limits of this volume have forced us to omit or, at least at times, to pass over cursorily. This, then, is an admittedly limited intervention but, we are convinced, a timely and necessary one so far as a radical empirical approach can reveal certain hidden potentialities of field research. Having now acknowledged some missing elements, I will outline our positive contributions.

Part I

Our first section comprises chapters by Michael Jackson, Vincent Crapanzano, James Davies, and Francine Lorimer. Each chapter applies varying psychoanalytic and psychological ideas to the understanding of the researcher's subjectivity in the field. In this they show how psychological theory can inform anthropology in novel ways—not in the traditional sense of aiding research into the origins and meanings of social and cultural phenomena but in illuminating how certain field experiences may be rendered methodologically pertinent. Even those who argued that psychology had little to offer sociology or anthropology (e.g., Emile Durkheim and *L'Année sociologique*, we recall, held that as society was more than the sum of its individual parts it could not be reduced to psychology) would be hard-pressed to dismiss the relevance of psychology in aiding understanding into the researcher's subjectivity—for researchers, after all, are psychological beings, and by Durkheim's own admission "subject matter" for psychology. Using psychology in this way nonetheless raises certain problems: how far can psychology go in assisting our understanding when certain psychologies may presuppose "concepts of the person" which are to some extent situational? In this sense, if we do interpret our field experiences in terms of a favoured psychological perspective, is there a danger that when in the field we will create ourselves in this perspective's image rather than in the image of the person embodied by our hosts?

This is one question among others addressed by Michael Jackson in his opening chapter. Jackson shows that in using psychology, anthropologists need not necessarily do violence to local facts by reducing all field experience to these homegrown understandings. One can use both psychology and local epistemologies to unravel field experience (the use of the local, after all, has always been an important learning resource). Jackson shows this by building upon George Devereux's idea that much anthropological knowledge is an outcome *both* of disinterested observation *and* of the observer's struggle to allay his anxieties and find his bearings in a new environment. Jackson focuses on what he calls fieldwork's "liminal phase"—that psychological phase marking the period between separation from our familiar lifeworld and our more comfortable integration into the new environment. The stresses of liminality, disabling and disorienting, are often unconsciously managed by researchers. One common way to manage the unstructured morass is to precipitously objectify and intellectually systematise the disorienting scene. While that strategy may help to "magically reorient ourselves to situations that seriously undermine our sense of self," when used defensively it can impede those insights that often arise when we allow ourselves to experience, slowly and non-defensively, the struggle to adapt. Jackson shows how, by turning to Kuranko oneiromancy to assuage liminal anxieties (rather than turning to objectification), he was able to understand the importance of dreams and portents in Kuranko life as well as to apprehend one situated, cultural solution to the general human experience of not-quite-fitting-in. He thus ventures beyond Devereux by showing that insights won through personal attempts at adjustment can illumine not only aspects of oneself and the world to which one is adjusting but also dimensions of the human condition itself: "In this view, the hermeneutic circle encompasses *three* horizons: that of one's own world, that of the society one seeks to understand, and that of humanity" at large.

Jackson's emphasis on learning by both studying our internal reactions and using local epistemologies is developed in a different direction by Vincent Crapanzano (chapter 2). Crapanzano starts by contesting those circumscribed and incomplete notions of participant observation that under-emphasize the importance of taking seriously our emotional responses. This reflective stance must consider both how field emotions affect the data we collect, frame, and interpret and how emotions are often structured by, and arise from, the field encounters themselves. Thus there are times when we can understand our emotions "transactionally": not as private phenomena but as "shared" or quasi objects that hover "in the between of an encounter." Here Crapanzano develops previous work on intersubjectivity by arguing that it is often framed by what he and recent psychoanalysts have called "the Third"—namely, a "meta-pragmatic" ordering principle, authorising the various "pragmatic, indexical, communicative, and interpretive maneuvers defining the encounter." The Third may be dominated by an overriding cultural concept, by a symbol (a god, a totem) or by one of the subjects of the encounter. Whatever dominates, the Third will influence what and how things are experienced by all parties to the encounter. Emotions do not necessarily emerge only out of "self," or even out of self in interaction with other (intersubjectivity); they may also emerge out of the structures that surreptitiously shape these intersubjective interactions. By recognizing that our emotions are thus influenced, we can direct our analytic attention to discerning the nature of the very structures that structure these interactions.

James Davies, in chapter 3, accepts two principles developed by Jackson and Crapanzano: firstly, following Jackson, that if methods are used solely to stabilise the self they can obstruct anthropological learning; and secondly, following Crapanzano, that participant observation as a method should oblige an interest in our states of being during research. Davies shows through the analysis of one so-called "anomalous" field experience that the disorientation it brought, the way in which the fieldworker managed his disorientation, and how the disorientation altered his perception of the field, all point to experiences more widely encountered in field research than is generally acknowledged. Dwelling on the strategies by which we often manage unfamiliar and uncomfortable states and experiences (such strategies may include Jackson's "objectification"), Davies argues that what should concern us is not that anthropologists regularly perform such strategies in the field, and that these strategies are differently employed by individual ethnographers at different times, but that these "strategies of withdrawal" are often performed spontaneously, without either the full recognition of the fieldworker or a full appreciation of the methodological implications. To the extent that this spontaneous and unconscious use of protective fieldwork strategies remains oblique, masked and under-formulated, our ability to learn is significantly impaired, for such strategies often inhibit the immersion which is essential for anthropological understanding.

Francine Lorimer, in the section's final chapter, rather than discussing certain obstacles to knowing (Jackson, Davies), takes forward Crapanzano's call for emotional reflexivity by showing how the psychoanalytic concept of transference can be used to translate so-called uninformative emotions into revealing facts. One method of obtaining social insight she identifies as reflecting upon our "countertransference" reactions—i.e., our emotional responses to the researched. During her fieldwork in a psychiatric hospital in Denmark, Lorimer's countertransference to the patient, Caroline, helped her grasp how the relationships fostered between patients in the ward created insidious cycles of relatedness which, although promoting contact between patients, sustained certain self-destructive styles of relating that these very patients entered the clinic to overcome. Here the psychiatric space engendered clinical outcomes opposite to those it worked to attain. Lorimer thus questions whether the true value of antidepressants resides in changing our biochemistry in ways that blunt the habitual and destructive styles of relating that can sustain clinical depression.

Lorimer shows through grounded examples how she reached these insights into sociality by identifying the visceral reactions that patients evoked within her and by reflecting upon how these reactions related to patients' emotional states.

Part II

While each chapter in our first section is concerned with how psychological perspectives can inform anthropological methodology and thus help us draw insights from the personal dilemmas and reactions arising from our struggles to adapt and understand, in the second section Ghassan Hage, Elisabeth Hsu, Linsday Smith, and Arthur Kleinman explore what emerges for fieldworkers when the sites they enter are themselves traumatised and politically fraught. Through investigating their emotional parity with different social worlds in varying states of crisis, they offer new understandings of how in emotionally loaded situations the political and the personal can affect each other in powerful and informative ways. Both researcher and researched can be blended into a shared subjective space as well as implicated in each other's lives, in the production of ethnographic knowledge, and in the political struggle at hand. Sites in crisis are not always to be avoided, as the heightened atmosphere can intensify affiliations and understandings as well as awaken buried obligations to act.

In the first chapter of the section Ghassan Hage scrutinises the anti-Israeli hatred he felt during Israel's bombing of Lebanon (2005), showing how these feelings represented "political emotions" that he shared with his informants. By reflecting upon his shared emotion, he refines Benedict Anderson's concept of the "imagined community": "If 'Israel is seething' and 'Palestine is weeping' and I am a person identifying with either of these two nations, I will feel that I am seething or weeping too. This makes the experience of national identification more than just an imagining. . . . We can call it emotive imagining." However, this sharing of emotions (participation) is disrupted by occasions of analytic distance (observation) as well as compulsions to act politically (practice). Thus participant observation in politically fraught contexts asks us to negotiate between not two but three modes of participating in reality: the emotional, the analytical, and the political. The emotional ambivalence generated by this negotiation Ghassan calls "ethnographic vacillation": "It is not like the famous image of the swing, used by some anthropologists to [symbolise the movement between two cultures. It] is more like being a table tennis ball on the beach being drawn in and out by the waves, with the sandy beach representing the informants' culture and the water the cultural world of the anthropologist."

Vacillation creates a third set of emotions born of this friction between the emotive, the analytic, and the political—a friction which, if not identified and understood, can confuse these three aspects of participatory research.

Of the three domains that Hage discusses, Elisabeth Hsu's contribution focuses on the emotional, providing an example of some powerful responses that fieldworkers can experience in the midst of any political crisis and exploring how these can be used to facilitate understanding. Reflecting upon her fieldwork experience in China during the military crackdown on Tian'anmen in June 1989, she asks how the political oppression following the protests provoked in her almost complete amnesia. In contrast to the psychoanalytic literature that locates the origins of forgetting in the repression of anxiety-provoking memories (Rycroft 1995; Ogden 2009; Singer 1995), she takes a less psychologistic position by asking whether it was the undeniable social repression experienced during the months after Tian'anmen that led her to banish from her memory many key events: had "the silently existent pressure on the social body . . . affected my individual body?" If this remains difficult to answer, what is clear is that her submersion into the body politic deepened her emotional affiliation with her informants. In retrospect, she analyses how the emotional parity she shared with them during the upheaval made possible the extremely revealing one-hour interviews six months later. In Hage's terms, the "emotional" thus assisted the "analytical." The experience indicated that "what makes a fruitful personal encounter and mutual understanding possible across boundaries of class, culture, gender, age, is located in an entirely different sphere of human experience, which makes any 'fieldwork method' [that ignores this] look hopelessly superficial. Sometimes the application of methods that allow systematic and quantitative assessment can even be detrimental." Hsu concludes that anthropologically relevant knowledge is not out there to be discovered in a purely systematic way, even if it may feel so to the fieldworker, but is created in moments, in heartfelt mutual interaction, in the emotive and unstructured conditions of the field to which we are all invariably subject.

If Hsu's chapter focuses on the emotional aspect of Hage's tripartite distinction between the emotive, the analytic and the political poles, then Lindsay Smith and Arthur Kleinman's chapter concludes the section by focusing on the political pole, how it is provoked or inhibited. They imply that the "analytical," by being overly concerned with proper method and analysis, can actually limit the emotional affiliation born of deep field engagement—an affiliation provoking moral impulses to act politically. For example, drawing upon their respective ethnographic research on China's Cultural Revolution and Argentina's children of the disappeared, they illustrate how engagement with others ("engagement" understood in Levinas' terms as including a sense of ethical responsibility to the "Other") emerges less from overt ethical or analytical decision making than from fundamental emotional affiliations born from empathic and human involvement. Conceived in this way, the consequences of engagement (feelings of guilt and injustice in their examples) also include the production of moral impulses to act. By broadening our understanding of engagement to include and normalise feelings of spontaneous ethical obligation, Smith and Kleinman transcend conventional ideas of the participant observer whose aim has been primarily conceived as intellectual/analytic and academic, not political or pragmatic. Their work implies a novel response to questions about why anthropologists are rarely political actors, and why, in Hage's formulation, the political pole is often ignored—the political is ignored by a narrow notion of engagement, which, by transfiguring moral emotions into distractions and artefacts, discourages, conceals, and thus ultimately dissuades the impulses that such emotions provoke and the political actions that these impulses occasionally propel.

Part III

While the first section explored how psychological perspectives can inform field methodology and the second dwelt on how political emotions arise in response to sites in crisis and create strong affiliations, identifications, or compulsions to act, in the final section Kirsten Hastrup, Tanya Luhrmann, and Joanna Cook dwell specifically upon what Luhrmann calls "non-cognitive modes of learning"—the bodily, emotional, or imaginal modes of learning which can provide entrées into knowing. Whether these modes evoke experiences that are sudden and flashing (Luhrmann; Hasturp) or more gradually emergent (Cook), they often illuminate the limits of cognitive learning by showing how sudden or "raw" emotive moments can be informative. In this sense these chapters directly challenge the mind/method link that I discussed earlier, which ignores how methods both affect and are affected by wider human experience, practice, and proclivity, not to mention the environment to which one is subject.

This latter point is explored by Kirsten Hastrup in her exemplification of how intersubjectivity denotes more than an encounter taking place in the human domain. Emotions in fieldwork emerge not only through relations between subjects (the intersubjective) but also through relations that exist between researching subjects and the material environment of the field. She shows how the presence of landscape can affectively be as psychologically significant as immersion in new systems of social and human life. The sudden "raw moment" she experienced while walking alone (and lost) in the icy expanses of her Icelandic field site provided an intimate entrée into the importance of landscape in the Icelandic world-conception. Whether what materialised through the mist was a piece of landscape or a person remains totally ambiguous, but what was clear was that her relation with materiality was significant. Hastrup develops work on both intersubjectivity and the anthropology of place by showing how the intersubjective is mediated by place—thus place itself contributes to the emotional marking of the field. In Crapanzano's terms, "place" may constitute a "Third"—a structure structuring our interactions. Here the *total* research site is rendered constitutive of experience and knowing, and thus warrants deeper epistemological elaboration in any discussion of field methods.

From the standpoint of the next chapter, by Tanya Luhrmann, we would class Hastrup's "raw moment" as what Luhrmann calls a "non-cognitive" field experience. These are visceral, emotional, highly unpredictable. But insofar as they illuminate the lifeworlds of others, they expose the limits of purely cognitive modes of learning. During fieldwork, she argues, learning other peoples' "discourses" (i.e., their cognitive models and representations of their world) is not enough. It was her own non-cognitive experience when researching witchcraft covens in London that revealed the limits of cognitive learning. One must also learn through practice: a deep participation which can potentially yield informative experiences. To these two modes of learning (explicated in her model of interpretative drift [Luhrmann 1989]) she here annexes a third essential mode—proclivity. Through her study of religious adherents in the United States she argues that individuals do not experience the ideas of their culture in the same way: "They must have something else: a willingness, a capacity, perhaps an interest in allowing those cultural ideas to change their lives." Some do, some don't; it is having the capacity which makes the difference. That personal proclivity affects the way individuals respond to cultural models and social practices she insists is as true for ethnographers as it is for those they study. This offers an important message for methodology: "If psychological and bodily proclivities make a difference to the way people use and understand cultural models, it is to the advantage of the anthropologist to understand their own proclivities and the way those proclivities may shape the way they learn about culture in the field." As the bodily, emotional, and psychological characteristics may be essential qualities affecting how we engage with and represent culture, a consideration of their affects must take up a more central place in our methodological considerations.

In the final chapter Joanna Cook, reflecting upon her research in a monastery in North Thailand, considers how doubt and anxiety in fieldwork can be potentially enabling aspects of research. She draws a comparison between the learning processes at the heart of participant observation and those involved in becoming a Thai Buddhist nun. She argues that in each a consideration of doubt as an aspect of the learning process enables the practitioner to learn *from* doubt rather than being inhibited *by* it. The doubts that she compares in the chapter are those of the researcher (regarding her competence) and those of the committed monastic (am I heading in the right direction?). She demonstrates how such doubts informed her own experience and how a consideration of doubt as an inherent and welcome aspect of fieldwork may help anthropological researchers more generally. Thus, rather than seeing the researcher as detached from the fieldwork process (via strategies of systemisation and objectification), she suggests that the ongoing subjective negotiation of the fieldworker in the field and the incomplete nature of many field experiences are themselves opportunities for learning—experiences which, if subjected to sustained reflection, may reveal dimensions of the studied community that would have otherwise remained concealed.

Radical Empiricism

While mainstream anthropology now comprises many fieldwork memoirs and confessions in which emotion is clearly acknowledged and expressed, what it still lacks are analytical works which *together* build a more comprehensive epistemology in terms of which field emotions and their methodological pertinence may be more consistently and systematically researched. What anthropology therefore requires is an epistemology whose first principles can be clearly stated, whose rules of method can indicate how to study field emotions more consistently and systematically in the future, and into whose framework existing subaltern work on field emotions can be more effectively related and integrated. It is therefore my aim in the final section of this introduction to outline such an epistemological framework, and in consequence to help bring to mainstream anthropological awareness not only the viability and necessity of this realm of research but also the guiding principles in terms of which it may be more effectively conducted in the future.

As I emphasised at the outset of this introduction, we call the particular framework advanced in this volume "radical empiricism"—a position first articulated by William James and later significantly developed in the realm of anthropology by Michael Jackson (1989). Here we understand radical empiricism in two separate senses. Firstly, in the sense that the *relations between things* are just as much matters for empirical study as are things themselves. In our case this includes the relations between *person and person(s)* (intersubjectivity), between *person and method* (inter-methodology), and between *person and materiality/environment* (inter-materiality). In this volume we specifically concentrate on the emotions and experiences that such relations evoke within fieldworkers and how these emotions, when translated through reflection into anthropological insight, can be proven to have definite empirical worth. Our second understanding of radical empiricism sees it as a methodological standpoint which takes as critical those periods during fieldwork when we are not applying a self-contained method (defined as a method productive of formal interview, statistical, or inventory data). This is to say, the subjective postures that self-contained methods oblige (e.g., "detached," "professional," "non-disclosing" postures), if ever completely realised at all, are realised only for the period of time during which the methods are being used. In this sense the postures that these methods coerce are temporary. Radical empirical enquiry thus begins at the point when our temporary adaptation to a self-contained method relaxes, when our personality or posture, so to speak, bends itself back to its habitual form. A radical empirical approach is therefore concerned with showing how the spaces between each separate adoption of a self-contained method contain happenings of critical and factual value. After all, these spaces absorb the majority of time spent in the field and generate personal postures and experiences at least as critical as those shaped by self-contained methods alone.

Radical empiricism, as a guiding framework, is therefore best conceptualised as a methodological position concerned with the *spaces between*—between things in relationship, on the one hand, and between each separate use of a self-contained method, on the other. Thus understood, radical empiricism need not necessarily stand in antagonistic relationship to the traditional empirical emphasis on using self-contained field methods. There is no need for an either/or—for both approaches may be used in any one season of research. As long as we are clear about how radical and traditional empirical approaches can affect each other in the domain of research (e.g., how codification may inhibit radical learning and how radical learning may impede codification), these approaches may be understood as complementary (as Tanya Luhrmann aptly demonstrates in her chapter, which makes use of both approaches). Such complementarity rests on the principle that each approach (the traditional and the radical) attains facts, via its particular techniques and modes of learning, that are inaccessible to the other.[14]

If unlike traditional empiricism, radical empiricism creates a framework in which emotion can epistemologically count, let me close by finally clarifying the central assumptions that inform how we study these now permitted emotions. Three assumptions, developed by Jackson in his chapter, could be said to underpin this volume more broadly.[15] The first is that "there are no emotions that are unique to anthropological fieldwork, which means that our task is one of identifying situations both in and out of the field that may be usefully compared and that shed light on one another." Identifying comparable experiences enables the use of existing psychological and anthropological theories of emotion to elucidate the methodological pertinence of the researcher's experience (Lorimer uses "countertransference"; Crapanzano, the "analytical Third"; Jackson, ideas of "separation" and "liminality"; Davies, analytic concepts of "mourning"; and Hsu, ideas of the "social and individual body"). It also permits the development of new explanatory concepts (in this volume these include Luhrmann's "proclivity" as influencing what can be known; Hastrup's "raw experience" as a powerful type of non-cognitive learning; Davies' "dissonance," which creates cycles of disorientation and withdrawal; and Hage's "vacillation" as capturing the movement of participant observation). Finally, to assume that there are no emotions which are unique to fieldwork challenges the old functionalist idea that fieldwork transpires in a distant realm of the "Other" or the exotic, or, psychologically speaking, of "exotic experience." This othering of field sites has in the past made the geographical distance that one travels to the field the measure of its validity as a site of research. The farther we journey, the more anthropological the study, or so the claim is made. But as soon as the concepts of "home" and "field" are understood in psychological rather than geographical terms, then "home" and "field" become wherever one *experiences* them to be, irrespective of their actual physical location. There is no reason why we should feel more affinity with a group situated 20 miles away than with one situated at 2,000 miles away; or why we should feel less at home in a geographically remote tribe than in a professional tribe located across the street. This is to say, if physical distance rather than human experience is privileged as defining what constitutes "the field," then whole ethnographic domains are depreciated in their legitimacy as valid sites for field research. Understood from this standpoint the "anthropology of home" is simply an outworn and unnecessary category, because by understanding "home" in terms of what is physically rather than psychologically proximate, it mistakenly privileges the dynamics of distance over the more meaningful dynamics of experience.

Our second assumption is that "emotions are but one aspect of any human experience, and we do violence to the complexity of lived experience when we make analytical cuts between emotion and thought, or emotion, the senses, thought and action." To adopt a self-contained method (one restricting how you should *be* when conducting research) is to assume a pre-defined and tightly controlled human *posture* towards the studied phenomenon. Methods delimit how and what aspects of subjectivity are said to generate the "purest" forms of knowledge. In this sense they try to shape and bend our subjectivity into a specific kind of research tool. These mouldings of self into instruments of data production not only privilege certain kinds of knowledge (essentially those which these tools can reveal) but also privilege what aspects of subjectivity and what kinds of experience epistemologically count. By implication they pronounce, jury-like, upon what aspects do not. But where methods artificially cut from research the so-called epistemologically corrosive subjective states, they oversimplify and warp the complex nature of how we as researchers learn. Experiences such as doubt (Cook), lust (Crapanzano), hate (Hage), mourning (Davies), raw experience (Hastrup), illumination (Luhrmann), loss (Jackson), compassion (Smith and Kleinman), and forgetting (Hsu), for example, can all provide entrées into knowing if only we know how to translate them. When traditional empirical partitions divide and view these experiences only negatively (i.e., as corrosive), they devalue those potential modes of learning which transcend the purely cognitive.

Thirdly, we reject the prevailing view that "the most significant thing that anthropologists have to say about emotions is that they are socially constructed and performed, for the brute reality is that many overwhelming feelings simply cannot be reduced to either culture or phylogeny." Emotions also arise out of experiences generated between things in relationship (Hastrup; Jackson; Crapanzano)—new combinations can create new experiences which go beyond old patterns of experience established by socialisation and set by culture (Davies; Hage; Luhrmann). Cultural or phylogenic reductionism thus does violence to lived experience through bypassing immediate human relations and the experience (often new and surprising) arising therefrom.

Conclusion

In the end, the structure of radical empiricism framing this volume, and our assumptions about field emotions which this structure permits, provides a complement to traditional empiricism's tendency to normalise the reduction of fieldwork to a series of neat research strategies (captured in proscriptive and positivistic "research guidelines"), strategies underpinned by a philosophy that is sceptical as to the heuristic value of emotion. Understanding fieldwork from only the traditional standpoint marginalises, expels, or simply ignores the wider domains of experience, action, and interaction which fall outside its methodological competence. Thus any position arguing for the relevance of these disowned phenomena is a position which, in an era of growing codification, not only provides a corrective to the unchecked expansion of codified research but re-emphasises those alternative modes of learning which have always rendered participant observation a singularly unique and powerful method in the sphere of human and social research. Having offered these comments, I now have only to say that if radical empiricism is to balance its traditional counterpart by better articulating the mechanisms by which it may deepen our understanding of other lifeworlds, then its object of enquiry, the human reaction, must be brought more fully within the scope of our methodological concerns. It is with this final thought that the following authors apply fresh modes of reflexivity to their own and to others' reactions and emotions evoked in the field. The study of these, while often testing, we believe is intellectually and methodologically compelling to the degree that it will further realise the rich potential of fieldwork research.

References

Adler, P. A. 2000. "Observational Techniques." In N. Denzin and Y. S. Lincoln, eds., *Handbook of Qualitative Research.* London: Sage.

Anderson, B. G. 1971. "Adaptive Aspects of Culture Shock." *American Anthropologist* 73:1120–1125.

Behar, R. 1996. *The Vulnerable Observer: Anthropology That Breaks Your Heart.* New York: Beacon.

Bernard, H. R. 2006. *Research Methods in Anthropology: Qualitative and Quantitative Approaches.* New York: Altamira Press.

Berreman, G. D. 1962. *Behind Many Masks.* Ithaca, NY: Society for Applied Anthropology.

Bowen, E. S. 1954. *Return to Laughter.* New York: Harper and Brothers.

Bruyn, S. T. 1966. *The Human Perspective in Sociology: The Methodology of Participant Observation.* Englewood Cliffs, NJ: Prentice Hall.

Bryman, A. 2001. *Ethnography*. London: Sage.

Casagrande, J. B., ed. 1967. *In the Company of Men*. New York: Harper and Row.

Cesara, M. 1982. *Reflections of a Woman Anthropologist: No Hiding Place*. New York: Academic Press.

Clifford, J., and G. E. Marcus, eds. 1984. *Writing Culture: The Poetics and Politics of Ethnography*. Berkeley: University of California Press.

Crapanzano, V. 1980. *Tuhami: Portrait of a Moroccan*. Chicago: University of Chicago Press.

Denzin, N. K. 1996. *Interpretive Ethnography: Ethnographic Practices of the 21st Century*. Thousand Oaks, CA: Sage.

de Vaus, D. 2001. *Research Design in Social Research*. London: Sage.

Devereux, G. 1967. *From Anxiety to Method in the Behavioural Sciences*. The Hague and Paris: Mouton.

DeWalt, K. M., and B. R. DeWalt. 2002. *Participant Observation: A Guide for Fieldworkers*. Oxford: AltaMira Press.

Dumont, J. P. 1978. *The Headman and I: Ambiguity and Ambivalence in the Fieldworking Experience*. Austin: University of Texas Press.

Evans-Pritchard, E. E. 1973. "Some Reminiscences and Reflections on Fieldwork." *Journal of the Anthropological Society of Oxford* 4:1–12.

Freilich, M., ed. 1970. *Marginal Natives: Anthropologists at Work*. New York: Harper and Row.

Golde, P., ed. 1970. *Women in the Field*. Chicago: Aldine.

Gottlieb, A., and P. Graham, eds. 1993. *Parallel Worlds: An Anthropologist and a Writer Encounter Africa*. New York: Crown.

Goulet, J., and B. G. Miller. 2007. *Extraordinary Anthropology: Transformations in the Field*. Nebraska: University of Nebraska Press.

Green, L. 1999. *Fear as a Way of Life*. New York: Columbia University Press.

Handwerker, W. P. 2001. *Quick Ethnography*. Walnut Creek, CA: AltaMira Press.

Hastrup. K. 1995. *A Passage to Anthropology: Between Experience and Theory*. London: Routledge.

Heald, S. 1989. *Controlling Anger: The Sociology of Gisu Violence*. Oxford: Ohio University Press.

Hill, C. 1974. "Graduate Education in Anthropology: Conflicting Role Identity in Fieldwork." *Human Organisation* 33:408–412.

Hume, L., and L. Mulcock, eds. 2004. *Anthropologists in the Field: Cases in Participant Observation*. New York: Columbia University Press.

Hymes, D., ed. 1972 [1969]. *Reinventing Anthropology*. New York: Pantheon.

Jackson, M. 1989. *Paths Towards a Clearing*. Bloomington and Indianapolis: Indiana University Press.

James, W. 1995. *Selected Writings*. London: Everyman.

Jorgensen, D. L. 1989. *Participant Observation: A Methodology for Human Studies.* New York: Sage.

Kimball, S. T., and J. Watson, eds. 1972. *Crossing Cultural Boundaries: The Anthropological Experience.* San Francisco: Chandler.

Klandermans, B., and S. Staggenborg. 2002. *Methods of Social Movement Research.* Minneapolis: University of Minnesota Press.

Kleinman, S., and M. A. Copp. 1993. *Emotions and Fieldwork.* London: Sage.

Laine, M. de. 2000. *Fieldwork, Participation and Practice: Ethics and Dilemmas in Qualitative Research.* London: Sage.

Lee, R. M. 1995. *Dangerous Fieldwork.* London: Sage.

LePlay, P. G. F. 1885. *Les Ouvriers Européens.* Paris: Tours.

Lévi-Strauss, C. 1963. *Tristes Tropiques.* New York: Atheneum (originally published in French in 1955).

Luhrmann, T. 1989. *Persuasions of the Witch's Craft: Ritual Magic in Contemporary England.* London: Blackwell.

Lutz, C., and L. Abu-Lughod, eds. 1990. *Language and the Politics of Emotion.* Cambridge: Cambridge University Press, 1990.

Lyotard, J. 1984 [1979]. *The Postmodern Condition: A Report on Knowledge.* Manchester: University of Manchester Press.

Macquarrie, J. 1972. *Existentialism.* London: Penguin.

Malinowski, B. 1960 [1922]. *Argonauts of the Western Pacific.* London: Routledge and Kegan Paul.

————. 1967. *A Diary in the Strict Sense of the Term.* London: Routledge and Kegan Paul.

Mills, C. W. 2000 [1959]. *The Sociological Imagination.* Oxford: Oxford University Press.

Nash, D., and R. Wintrob. 1972. "The Emergence of Self-Confidence in Ethnography." *Current Anthropology* 13:527–542.

Obeysekere, G. 1990. *The Work of Culture: Symbolic Transformation in Psychoanalysis and Anthropology.* Chicago: University of Chicago Press.

Ogden, T. 2009. *Rediscovering Psychoanalysis: Thinking and Dreaming, Learning and Forgetting.* London: Routledge.

Powdermaker, H. 1966. *Stranger and Friend: The Way of the Anthropologist.* New York: Norton.

Quinn Patton, M., ed. 2002. "Fieldwork Strategies and Observation Methods." In M. Quinn Patton, *Qualitative Research and Evaluation Methods.* 3rd ed. London: Sage.

Rabinow, P. 1977. *Reflections of Fieldwork in Morocco.* Berkeley: University of California Press.

Read, K. E. *The High Valley.* New York: Charles Scribner's Sons, 1965.

Robben, A. C. G. M., and J. Sluka. 2006. *Ethnographic Fieldwork: An Anthropological Reader.* London: Blackwell.

Rosaldo, R. 1980. *Knowledge and Passion: Illongot Notions of Self and Social Life*. Cambridge: Cambridge University Press.

Rycroft, C. 1995. *A Critical Dictionary of Psychoanalysis*. London: Penguin.

Spradley, J. P. 1997. *Participant Observation*. New York: Holt, Rinehart, and Winston.

Storr, A. 1960. *The Integrity of the Personality*. London: Heinemann.

Taussig, M. 1992. *The Nervous System*. New York: Routledge.

Ulysse, G. 2002. "Conquering Duppies in Kingston: Miss Tiny and Me, Fieldwork Conflicts, and Being Loved and Rescued." *Anthropology and Humanism* 27 (1): 10–26.

Walsh, D. 2004. "Doing Ethnography." In C. Seale, ed., *Researching Society and Culture*. London: Sage.

Notes

1. "Traditional empiricism" I define, following William James, as firstly that methodological approach which is more concerned with studying "things themselves" than the *relations* between things, and secondly—and consequently—as an approach that treats subjectivity in both quantitative and qualitative research as something to be controlled and restrained. The investigator's emotions and experiences from this standpoint are viewed as corrosive elements in research, not as elements integral to the research process or elements whose study can be empirically informative.

2. For example, Casagrande wrote in his introduction: "Field research is a challenging scientific undertaking, an adventure of both mind and spirit. It is also a memorable *human* experience, yet most anthropological writings tend to obscure the fact" (Casagrande 1960:xii).

3. Freilich went on to explain this partition in terms of "a fieldwork culture that underemphasises methodology and supports private rather than public communications of field experiences, and second, the 'rewards' field workers receive for keeping their errors and their personalities hidden and for maintaining a romantic attachment to the fieldwork mystique" (1970:36).

4. With these we could include George Spindler's edited volume *Being an Anthropologist* (1970), which contains personal accounts of what anthropologists do in and around the field.

5. Meyer Fortes (1963:433) epitomised this position when he remarked that psychological adjustment in the field is largely a "peripheral" issue, while at the same time being notorious for criticising academic faculty psychology.

6. John Macquarrie makes this point in his *Existentialism* (1972:155).

7. To be correct, Jackson uses this phrase to account for our use of conceptual models to order reality into ideas manageable for *us*. But he also thinks in these terms about our use of methods: "Given the arduous conditions of fieldwork, the ambiguity of conversations in a foreign tongue, differences of temperament, age, and gender between ourselves and our informants, and the changing theoretical models we are heir

to, it is likely that 'objectivity' serves more as a magical token, bolstering our sense of self in disorientating situations, than as a scientific method for describing those situations as they really are" (Jackson 1989:3).

8. These streams stem from various sources—one issues from classic psychological anthropology such as Devereux's *From Anxiety to Method* and now includes more recent psycho-cultural studies (particularly studies that use phenomenological approaches, i.e., Csordas and Dejarlais); a second might be said to flow from anthropological work closely aligned with postcolonial and subaltern studies from Green (1999) and Dominquez (2000), and a third from feminist anthropology (Luz 2001), Ulysse (2002).

9. These have been joined by recent and highly admirable compilations of classic papers on fieldwork—we think here of Bryman's (2001) and Robben and Sluka's (2006) edited volumes, which are highly readable collections although they contain only one or two papers that consider emotions in the field.

10. There is a long history of viewing women and non-Caucasian Euro-Americans as irrational and unable to control emotions, and thus more susceptible to hysteria, depression, culture-bound syndromes (such as anorexia, *latah, windingo, koro,* amok), and violence. This history of emotion and pathology may be part of the reason that female and non-Caucasian researchers have championed emotional reflexivity and the usefulness of emotional understanding in everyday life situations (as opposed to the "pathological," later spun into the "extraordinary").

11. To provide but one example—the Economic and Social Research Council has now refused to fund anthropology doctoral candidates in Britain unless they can first demonstrate competence in using qualitative and some quantitative methods. Departments like the Institute of Social and Cultural Anthropology at Oxford, for example, while having largely defined how anthropology has been taught there for the past 100 years, are increasingly subject to an external research culture to whose values it must be seen to at least partly correspond.

12. For whatever prevailing zeitgeist we are "subject to" in the academy will affect how we proceed in the field, as what aspects of "self" or subjectivity are deemed relevant to knowledge construction are largely determined by the empirical values we internalise in the academic space. Following Adorno, the "subject to" and the "subjective" are always indivisible, always mutually entailed. And thus enfolded in subjectivity reside the multifarious and manifold coercions of culture guiding individual and professional activity in ways consistent with these internalised demands.

13. Of course we have not entirely ignored these considerations. In short, we can say that this volume broadly defines "subjectivity" as both an empirical reality and a conceptual category. In this we follow the definition offered by Biehl, Good, and Kleinman in their recent edited volume *Subjectivity* (2008). Here they view subjectivity as "patterned and felt in historically contingent settings and mediated by institutional

processes and cultural forms" (5). In this sense subjectivity is understood as a synonym not only for inner-life processes and affective states but also for states or "inner-life processes" that by being "refracted through potent political, technological, psychological and linguistic registers . . . capture the violence and dynamism of everyday life" (5).

With respect to the category of "field," we define it less in spatial and geographical terms than in psychological (see pages 24–5 for elaboration). When we understand concepts of "home" and "field" in psychological rather than geographical terms, then "home" and "field" become wherever one experiences them to be, irrespective of their location. In this sense all geographic delineations of the field are simply arbitrary constructs—lines drawn which may have little bearing on internal subjective states.

Finally, while the category of emotion shall be treated in greater depth in the conclusion, for now we may say that emotion here refers to those affective phenomena which can be differently expressed, repressed, managed, and conceptualised in different sociocultural settings.

14. Thus while in a practical sense these two positions are complementary, this is not to say that their underlying epistemologies are consistent. As we have seen, radical and traditional empiricism both undermine the conceits and excessive claims of each other. But they may also do this without totally effacing the other's value and importance. The balance is found in the spirit of compromise, where each recognises the other's ability to discern facts debarred to the other and where each is able to attain a kind of relativistic position with respect to its own epistemological status.

15. The first assumption does not apply to Ghassan Hage's chapter. He argues that ethnographic vacillation creates a "friction" particular to fieldwork, a friction which generates its own unique experiences.

Psychology of Field Experience

1

From Anxiety to Method in Anthropological Fieldwork

An Appraisal of George Devereux's Enduring Ideas*

Michael Jackson

> *The subjectivity inherent in all observations [is] the royal road to an authentic, rather than fictitious, objectivity . . . defined in terms of what is really possible, rather than in terms of "what should be."*
>
> **George Devereux**,
> *From Anxiety to Method in the Behavioural Sciences* (1967:xvii)

THIS CHAPTER IS INFORMED BY THREE ASSUMPTIONS. First, I take the view that there are no emotions that are unique to anthropological fieldwork, which means that our task is one of identifying situations both in and out of the field that may be usefully compared and that shed light on one another. Second, I contend that emotions are but one aspect of any human experience and that we do violence to the complexity of lived experience when we make analytical cuts between emotion and thought, or emotion, the senses, thought, and action. Third, I repudiate the prevailing view that the most significant thing that anthropologists have to say about emotions is that they are socially constructed and performed, for the brute reality is that many overwhelming feelings simply cannot be reduced to either culture or phylogeny.

My starting point here is the ambivalence and anxiety that I experienced when beginning fieldwork among the Kuranko in northeast Sierra Leone more than thirty-six years ago. My initiation into anthropology, however, depended not only on fieldwork but also on the intellectual mentorship of George Devereux, whose work proved crucial to the evolution of my approach to comparative method, anthropological theorising, and ethnographic writing. I therefore begin this chapter with a personal reminiscence of my relationship with Devereux, whose work, in my judgement, remains fundamental to any exploration

---

* Material in this chapter was adapted from "From Anxiety to Method: A Reappraisal," in Michael Jackson, *Excursions* (Durham, NC: Duke University Press, 2007).

of the relationships between observer and observed in the behavioural sciences. This then sets the theoretical scene for an account of how I addressed the anxieties of first fieldwork among the Kuranko by having recourse to local techniques of dream interpretation and divination. I then proceed from questions of anxiety to matters of comparison, arguing that insights that turn out to be *personally* useful may also illuminate the *transpersonal* and *interpersonal* life-worlds that one is seeking to understand.

George Devereux

In the antipodean summer of 1973–74, thanks to an initiative by my friend Michael Young, whom I had gotten to know at Cambridge a few years earlier, I spent about eight weeks in the Department of Anthropology in the Research School of Pacific Studies (RSPacS) at the Australian National University in Canberra. Derek Freeman, then head of the anthropology programme at RSPacS, had brought together an exceptional group of anthropologists, including George Devereux, Meyer Fortes, Adam Kendon, and Peter Reynolds, whose research interests encompassed biological anthropology, human ethology, kinesics, and psychoanalysis. Though these fields were all comparatively new to me, it was George Devereux's work that made the most profound and enduring impression.

Like Meyer Fortes, George Devereux was only a short-term visitor, and I had already been in the department for several weeks before he arrived. During those weeks, his book *From Anxiety to Method in the Behavioural Sciences* was passed around. Everyone appeared nonplussed by it, and I don't think anyone bothered to read it from cover to cover. But when the book came into my hands I was instantly and completely enthralled. Here at last was an anthropologist who sought the universal in the particular, yet did justice to the idiosyncratic and cultural contexts in which the universal is actually lived. Other thinkers possessed the same scholarly breadth and erudition as Devereux, but none, to my mind, so successfully showed how one might integrate social and psychological approaches to human reality. I felt as though Devereux was addressing and offering solutions to the very problems I had been struggling with—methodological as well as philosophical—in my own work. First was the question of reflexivity—of the reciprocal interplay of one's relationship with oneself and with others—or, as I phrased it at the time, the twofold movement that takes one out into the world of others and returns one, changed, to oneself. For Devereux, understanding this dialectical movement was imperative if anthropology was going to be truly methodical, but it had to be managed and monitored by techniques that involved the *complementary* use of psychological *and* socio-logical models. In other words, true reflexivity demanded scientific discipline, not artistic license or confessional impulse. Second, I found myself in com-plete accord with Devereux's insistence on the value of Heisenberg's uncer-tainty principle for anthropology: *interactions* between observer and observed, object and instrument, are constitutive of our knowledge of all phenomena. This meant that anthropologists had to make choices of method and theory not on the basis of an objectivist principle of *representing* reality but on the basis of ethical, political, and artistic commitments to practical truths—truths that might make for a more equitable society or that held out the promise of enriching rather than impoverishing our lives. Third, I was impressed by Dev-ereux's notion that much of the experience-distant rhetoric and theoretical model building we do in anthropology may be understood through an analogy with intrapsychic defence mechanisms—subterfuges for coping with the stress-ful effects of fieldwork and the unsettling complexity of life. Anthropological systematising could be placed on a par with pretty much anything human be-ings do to bring an illusion of order to their lives—attributing causation to inanimate things, furnishing a house, making a garden, writing a book, build-ing a nation. In other words, whatever their different epistemological values, scientific and magical reasoning provide alternative strategies for coping with the panic that all human beings experience when confronted by the unrespon-siveness of matter—the sheer otherness, non-humanness, and unmanageabil-ity of many of the forces that impinge upon us. Fourth, I found in Devereux's psychoanalytic arguments for the psychic unity of humankind a justification for the kind of anthropology I instinctively wanted to do—"the principle that each person is a complete specimen of Man and each society a complete speci-men of Society" (1979:23). Fifth, and perhaps most momentously, I found in Devereux's focus on the politics of how ego boundaries are revised and drawn (rather than on how egos may be defined) a way around the static schemata of bounded entities—selves, social groups, tribes, cultures, nations—that domi-nated cultural anthropology in the 1970s.

Nothing is more sure to undermine one's social confidence than regard and respect, so when I was first introduced to the man whose work had already made such an impression on me, I was abashed and tongue-tied.

I remember the day vividly. A group of us were sitting around a table in the garden at University House, eating lunch. George had only just flown in from

France, and in the dazzling sunlight that filled the garden he looked etiolated, jetlagged, and utterly out of place. I sat close to him, wanting to hear what he had to say. He grasped an unlit cigarette in a tortoiseshell holder, and his first remark was a request: Did anyone know where one could buy a Cricket lighter? His had run out of fuel. I volunteered immediately, and spent the next half hour going from one kiosk to another in the city until I found a Cricket.

Years later, reflecting on this afternoon of his arrival, George would use his disoriented frame of mind—"a combination of influenza and severe jet-lag"—to illustrate how consciousness continually moves between focused and diffuse extremes, between modalities of engagement and detachment:

> My total stimulability, my capacity to apprehend situations multidimensionally, was almost abolished. The moment I was able to entrust myself to my host's kindly care, I observed first an incapacity to operate in the framework of a time-span exceeding a few minutes. On talking over afterwards my behaviour while in a state of jet-lag exhaustion, my host told me that I had spoken rationally, but also that what I had said had no real continuity. I appear to have skipped from one thing to another, in response to the stimulus of the instant. My "temporal ego" had been momentarily impaired.
>
> On another level, I noted that whenever I was not the recipient of a stimulus directly addressed to me—that is, whenever I was not directly spoken to—part of my mind began to dream. Thus, I knew that I was sitting at a table and eating; I was also aware of my host's presence, but only in a remote sort of way. With my eyes open, part of my mind was periodically slipping "sideways", into a dream-like, at least hypnagogic, state—for the first, and I hope the last, time in my life, for it was not a pleasant experience. Also, though I was able to set in motion the machinery of my good upbringing, I could hear myself say "please" and "thank you" as if I were only a suitably programmed computer. At least twenty-four hours elapsed before I could once more apprehend those I met as multidimensional persons and not as mere "partial objects". So far as I know, I did nothing silly during the first twenty-four hours, but I also know that every person and thing I encountered during that period was experienced as unidimensional and non-symbolic and that successive events were apprehended as discrete: not as sequential, not as components of a temporal pattern. My time perception was not that of the historian but that of the chronicler. (1979:28–29)

Despite seeing me as unidimensional and non-symbolic, George must have divined in my eagerness to place myself at his disposal a desire for intellectual apprenticeship or affiliation. In any event, this is what happened. I accompanied him back to his third-floor room in University House—realising, as he rested a while on each landing and complained about the stairs, that he suffered from acute emphysema. And I devoted myself to proofreading articles and running errands for him, and hearing him out as he regaled me with stories of academic politics in Paris, of the indifference and dismissiveness of the university establishment to his ideas, and of his current psychoanalytic explorations of dreams in classical Hellenic literature.

Perhaps, too, I sensed some distant kinship, born of our isolated childhoods, though the vexed circumstances of his were more "political" than "familial." He was born in 1908 in the trilingual, tricultural town of Lugós, then part of Hungary. At the end of World War I, the town passed into Romanian hands and George's lycée became officially Romanian. This meant that one year he was told that the Hungarians had defeated the Romanians; the next, he was taught the opposite. Experiencing a growing sense of cultural contradiction, and an abhorrence of the hypocrisy of identity politics, he found "affective sincerity in great music" and turned, for objective truth, to the study of mathematical physics at the Sorbonne in 1926. But one year before Heisenberg's breakthrough, he abandoned physics for anthropology.

I think I also identified with George's sense of marginality—of often finding himself in countries where he did not feel completely at home, of often seeming to go against the grain of what was considered important or fashionable in his field. "One of the reasons for my huge written output," he once confided to a friend, "is the fact that for all those years I had no one to talk to. So I wrote" (1979:15). And elsewhere, and for me, as it turned out, presciently: "Considering all things—even the years of actual starvation, the lifelong insecurity of employment, no retirement income . . . thirty-five years in outer limbo, I deem myself fortunate on two capital scores: I have made no compromises and I have done work that passionately interested me" (1978:402).

After Canberra, I saw George again twice, on visits my wife and I made to Paris in 1979 and 1982, and of course we corresponded frequently. One afternoon, he entertained us (more accurately, I should say, overwhelmed us), by playing one of his own compositions on his grand piano. On another he showed me some his old fieldnotes—evidence of how much work he had still to do. But most memorable is that long ago Austral summer, when ideas seemed to materialise out of thin air, bubble up out of the earth, as from a spring, and come in dreams, when the intense, undisturbed heat of the afternoons was filled with the brittle odour of eucalyptus, the screech of *gallahs* and parakeets, and the *chug-chug-chug* of water sprinklers on dark green lawns.

On the Margins

Devereux's pioneering work on the effects of countertransference[1] in the behavioural sciences, particularly the way we readily fall back on strategies of pseudo-objectification, intellectual systematizing, selection, scotomization, and simplification in order to magically reorient ourselves in situations that seriously undermine our sense of ontological security, implies for me that the viability of any human life depends on one's sense of being able, in some small measure, to comprehend and control one's immediate circumstances. As Bowlby (1973) and others have shown, the situations most devastating to our ontological security and sense of identity involve traumatic separation and loss. Though the prototype of all separation is separation from the mother, the bereavement reaction is grounded in our biogenetic evolution and has universally identifiable elements. This does not mean, however, that the familiar experiences of anger, protest, withdrawal, and acceptance conform to a strict behavioural sequence—a lineal progression in which each stage eclipses the one before it. Human beings seldom suffer grievous losses without some conceptual and creative response. And recovery depends not just on phylogenetically determined processes but on social imaginaries, cultural pre-understandings, and idiosyncratic experience (Friedman and Silver 2007:288). Existentially speaking, separation anxiety involves a fear of losing one's hold on the world around—of being reduced to passivity, aloneness, and childlike dependency, at the mercy of forces that are unresponsive to one's needs or persons who are hostile or indifferent to one's humanity. The recovery of a sense that one can, in some way and to some extent, comprehend and control one's situation—may be achieved in a variety of ways—telling stories in which we retrospectively recast ourselves as acting subjects rather than abject sufferers, having others confirm our wild guesses as to what is happening and why, seeking out familiar objects that symbolically restore our relationship with the world we have lost, and even imagining bonds of kinship or friendship with those who have, albeit innocently, made us feel so insecure, so that we later extol their virtues out of a misplaced gratitude for their having saved our face and recognised our humanity in a place and at a time when these were imperilled (La Barre 1972:52).

Reorientations

In what follows, my focus is the liminal phase of fieldwork—after separation from one's familiar lifeworld but before one finds one's feet and feels at home in one's new environment.

In retrospect, three things troubled me during my first few weeks in northern Sierra Leone: the first was my dread of interrogating strangers in a language I had only a smattering of; the second was an anxiety that I would never amass enough data in a year to write a Ph.D. dissertation; the third was a deep disquiet about having brought my wife, three months pregnant, to a place so remote from emergency medical services. While this last concern found expression in a generalised sense of moral uncertainty, the first two came into focus in my dreams.

A few weeks after beginning fieldwork, I had a disturbing dream that I felt compelled to record immediately upon awakening. The dream comprised two episodes. In the first I found myself in a bare room, reminiscent of one of the classrooms at the District Council Primary School in Kabala where I had first met Noah Marah (a teacher at the school, who later became my field assistant). A corrugated iron door was opened into the room and a book was passed into the room by an invisible hand or by some other invisible agency. The book hung suspended in midair for several seconds and I identified a single word in bold type on its cover: "ETHNOGRAPHY." I had the definite impression that the book contained only blank pages. In the second episode I found myself again in the same room. Again the door opened. I felt a tremendous presence sweep into the room. I felt myself lifted up bodily and, as if held in the hands or by the power of a giant, I was taken out of the room. The hands and arms of the giant exerted such pressure against my chest that I could not breathe easily. I was borne along aloft, still being squeezed. At this point I awoke in fear from the dream.

The dream obviously manifested several of my anxieties at that time: my concern that I would not prove capable of carrying out the research for a thesis or book on the Kuranko; my dependence upon my field assistant, who at that time mediated all my relationships with Kuranko people and was instructing me in the language; the mild paranoia, vulnerability, and estrangement I experienced in the villages, surrounded by people I did not know and by talk I did not understand.

The day after this dream I made a trip to Dankawali (a village about twenty-five miles from Kabala), where I met the brother of Alpha Kargbo II, a Kuranko elder with whom I had spent some time in Kabala during the preceding weeks.

Upon learning that Alpha's brother, Fode, knew something of dream interpretation, I recounted my dream to him. He was puzzled, and the dream was discussed among other elders who were present. I was asked whether the giant flew up into the sky with me and whether or not he had placed me back on the ground. After I had answered these questions Fode announced the meaning of the dream: it signified importance; it meant that if I were a Kuranko man I would be destined to become a chief. Fode added, "You will become a very important person; I do not know about you because you are a European, but for us the book means knowledge, it came to reveal knowledge." Some confusion had followed from my reference to a giant since that word cannot be translated exactly into Kuranko (and I had relied, in this conversation, on my field assistant to interpret for me). The nearest equivalent to our word "giant" is *ke yan* (lit. "long man"), which designates a tall bush spirit which sometimes allies itself with a hunter. I was told that if this bush spirit appears in a dream, it wishes to help the dreamer.

Despite Fode's caveat (that he might not be able to interpret correctly a European's dream using Kuranko hermeneutics), his elucidation of the meaning of the dream was quite consistent with orthodox Kuranko readings. Thus, a book signifies knowledge; being in a strange place among strange people signifies good fortune in the near future; being in a high place signifies the imminent attainment of a prestigious position; flying like a bird signifies happiness and prosperity. Where Fode's interpretation differed from my own wasn't only at the level of exegesis; it was in his conviction that the dream presaged future events rather than revealing present anxieties. Nevertheless, his assurances did help to allay my anxieties, and I felt that his interpretation of my dream consisted of more than pat references to commonplace Kuranko images—a fish with scales foretelling the birth of a son, a fish without scales foretelling the birth of a daughter, being in a dark forest or a swamp signifying a conspiracy, and so forth. Fode's interpretation suggested conscious or unconscious sympathy for my situation as a stranger in his society. Indeed, from subsequent conversations with many informants, I became convinced that while a great number of dream events have a standardized significance attached to them, the dream interpreter "negotiates" a commentary that speaks directly to the client's situation. In other words, although dream interpretation is inductive (according to the official Kuranko point of view), it probably involves unconscious and inadvertent introjections by both analyst and analysand—i.e., it is largely intersubjective, interpretive, and intuitive. This intuitive element in dream analysis may make it more likely to be abused. On one occasion I met a man who told me that he had dreamed the previous night that a European came and gave him some money (to distribute to others) and a multicoloured collarless shirt. He added that he had woken up that morning and given money to others, and therefore I owed him that amount. I knew him well enough to suspect that his "dream" was probably a ruse to extort money from me.

By turning to Kuranko oneiromancy, I not only went some way toward alleviating my anxieties about doing fieldwork, but my eyes were opened to the importance of dreams and portents in Kuranko life—a subject that I researched during my fieldwork in 1969–70 and am now researching among expatriate Sierra Leoneans in London.

A similar transformation of self-centred reflections into research concerning the lifeworlds of others followed from a consultation with a Kuranko diviner not long after I began fieldwork in the village of Firawa in late December 1969.

. . .

During my first few weeks in the village, I found myself so captivated by the things I heard and saw around me that it was all too easy to believe I intuitively understood them. But understanding is never born of enchantment, any more than initiation is consummated in newness alone. Understanding comes of separation and pain. To understand is to suffer the eclipse of everything you know, all that you have, and all that you are. It is, as the Kuranko say, like the gown you put on when you are initiated. To don this gown you must first be divested of your old garb, stripped clean, and reduced to nothingness.

I would begin my days at Abdul's house. The porch was of mud and dung, its floor as burnished as a river stone. Sitting with my back against the wall, I could observe the comings and goings in the compound and ply Noah and Abdul with questions. Abdul was ensconced at a treadle sewing machine at the other end of the porch, putting the finishing touches to the white country-cloth gown his niece would wear for her initiation. He was a taciturn man at the best of times, and I suspected that the row of pins he held tightly between his lips was a pretext for ignoring my questions. So it was Noah who bore the brunt of my incessant curiosity, as groups of strangely attired women performed before the house before receiving a dash and moving on, or groups of pubescent girls, their hair braided, beaded, and decorated with snail-shell toggles, their waists encircled with strings of beads, danced out the last days of their childhood. But behind the drumming that lasted long into the night, and the air of festivity, there were deep shadows. I was told of the neophytes' vulnerability to witches, and of the dangers attending cliterodectomy. I heard of fearful encounters with bush spirits and arduous hazings. And I wondered how these young girls would feel, returning after weeks of sequestration in the bush and going not to the security of their parental homes but to the uncertainties of life as newlyweds in the houses of strangers.

If I empathised with the neophytes, it was, I suppose, because I was also like a child, and because the shock of too many new experiences—a language I could not grasp, food I often found unpalatable, customs I could not understand, afflictions I could not cure—was beginning to erode my own self-confidence and make me vaguely paranoid. As the days passed, I began to miss Pauline and worry about her.

One evening I went out to the latrine that stood in the grassland behind the house where I was staying. For a while, the silence around me was broken only by the repetitive piping of a *sulukuku* bird. Then suddenly I was startled by the presence of several Senegalese fire finches flitting above me. Aware that for Kuranko these small crimson birds embodied the souls of children who have died in infancy, I became convinced that something was amiss in Kabala—that my wife had had a miscarriage, that her life was in peril.

That night I slept badly, and in the morning confided my anxieties to Noah. He too was missing his children, and wondering about his wives back in Kabala. Perhaps it was time for us to return.

But I was determined to stay, at least until the initiates entered the *fafei*—the bush house where they would live for several weeks after their operations, receiving instructions from older women.

It was at this time that I consulted my first Kuranko diviner. His name was Doron Mamburu Sise. Noah had sought his advice, and allowed me to sit in on the consultation, and so, a couple of days later, without thinking too much about it, I asked if I might follow suit.

"The *tubabu* wants to know if you can look at the stones for him?" Noah
     asked.
Doron Mamburu gestured that we should go inside his house.
Stooping, I followed Noah through the low doorway into a house that smelled
     of stale woodsmoke.
Doron Mamburu dragged shut a rickety cane door whose daubing of mud had
     all but flaked off. He then sat and waited, his eyes becoming accustomed to

the gloom, before spreading out a mat on the earthen floor and ordering me to sit down opposite him.

"Why have you come?" he asked.

Noah spoke for me. "He wants to find out about his wife," he said. "She is expecting a child. He is worried about her. He wants to know if all is well, if all will be well."

The diviner emptied some stones from a small monkey-skin bag and with the palm of his hand spread them across the mat. Most were river pebbles: semi-lucent, the colour of rust, jasper, and yellow ochre. Among them were some cowrie shells, old coins, and pieces of metal. When I handed Doron Mamburu his fifty cents consultation fee, he mingled this with the other objects.

"What is your wife's name?"

"Pauline," I answered, pleased to have understood the question.

Doron Mamburu found difficulty with the name but did not ask for it to be repeated. In a soft voice he addressed the stones, informing them of the reason I had come. Then he gathered up a handful and began to chant. At the same time, with half-closed eyes, he rhythmically knocked the back of his cupped hand against the mat.

With great deliberation he then laid out the stones, some in pairs, some singly, others in threes and fours.

"All is well," Doron Mamburu said quietly, his attention fixed on the stones.
"Your wife is well. She will have a baby girl."

Without a pause he proceeded to lay out a second pattern.

"There is nothing untoward. The paths are clear. The birth will be easy."

In order to see what sacrifice I should make, Doron Mamburu laid out the stones a third time.

"Your wife must sacrifice some clothes and give them to a woman she respects. You must sacrifice two yards of white satin and give it to a man you respect. When your child is born, you must sacrifice a sheep."

The diviner looked warily at me, as if wondering whether I would do as the stones suggested.

"To whom must I address the sacrifice?" I asked in English. Noah translated.

"To your ancestors," Doron Mamburu said flatly. Then, seeing that I was still nonplussed, he added: "You must give those things away, do you see?"

Doron Mamburu began to gather up his stones. He had been working on his farm since first light and was famished. The dull clang of a cooking pot in

the yard had already distracted him, and I caught a whiff of chicken and
red pepper sauce.

Reassured by the diviner's insights, I nonetheless remained sceptical.

"How can the stones tell you what you told me?" I asked, again relying on
Noah to translate.

"They speak, just as we are speaking now. But only I can hear what they are
saying. It is a gift that I was born with."

"Could I acquire that gift?"

"A person cannot tell if a bird has an egg in its nest simply by watching it in
flight."

I told Noah that I did not understand.

Doron Mamburu fetched the loose sleeve of his gown up onto his shoulder
and frowned. "You cannot go looking for it. Not at all. It comes to you."

There was a silence.

"Eat with me," Doron Mamburu said, climbing to his feet. He stowed his bag
of stones between a rafter and the thatch, then wrenched the door open.
The sunlight blinded me.

When we were seated in the yard, Doron Mamburu's wife brought us rice and
sauce in a chipped calabash. But I had more questions.

"How did you get the stones?" I asked. "And the words you say to them—
surely someone taught them to you?"

Doron Mamburu finished his mouthful of rice. Then, as if amused by my curiosity, he said cryptically: "If you find fruit on the ground, look to the tree."

I must have looked very perplexed. Doron Mamburu continued. "In my case,
I began divining a long time ago, in the days of Chief Pore Bolo. I was
favoured by a djinn. I saw a djinn, and the djinn told me it was going to
give me some stones so that I would be able to help people."

"Where did you see the djinn?"

"In a dream. They came in a dream. There were two of them. A man and
a woman. They had changed themselves into human beings and were
divining with river stones. They called to me and told me their names.
They said, 'We are going to favour you with a different destiny.' They
showed me a certain leaf and told me I should make it into a powder
and mix it with water in a calabash. Then I was to get some stones from
the river and wash them in that liquid. When I woke up next morning I
went at once to the Bagbe river and found that leaf and those stones. I did
everything the djinn told me to do."

"Would I be able to find that leaf?"

"Eh! I cannot tell you about that."

"The djinn, then, did you see them again?"

"Yes, I see them often. Every Thursday and Friday night they appear to me in a dream. Sometimes they say to me, 'Are you still here?'"

"Do the djinn speak to you through the stones?"

"Yes," said the diviner emphatically, as if pleased that I had finally understood something of what he was telling me.

"When you address the stones, you are not speaking to the djinn?"

"No! I am speaking to the stones." Again a frown creased Doron Mamburu's forehead. Hitching up his sleeve, he scooped a ball of rice from the calabash and slipped it deftly into his mouth.

I had finished eating, but not my interrogation. "Do you ever give anything to the djinn?"

Doron Mamburu swallowed the rice and washed it down with some water.

"From time to time I offer them a sacrifice—of white kola nuts."

I could see Doron Mamburu was tired, and that Noah was exasperated by my questions and the difficulty of translating them. I got up to go. "I have eaten well," I said.

"You are going?"

"Yes, I'm going to my house."

In those first weeks of fieldwork in Firawa, the seeds of almost all the ideas that would shape my thinking over the next thirty years were planted. I was now convinced that the justification of anthropology lay not in its potential to explain social phenomena on the basis of antecedent causes or underlying laws—evolutionary, structural, or psychological—but in its capacity to explore, in a variety of contexts, the ways in which people struggle, with whatever inner or worldly resources they possess, to manage the immediate imperatives of *existence*. Though worldviews differ radically from society to society and epoch to epoch, our everyday priorities, as well as our notions of what makes us quintessentially human, are remarkably similar wherever one goes. To participate in the lives of others, in another society, is to discover the crossing-points where one's own experience connects with theirs—the points at which sameness subsumes difference. It may be that this savoir faire, more than abstract ideas, promises the best basis for practical coexistence in a plural world.

As for Kuranko divination, I published my account of it in 1978, four years after my auspicious meeting with George Devereux, who had encouraged me to write about the interface between my own subjectivity and the subjectivities of others. In this paper (Jackson 1978, republished 1989), I included an account of my own consultations with diviners like Doron Mamburu, as well as what I learned from extensive conversations with other diviners (some of whom used techniques other than pebbles) and with clients, about why they sought the insights of diviners and why they did or not follow the courses of action and kinds of sacrifices prescribed to avert misfortune or secure a safe outcome of a journey, an initiation, a marriage, a childbirth, a course of medical treatment, a business venture, the building of a house, or the clearing of a farm. At the time when I wrote my paper the orthodox anthropological approach to divination was intellectualist in character and under the influence of the rationality-irrationality debate. Anthropologists sought to explain how diviners maintained credibility and protected the plausibility of a diagnostic system that is so hit and miss. Arguing against this intellectualist bias, I focussed on the existential situations in which clients found themselves—the vexing uncertainty, enforced passivity, and conceptual confusion into which circumstances had thrown them. I argued that insofar as I had not felt any need to embrace Kuranko beliefs about spirits in order to enter into the spirit of a divinatory séance, Kuranko probably did not have to commit absolutely to the tenets of their belief system in order to use them in coping with adversity—though reifying and ontologising these beliefs undoubtedly invests them with the kind of power or aura without which some people might deem them inefficacious.

My focus, however, was not belief per se but the mixed emotions, the fragmented thinking, the hallucinatory images and wild imaginings that are associated with separation anxiety. I approached the phenomena in two ways. First, I explored how, in the divinatory séance, subjectivity gives ground to some form of objectification in which the problem can be grasped or handled as if its locus were outside rather than within the self. Objects (or words) are invested with the emotions that have proved refractory to conscious organization; the objects (or words) are then organized and manipulated in order to achieve a mimetic or vicarious mastery over the emotions and events they stand for. This process of externalization entails two parallel transitions: (1) the consultor surpasses the chaotic and inchoate state in which he finds himself and, through social action, is enabled to assume responsibility for and determine his own situation; and

(2) the consultor's situation is classified according to collective dogmas of causation and, as a consequence, the consultor's group (family, subclan, or village) is enabled to act decisively to determine its situation. The diviner's role can thus be understood as one which ritualises the transition from inertia to activity, on the one hand, and from private experience to shared experience, on the other.

My second approach was to emphasise the instrumental, or praxeological, rather than the expressive or semiotic aspects of divination. The diviner's analysis transforms uncertainty into a conditional certainty, and his instructions for an appropriate sacrifice enable the consultor to regain his autonomy—to act upon the conditions that are acting upon him. This autonomy precludes anxiety. I argued that these psychological and existential changes are immediate and positive and that the ultimate outcome of any prognostication or sacrifice does not necessarily inspire retrospective interest in the truth or falsity of the diviner's original propositions. The reassurances that follow from and the activity enabled by the consultation entail a suspension of disbelief. This pragmatist interpretation had, I argued, the added advantage that it was consonant with Kuranko attitudes toward belief. What is imperative for Kuranko is not whether a story told, a prognosis offered, or a sacrifice made will give intellectual satisfaction but whether it will improve one's lot, enable one to act, strengthen one's bonds with others, and minimise the risks of misfortune. As William James puts it: truth is what "*happens* to an idea. It *becomes* true, is *made* true by events. Its verity *is* in fact an event, a process" (1978:97).

Borderlands

I began this essay with Devereux's assertion that anthropological knowledge is an outcome of *both* disinterested observation *and* the observer's struggle to allay his or her anxieties and get his or her bearings in a bewilderingly new environment. But in making reflexivity essential to ethnographic method, I have perhaps ventured further than Devereux in claiming that insights gained in the course of one's personal attempts to adjust to a strange new world may afford insights not only into that world but into the human condition itself. In this view, the hermeneutic circle encompasses *three* horizons: that of one's own world, that of the society one seeks to understand, and that of humanity. In what follows, I sketch out what this universalising claim entails.

I begin with the observation that separation anxiety, whether experienced by an anthropologist embarking on fieldwork or by any human being suffering a devastating disruption of his or her lifeworld, may be understood as a particular instance of boundary-disruption—a sudden loss of the normal balance between inside and outside. In *Beyond the Pleasure Principle* (1961:30–35), Freud noted that all organisms, from the lowly amoeba to human beings, need to *both* absorb elements of the world beyond their boundaries *and* protect these boundaries from invasive and life-threatening forces. Filtering, monitoring, and controlling traffic across body boundaries, through either practical or imaginative strategies, is thus crucial to the life of any organism and constitutes what Vincent Crapanzano has called Hermes' dilemma. Wherever microcosm merges with macrocosm, anxiety begins, and it is at the threshold between the familiar and the foreign that ritual, taboos, mixed emotions, and intellectual concern are concentrated.

As I became aware of the working of this subjective dialectic between being open to the Kuranko world and protective of my own sense of self, I began to see evidence of the same dialectic in Kuranko social life. Let me explain.

A few months before I left England, NASA succeeded in putting two men on the moon. I sat up all night at my Cambridge college watching the television coverage, and by the time the two silvery-grey, bulky figures of Armstrong and Aldrin finally ascended the ladder to the LEM and "achieved re-ingress," dawn was breaking. Walking back to my flat, wearied by the clichés of the night, I warmed to the sight of the sun coming out of the mist and the noise of birds.

It so happened that when my wife and I arrived in Sierra Leone, the country was in the grip of a conjunctivitis epidemic. Locals called the eye disease Apollo, though when a second wave of the epidemic swept the country a distinction was made between Apollo 11 and Apollo 12. "What was the connection?" I asked people. The American moon landings had disturbed the dust on the surface of the moon, I was told. Just as the sand-laden harmattan blows south from the Sahara in the dry season, filling the air and irritating one's eyes, so this cosmic dust had brought its own discomforts and disease.

Given my curiosity, people were then eager to have me clarify some of the anomalies in the accounts they had heard of the Apollo missions. Some suspected that these accounts were untrue; no one could travel to the moon. Others (ignorant as to how far away the moon was and believing it to be just overhead—no bigger than it appeared in the night sky) asked me to explain how a rocket large enough to hold three men could come to a standstill alongside the moon and allow the men to get out and walk about on its surface. Still others demanded to know why the Americans wanted to go to the moon in the first place; what sinister designs and global repercussions did this presage? I had already noted this same suspicion of America in local people's refusal to allow Peace Corps volunteers to photograph them. Anxieties clustered around the rumour that photos showing village women with bare breasts would be used by whites in the United States as racist propaganda, a way of arguing for the oppression of African Americans on the grounds that their origins and essence were incorrigibly primitive. In many ways these anxieties anticipated the fears of a later generation: that just as Americans had once sought to steal people's vital essence by capturing their likenesses in photographs, so foreigners were now out to steal and traffic in human body parts and vital organs.

But getting back to Apollo, the questions that people in Firawa and Kabala put to me should not be read too literally. People were less interested in grasping intellectually the truth of the Apollo programme than in how to resolve an old existential dilemma that it had brought to mind. This was the dilemma of how to control traffic across the borders of their own local world, such that it would be perennially revitalised by imports from the outside world—including magical medicines, women, and commodities like salt, cloth, kerosene, and seeds—without its integrity being endangered or undermined by foreign influences that they were powerless to control. It was not that Kuranko had hitherto lived in isolation but rather that the post-Independence period had brought increasing hardship in negotiating relations with the outside world that were to their advantage. While villagers were building roads to get access to markets, young men going south in increasing numbers to work in the diamond districts, and Muslim converts making the pilgrimage to Mecca, the Kuranko were coming to see that the outside world was much larger, much more complex, and probably much less manageable than it had been for their forefathers. The Apollo stories encapsulated this pervasive suspicion that the might of a foreign power of which they knew very little could cause things to happen in their own backyard without their consent, without their comprehension, and without their control.

The fear of uncertainty and loss is part and parcel of the human condition, and no human being is indifferent to the real or imagined forces that threaten his or her sense of ontological security—whether these take the form of an oppressive state, a foreign invader, viral or bacterial threats (e-coli, SARS, HIV-AIDS), terrorist attacks, witchcraft, the infirmities of age, or natural disasters. When I first lived in the United States, I observed the Stars and Stripes outside homes, the ubiquitous security systems, the preoccupation with hygiene, the ownership of firearms, the massive vehicles, and the bumper stickers supporting American wars on foreign soil, and was reminded of the white flags that Kuranko villagers hung outside their houses on the advice from diviners, or the various fetishes on lintels and farm fences or worn on the body—magical techniques for bolstering one's own sense of well-being and at the same time warning away the forces of darkness beyond the perimeter of one's hearth and home.

Different people, and different peoples, have different thresholds of tolerance for otherness and unfamiliarity. Children who experience constant assaults on their sense of self-worth will tend to behave self-protectively as adults, cautious in their relationships and less trusting and giving than their peers who were praised by parents and acquired a more confident capacity to brave the uncertainties of the world. Just as my own susceptibility to separation anxiety reflects the circumstances of my early childhood (Jackson 2006:16), so the excessive secrecy and suspicion in rural Sierra Leone may reflect slave-raiding and endemic warfare in the past (Ferme 2001; Shaw 2002). But enculturation may, in many circumstances, hold the key to how people cope with suffering. Among the Kuranko, for example, children are taught to accept adversity and to endure it. This is the overriding lesson of initiation, when pain is inflicted on neophytes so that they may acquire the virtues of fortitude and imperturbability. Pain—like anxiety—is an unavoidable part of life; it can be neither abolished nor explained away. What matters most is how one suffers and withstands it. This is nicely expressed in a Kuranko proverb that exploits the fact that the words "load" and "world" are near homonyms—"The name of the world is not world; it is load, and everything depends on how you carry it." Accordingly, Kuranko are probably better at inhibiting socially counterproductive thoughts and feelings than someone raised in a European middle-class milieu, where self-expression often trumps social etiquette. But the range of variations within any culture is probably as great as the range of variation between cultures, and unique traits never cluster in such numbers as to warrant the ascription of significant discontinuities to the relations between individuals, nations, or cultures. A common mistake in social analysis is to assume that the terms that define one's *field of study*—"culture," "history," "religion," "class"—also delimit a *phenomenal* field, so that one's analysis is fully justified in reducing everything to one's preferred concept or professional jargon, or in privileging such substantives in the framing of the analytical project. Empirically, however, we encounter neither cultures nor individuals but what Walter Benjamin and Theodor Adorno call "constellations" (Rose 1978:90–91)—unstable clusters of experiences and events that are never identical with the terms with which they are represented or objectified and that cannot be analysed in terms of some hierarchy of causes. Accordingly, our analytical strategy must be opportunistic— availing itself of cultural, psychological, and even aesthetic models to grasp a reality that is never one-dimensional or static. Like Devereux, I argue that what is all too often left unexplored is the dynamic interplay of observer and observed, and the co-presence of culturally specific and existentially universal elements within the same behavioural field.

References

Bowlby, J. 1973. *Attachment and Loss.* Vol. 2, *Separation: Anxiety and Anger.* Harmondsworth: Penguin.

Deluz, A. 1979. "George Devereux: A Portrait." In R. H. Hook and G. Devereux, eds., *Fantasy and Symbol: Studies in Anthropological Interpretation,* 11–18. London: Academic Press.

Devereux, G. 1967. *From Anxiety to Method in the Behavioural Sciences.* Mouton: The Hague.

———. 1978. "The Works of George Devereux." In G. D. Spindler, *ed., The Making of Psychological Anthropology,* 402. Berkeley: University of California Press.

———. 1979. "Fantasy and Symbol as Dimensions of Reality." In R. H. Hook and G. Devereux, eds., *Fantasy and Symbol: Studies in Anthropological Interpretation.* London: Academic Press.

Ferme, M. 2001. *The Underneath of Things: Violence, History, and the Everyday in Sierra Leone.* Berkeley: University of California Press.

Freud, S. 1961. *Beyond the Pleasure Principle.* Trans. James Strachey. New York: Norton.

Friedman, H. S., and R. C. Silver. 2007. *Foundations of Health Psychology.* New York: Oxford University Press.

Jackson, M. 1978. "An Approach to Kuranko Divination." *Human Relations* 31:117–138.

———. 1989. *Paths toward a Clearing: Radical Empiricism and Ethnographic Inquiry.* Bloomington: Indiana University Press.

———. 2006. *The Accidental Anthropologist: A Memoir.* Dunedin: Longacre.

James, W. 1978. *Pragmatism.* Cambridge, MA: Harvard University Press.

Jane, B. 1975. *Primate Behavior and the Emergence of Human Culture.* New York: Holt, Rinehart, and Winston.

La Barre, W. 1972. *The Ghost Dance: Origins of Religion.* New York: Dell.

Rose, G. 1978. *The Melancholy Science: An Introduction to the Thought of Theodor W. Adorno.* London: Macmillan.

Shaw, R. 2002. *Memories of the Slave Trade: Ritual and the Historical Imagination in Sierra Leone.* Chicago: University of Chicago Press.

Notes

1. Although this term has a specialized meaning in psychoanalysis (an analyst's emotional attitude toward a client, and his or her tendency to perceive and respond to the client through the lens of his or her predispositions and preoccupations), it also denotes our all-too-human tendency to see others solely in terms of our own entrenched interests, views, and values. Addressing the issue of countertransference is thus vital to reflexivity in fieldwork, sound empirical research, and genuine mutuality in our everyday relations with others.

2 "At the Heart of the Discipline"

Critical Reflections on Fieldwork

Vincent Crapanzano

"WE HAVE A JOB TO DO, SO LET'S GET ON WITH IT." These are the words of one of the most down-to-earth, most pragmatic anthropologists I have ever known. Mervin Meggitt and I were driving back to New York from Princeton, where I was teaching. Meggitt had given a talk there, and though I can no longer remember his subject, I remember our conversation vividly. He was describing how surprised he was when he came to the States by all the talk, the anguish, about fieldwork. "I never heard the word 'culture shock' in Australia." Culture shock was very much in fashion then, in the early seventies. It was with some impatience that Meggitt went on to say: "We have a job to do, so let's get on with it."

I remember thinking at the time how lucky Meggitt was. I was just beginning to write *Tuhami* and was struggling with the intricate dynamics of my encounter with a Moroccan tilemaker who believed himself to be married to a *jinniyya*—a she-demon (Crapanzano 1980). With some trepidation, I began to describe my project. Before I could finish, Meggitt interrupted: "I suppose it all depends on with whom you're working. The Aborigines and the Papuans are a very pragmatic people. The Moroccans don't seem to be." Clearly Meggitt had not read Geertz's "Islam Observed" (1968) or was simply dismissing Geertz's portrait of them as Wild West pragmatists. Meggitt had some unkind words to say about participant observation as well, but I don't remember exactly what he said.

I don't believe there was ever much fuss made about the nature of fieldwork, at least its psychological dimensions, in the United Kingdom. Nor was there in France. Nor, I believe, was there ever so much concern about methodology.

This concern with methodology reflects the position of American anthropology in terms of its "sister" disciplines in the social and psychological sciences, which have elaborated methodologies that are themselves responses in part to the hegemonic position of the physical sciences and their methodologies. It is also a response to the "scientific" criteria of granting agencies and in complex ways to American attitudes toward "hard" data, numbers, and literal meaning, all of which have influenced the American take on empiricism and positivism. It also reflects a particular epistemological stance that favors the universal, the general, over the particular. It accounts for an at times apologetic, at times defiant tone in anthropology's defence of itself. It may well account for American anthropologists' propensity to cling to one theoretical model or another, most often borrowed from other disciplines, with an intensity that borders at times on the religious, or at least the ideological. All of this affects the way American anthropologists have constructed and evaluated fieldwork.

I have stressed the "American" here and opposed it to the British and the French to call attention to important differences in national anthropological traditions. What I have to say about fieldwork reflects my training and my particular relationship to that tradition. Although I have attempted to preserve critical distance by assuming one external vantage point or another, I have to acknowledge that, even at a remove, my training echoes intellectually, stylistically, and emotionally in "my" research in often surprisingly uncritical, indeed unwitting, ways. "As a constraining conscience," I am tempted to add. I have placed "my" in "'my' research" in quotation marks to accent a propensity in anthropological research to take possession of that research's findings, often masking the complex interlocution at home and in the field which defines and gives direction to the research.

Fieldwork has been taken as the heart of the discipline, but it has not always had such a privileged position. In northern Europe, in Denmark until recently, fieldwork, as the task of the ethnographer, had a somewhat inferior status to interpretive and theoretical elaboration—the task of the ethnologist. Though it is at the heart of the discipline, it has, as Meggitt's words indicate, not received the critical reflection it deserves. To be sure, there has been a lot of talk about participant observation, but it is now recognized that "participant observation" does not adequately describe what occurs in the field. Its oxymoronic implication has been belabored, but it does call attention to a particular demand in anthropological research: the need to be critically conscious of what one is doing as one does it. This reflective stance refers not only to whatever activities one is engaged in—watching a ritual, mending a fence, measuring a field—but to verbal exchanges as well.

.   .   .

I want to look at a range of encounters in the field, not only to illustrate this range but to suggest how these encounters influence the data collected and how those data are construed. Before proceeding, I want to make twelve general observations. They are abstract but will be filled in further on in this essay, when I discuss concrete field situations.

1. Every field encounter determines in part the way in which the data collected, including the encounter itself, is framed, interpreted, and generalized. We usually focus on what is in-frame—what transpires in the field—and ignore, misperceive, or devalue what is out-of-frame, outside the field experience itself. In so doing, we disturb the day-to-day experience of those with whom we work.

A First Corollary

However sensitive we are to our informants, we have to recognize that fieldwork is at some level always a violation. We are rather like uninvited guests who hopefully, once welcomed, behave with consideration and perhaps even offer our hosts something they value. We gain nothing by denying this violation: the inherent violence of field research.

2. Every field encounter, and every encounter in the field, is a unique encounter. But insofar as it is thought to lay bare social and cultural generalities, the immediacy of the encounter is torn asunder by a telos alien to most ordinary encounters that are the ethnographer's idealized object of study. In other words, the immediacy, the spontaneity, the particularity of the encounter is corrupted by the generalizing goal of the anthropologist (and at times that of his informants). It is symptomatized. The ambiguity, the paradoxical nature of the ethnographic encounter, insinuates itself through all phases of research, analysis, interpretation, and textualization and the theory that is generated or implicated thereby. It demands—for lack of a better term—a deconstruction that assaults the normalized anthropological goal and produces defenses (denials) that are perhaps even more destructive of that goal or those goals (Devereux 1967).

3. Though the encounter influences the data, its influence is constrained both by psychological blinkers (blinders) and by the orientation—the conventions and assumptions—with which one approaches the encounter. In the words of Hans Georg Gadamer (1975), the encounter is influenced by pre-understanding and prejudice—the *Vorverständnis* and *Vorurteil*—with which one enters the field.

4. We tend to restrict these prejudices, this orientation, to those of our discipline. But in so doing, we may blind ourselves to the defensive structure, whatever its truth or efficacy, of these orientations. They may mask, for example, racialist assumptions that even if we are not racist affect how we construe the field situation.

5. There is in all fieldwork a struggle at both manifest and latent levels between openness to the new, to the exotic, to otherness and to our reductive loyalty to our orientations and prejudices. (I use "exotic" in a neutral but potent sense to refer to that which is foreign, unfamiliar, outside.) Our take on the data we collect is always a compromise between our acceptance of the risks posed by openness to the exotic and the comfort of reductive closure. It may be emotionally laden.

6. To be good fieldworkers—and none of us are always good fieldworkers— we require what Keats called negative capability—the ability to identify with a character (and, I would add, a point of view) without losing our own identity, our own point of view, the confidence of our position. But I hasten to add, lest you remark on a contradiction between this Keatsian assertion and the stress I have given openness, that one's own point of view is subject to modification without crashing.

7. Thus far I have stressed the researcher as though he or she were operating singly in an exotic field. But clearly this is not the case, for fieldwork consists of encounters with others, who come to the encounter with their own prejudices and orientations, including the value they put on openness and closure. It is interpersonal, interlocutory—a mini-drama of plays of power, desire, and imagination.

Two Corollaries

The first is that the casting of the field encounter in terms of power and desire reflects a culture-specific orientation—what Joel Robbins (2006), following the theologian John Milbank's (1990) re-visioning of the social sciences, calls a social ontology of violence and conflict. Milbank urges, as we might expect, an ontology that gives central place to peace, charity, and reconciliation. Does an ontology of violence preclude one of peace, charity, and reconciliation?

The second corollary concerns that barbarous neologism *othering*. What is the attraction today of othering, otherness, the other? Yes, it is abstract enough to play an important (post-Hegelian) generalizing, indeed universalizing, role in the construction of our socio-logics. With this I have no quarrel, provided we recognize that its abstractness precludes, or at least facilitates the preclusion of, the recognition of more nuanced qualities of relationship—loving, hating, seductive, dismissive, idealizing, derogating. All of these relate "self" and "other" in subtly different ways that are of immense social and psychological importance. They may promote engagement, closeness, identification, fusion, and even possession or disengagement, distance, rejection, isolation, and solitude. Of course, their consideration raises a set of moral issues that, no less present, are not as salient when we refer simply to othering, the dialectics of alterity, and otherness. We have to ask what we are excluding from consideration. Are we attempting to avoid the moral pressure of the intimate and the particular? Or, in another way, the epiphanous quality of the particular and all it opens up, including the aesthetic?

8. Fieldwork can produce deeply and sometimes troubling emotions in both the anthropologist and his or her informants, who, each in his or her own way, defend against them, say, through repression or by assuming a stoic stance. But fieldwork may also produce pleasurable emotions which we want, sometimes at our expense, to prolong. Here I want to stress that, though we in the West tend to locate emotions in the individual, not all societies conceive and experience them that way. They may understand them transactionally; the emotions may be thought to be shared or to hover as quasi objects in the between of an encounter. I myself have insisted on an interlocutory approach to emotions (Crapanzano 1992:229–238, 1994; Rosenberg 1990). What becomes significant is the transfer of emotions from interlocutor to interlocutor and their *dramatic* progression (Crapanzano 1994).

9. Fieldwork extends over time. To say that the anthropologist is a participant observer in research that may extend over years, decades even, carries detemporalization and simplification to absurdity. Extended over time, fieldwork is subject to the conventional and contingent course of life, as it is subject to all the moods and feelings of the fieldworker and his or her informants. Given our particular chronotope, this temporal dimension is

often spatialized and, as such, rendered static. We might, however, speak more dynamically of the centrifugal and the centripetal movement of the field experience.

Two Corollaries

The first concerns the importance of the contingent and accidental in fieldwork. I know of no anthropologist who has not recounted the contingencies that led him or her to settle in a particular village, live with a certain family, meet an especially insightful informant, or discover an aspect of the society or culture hitherto unknown to him or her. I myself could give countless examples. We do depend on the contingent from the moment we start our research, and this dependency affects the way we do our research. It may produce a particular sense of time or progression: a fragile, at times resigned, positive or negative, expectation verging on the atomistic, infused—as troubling as this may be— with a sense of fate or, less systematically, with chance. It may promote in reaction a strong sense of determination.

The second, related corollary concerns the importance of breakdowns in the field. Not only do they reveal responses that we might not otherwise discover, but they also convert our perspective and that of our informants from one of unthinking engagement, being lost in the flow of habitual activity, to a reflective, objectifying stance toward whatever has broken down and its immediate surround. Heidegger (1967:95 ff.) would understand this change as a shift from the *Zuhanden* (ready-to-hand) to the *Vorhanden* (presence-at-hand). I want to stress the importance of breakdowns in conversation, many of which we understand in terms of misunderstanding. These misunderstandings, as dangerous as they may be, are one of principal ways to ethnographic discovery—that is, if they are not ignored or dismissed. The arrival of the anthropologist may itself be understood as accidental by his or her informants and as a break—a breakdown—in their routine life. They may conceive of the arrival as fated, god-given, demonically inspired, or just a product of chance. Obviously it will affect their attitude toward the anthropologist.

10. For the anthropologist, the time of fieldwork is no doubt differently conceived and experienced than it is by his or her informants. To put it simply: the anthropologist's sense of time, marked as it is by a beginning and an ending—an arrival and a departure—is telic. It has a goal, in fact a moving goal: to come up with an array of findings that will eventually become a text, or texts, of one sort or another that will make a contribution to

the discipline, and ultimately (hopefully) to our understanding of being human. This goal, which is usually preformed (though expectably subject to change as the fieldwork progresses), affects the field experience in multiple ways. Among the most important of these is rendering it suspenseful and anxiety-provoking (Will I get the data?); curtailing time (Will I have sufficient time?); and extending time (I've got what I need, but I have to wait it out, don't I? Do I need more?). Often the goal leads to fishing for facts, which gives to the experience a staccato quality and in consequence a distortion of the shared experience of duration. It tests the anthropologist and his or her subjects' patience.

Two Corollaries

Note taking influences the progress of the field encounter by slowing it down, making it awkward, objectifying it, rendering it episodic and worthy of preservation. The notes extend the field experience in time as they reduce it by giving greater credence to the written word than to live—however, distorting—memory. As time goes on, the mnemonic force of the notes deadens even before its ultimate extinction with the demise of the note-taker. Under many circumstances, the privilege given (culturally) to the written word by the anthropologist clashes with that given to the spoken word, to the phatic dimension of interlocution, by the people under study. We might well consider King Ammon's (Thamus') response to Theuth's invention of writing in Plato's (1987:274d–e) *Phaedrus* as expressing one possible attitude toward the written and spoken word and memory. Socrates quotes the king: "If men learn this [the art of writing], it will implant forgetfulness in their souls: they will cease to exercise memory because they rely on that which is written, calling things to remembrance no longer from within themselves but by means of external marks: what you have discovered [writing] is a recipe not for memory, but for reminder." The shift from memory to reminder would affect the anthropologist's experience of time both during and after fieldwork in ways radically different from that of those informants who do not share his or her faith in the written word. Audio and visual recordings are no less intrusive. Though they suggest greater accuracy than note-taking, they delimit the progression of field research. Recorded, they cannot capture the immediacy of contact of the spoken encounter: engaged co-presence (Traimond 2008). The foreknowledge of departure affects the anthropologist and his informants in different ways. It may be looked forward to or dreaded by both. It imposes a burden on the anthropologist. It may produce a *crise de conscience*, a sense of responsibility for real or imagined disruptions that his or her interventions have effected, and a constellation of feelings that arise from the knowledge that remediation will no longer be possible. I stress the negative here—regret—not because I want to deny the positive consequences of the presence of the anthropologist for the people studied—they may well be significant—but because most anthropologists with whom I have spoken describe their departures with regret, sorrow, and guilt. Frequently departure ends with a promise to return, which may well never be kept (as both parties suspect), and whose breach will color the aftermath of fieldwork for both the anthropologist and his or her subjects for years.

11. In field encounters, genre, convention, and style, the permissible and im-permissible, what can and cannot be said and in what idiom are subject to complex negotiations. They open up imaginative horizons, as well as memories of the past, which may be received with enthusiasm or with fear and regret. To put it in language that is not usually used in discussing fieldwork, the anthropological encounter opens up transgressive possibili-ties that affect all parties to the encounter and the nature of the encounter in ways that extend beyond consciousness. The encounter demands a shift in perspective, or better, a continuing shift in perspective, by both the re-searcher and his or her subjects (Bachnick 1986). I want, especially, to stress the negotiation of *a* perspective, which I liken to the editorial perspective that we adopt as we revise what we have written. Of course, what we are to write, what we write and have written, all figure in the maintenance of this perspective—its artifice. As the relationship between fieldwork and writing has been more than amply discussed by the writing anthropology school, I will not discuss it here.

One Corollary

We usually assume mimetic intention in what our informants tell us without recognizing that their intentions may be not mimetic but rhetorical, pragmatic, phatic, ironic, comic, or aesthetic. Our assumption rests, as I have often sug-gested (e.g., 1992:12–18), on the priority that we give to the semantic, the ref-erential in our understanding of language usage, but it may be that in other linguistic communities, other linguistic *Einstellungen* are privileged. Where, for example, we assume that informants are describing their life-historical experi-ence as it happened, leading us to phenomenological or experiential under-standing, they may in fact be describing experiences that never occurred, or that occurred quite differently, in order to produce a desired effect in us or because they find those experiences aesthetically pleasing. These elaborations should not necessarily be understood in terms of fiction, for fiction itself is, conceptually, a product of our particular epistemological and axiological, indeed ontological, assumptions. It is by no means a universal category, as some of the writing culture proponents would have it. We have, I believe, at the earliest stage of fieldwork possible, to determine the prevailing take on language and by extension discourse and how that take affects what is said and interpreted.

12. In field encounters, particularly in their initial stages, the fieldworker and his or her informants are confronted with each other's opacity—with the inevitable fact that we can never know what is going on in the mind of our interlocutors, in what I have called shadow dialogues, those inner conversations that accompany the mentation we have as we converse (1990). (We do have to recognize, however, that solipsism—the problem posed by other minds—supports our culturally and linguistically embedded philosophies in ways that may not be stressed or acknowledged in other societies.) Of course—I am not sure how to put it—this opacity is, in its deadness, its intransigence, alive; for whatever lies behind that opacity is, as we conceive of it, an active agent, capable of apprehending us not as we know ourselves to be but as we are assumed to be. It is not simply a mirroring, as complex as that may be, but an appraisal—a projective appraisal over which we have but scant control. We tend to figure this appraisal in visual terms—terms that may not be shared in other societies. As we see, we are seen. Inherent in the gaze, as the Lacanians insist, is the look—the gaze—of the other. The eye of the other, so it seems to be taken nowadays, by Foucault for example, is penetrating, controlling, alienating in its effect. But, we have to remind ourselves, it may also be reflective, loving, mysterious, an allure, charming in both its positive and its negative senses.

The "fact" of the opacity of those with whom we engage, the terrible loneliness that accompanies its recognition, our mistrust of the "charm" of the other's eye, are shunted aside in most conventional encounters. But anthropologists and often enough their informants do not have such conventional support, at least during the initial stages of research, because of the strangeness, the alien, quality of their encounter. More important, the anthropological stance itself demands the preservation, to a surprising extent, of strangeness, alienation, what Brecht would call *Verfremdung*

(1982:94–96, 143–145) and the Russian formalist Viktor Shklovsky, *ostranenie* and in consequence loneliness (1992). The absence of such conventions and our professional commitment to defamiliarization call attention to the illusions of knowing, of seeing through, and the fact, perhaps, of their possibility.

These observations certainly do not do justice to many recent attempts—and some older ones—to account for how the field experience affects the data we collect, its framing, and the range of acceptable interpretations. Many of these efforts understand this influence in psychological terms that stress subjectivity—subjective understanding—and the distortions to that subjectivity, that understanding, that arise out of the field situation in both conscious and unconscious ways (Wengle 1988). Reference is often made to transference and countertransference without regard, I have argued (1992:115–135; Hunt 1989:58; Ewing 1987), to the significant differences between a psychoanalytic session and a field encounter (Devereux 1951, 1967; Parin, Morgenthaler, and Parin-Matthèy 1966, 1971; Kracke 1987). I don't want to pursue these differences here other than to note that informants do not normally seek out the anthropologist the way patients do the psychoanalyst. They do not share the same intentions, frames of understanding, figurations of the anthropologist or psychoanalyst, and thus resistances. Usually the anthropologist and the therapist, even psychoanalytic anthropologists, do not have the same therapeutic or research goals and relations with those with whom they work. I do want to stress that there are two profoundly different understandings of transference and countertransference: in the first—the more typical in Anglo-American psychoanalysis—each party to the encounter responds, individually, to the encounter in terms of his or her biography; in the second—the French—the fact is stressed that both parties to the encounter are caught within an overriding transference relationship which governs the way in which transference and countertransference are experienced and interpreted. The emphasis here is on the intersubjective. I suggest that this second understanding of transference calls attention, analogically, to the way in which our engagements in the field—indeed, our interpretations—are governed by subsuming intersubjective, or, if you prefer, interpersonal relations, established—circularly—in the engagements themselves. Of particular significance in appraising field research are the ways we seek to escape this subsumption, this entrapment.

· · ·

I want to turn now to certain of my field encounters to illustrate some of these points, especially those which I find worthy of elaboration, and to provide grounds for the beginning of their formalization. It's a tall order, and I will not be able to do justice to it in this essay, if ever I can. I apologize for using my own experiences. I do so neither out of egoism nor as confession, but because the consideration of field encounters requires intimate understanding. Of course, I can never have the critical distance necessary for the required objectivity, as "objectivity" has been conventionally stipulated. No matter. My lack of objectivity has itself to be seen as if not an objective fact, then a social fact or, as I prefer, a fertile fact in the manner in which Virginia Woolf understood it.

My first field experience, if it can be so called, was with Haitian refugees in New York City. It was part of a project for Margaret Mead's seminar on field methods at Columbia. Aside from being prayed for by several hundred people at a Seventh-day Adventist service—I'll have more to say about prayer later—I was forced into a drinking bout in which I consumed more than half a bottle of rum. It was a test—one I failed—and I was subjected to a lot of teasing, some of it good-natured and some of it, at least as I, humiliated, saw it at the time, malicious. I bring this first, initiatory experience up because it calls attention to two important relations one may have in the field: testing and humiliating.

Though humiliation plays an important role in many field encounters, I will only call attention to it, as responses to it vary significantly from person to person and situation to situation. It does reflect plays of power in the field situation. Testing, on the other hand, requires comment. A test is a way one's informant learns something about you. (I will restrict my discussion here to the anthropologist's being tested by the people under study.) It may involve physical prowess (as when, on the Navajo reservation, my stamina was carefully monitored as I helped build a thousand-foot fence); one's reaction to a food or practice that is assumed to be unpleasant or distasteful to outsiders; one's sexual capacity (so frequently challenged by Moroccan men); one's linguistic ability (often through punning); one's recollection of what one has been told (a prayer, the explication of a passage from the Bible); or what one really believes.

Sometimes one is immediately aware of the test and at others only later, upon reflection. When I was working with the Navajo, I was told, over the course of my brief stay, a set of stories, each of which I noted but did not link until long after I had left the reservation. The first of these was simply a joke: What is a Navajo family? It's a mother, a father, a bunch of kids, and an anthropologist. The second was about a psychologist who had visited the reservation a few months before my arrival and had paid the Indians a few dollars to tell him what they saw in a set of pictures he had shown them. It was, I believe, a thematic apperception test. He never told them why he was giving them the test or what it might mean. He simply left them hanging in the anxiety that such tests produce. Though they never quite put it this way, they inferred that the psychologist had stolen something—a secret—from them, but what it was, they did not know. Toward the end of my stay, the father of the family with whom I was living told me about a man—a drifter—who had arrived in the valley penniless one freezing winter day several years earlier. One of the valley families took him in, fed him, and befriended him. He spent the winter with them, and then in the spring, when it was warm, he raped and killed one of their daughters and stole what little money they had. I was asked by several other Navajos if I had been told the story. Clearly whether and when to tell it to me had been discussed. It was only when I read through my field notes, not even the first time, that I realized that each story was about a man who could have been me. Each, I believe, was about why the Navajo had been suspicious of me. Each marked a growing confidence in me. I was passing muster.

It is the testing of what one really believes that is most difficult to grapple with and leaves its mark, as a breakdown sometimes, on the course of fieldwork and its interpretation. Working on spirit possession among the Hamadsha, a popular Sufi confraternity in Morocco, I was asked one day what I thought of the *jnun*, the spirits. It was a general question asked by two young men whom I knew slightly. I sparred with them, saying such foolish things as "I find them interesting," "I find them dangerous." Quite rightly, none of my answers satisfied Moha and Driss. Finally, Driss asked if I thought the *jnun* existed (as if he and his friend hadn't suspected my disbelief). I was caught. If I said I did, they wouldn't believe me since *nasraniyya*—Europeans, Christians—do not believe in the *jnun*. If I said no, I might offend them and—more important—raise questions about why I was there asking about the spirits when I didn't believe in them. I would call attention to a hierarchical relationship, which I had done my best to counter, between Europeans and Moroccans. (The French protectorate had ended only a few years earlier.) What was I to say? Finally I admitted that I wasn't sure whether the *jnun* existed or not, quickly adding that I was deeply impressed by their power to strike and possess. Moha, who was more expressive than Driss, looked wounded; Driss said coldly, "We didn't think you did." I realized at that moment that most of the Moroccans with whom I was working were probably asking the same question and looking for signs of my belief or disbelief. I had to acknowledge a "display" quality—"we'll show you"—in some of the exorcisms I had witnessed. This seemed particularly true of one of the exorcists, Qandish, about whom I'll have more to say later. I had to concede that my stance might well have been experienced as objectifying, symptomizing, impersonal, put on, and insincere. I had to admit that my relations with many Moroccans were governed by my desire to avoid questions of my belief. Today, I recognize that I had rendered the role of belief rather more mechanical, more starkly factual, in my writings than it probably was. After this exchange, Driss and Moha avoided me, and when we finally met, they asked why I had been avoiding them. I didn't deny it. I said that I had felt uneasy, as I was sure they did, after our last conversation. Moha looked sheepish; Driss said nothing had changed, and the two of them walked off without another word.

None of the Moroccans ever tried to convert me. They preserved a distance when it came to their beliefs and practices. Though they sometimes told me about Europeans who had been possessed and cured by their healers, I did not find their stories a challenge to my presumed lack of belief or an admonishment. They assumed that *nasraniyya* were not usually subject to possession. Their attitude came as a relief—a relief I was to appreciate all the more when I worked with whites in apartheid South Africa, many of whom were participating in a revivalist movement, and with Christian fundamentalists in the United States (Crapanzano 1985, 2000).

The South African Pentecostalists made a concerted effort to convert me, my wife, and my eleven-year-old daughter (she had little patience with their attempts). The South Africans knew I was not a believer. They had been asking me about my beliefs—religious, social, racial, and political since I first arrived. Indeed, the attitude of many of them was curiously ambivalent. I should note that I had less trouble in telling the South Africans that I was a non-believer than in telling the Moroccans that I did not believe in *jnun*. Does this have to do with my perception of their religious commitment? With the differing role of doubt in their respective faiths? With my greater familiarity with one culture than the other? With a propensity—an imperial propensity—to infantilize peoples from an exotic society? Imperial assumptions aside, infantilization of the people one works with, especially those from so-called simpler societies but others too, can be a defense against the challenges of the "exotic other"—a defense, I should add, that has received both institutional and ideological support from the way anthropology conceives of itself, the anthropologist, the informant, and the society under study. I would suggest, but cannot support this suggestion on firm grounds, that the founding and now tabooed notion of the primitive (not to mention the savage) that defined anthropology's constituted subject until rather more recently than most anthropologists like to admit is not without influence today in the constitution of the anthropologist's turf even when that turf, those subjects, come from "complex" societies. Indeed, the very characterization of such societies as complex (however complex they may in fact be) evokes its opposite. My point here is that we, as individuals at least, should delve into those foundational assumptions of our discipline which have been set aside. Though silenced, the semantic, axiological, and emotional space that they occupy is never without effect. Indeed, as any rhetorician knows, the unsaid, the silenced, the paraleptic, can be more forceful than the said. I have made the same argument for anthropology's religious and romantic roots (Crapanzano 2004).

From the start, knowing that I had just come to South Africa, the South Africans asked me, nevertheless, what I thought of their country—as an expert, when clearly I wasn't—and took stock of what I said. It was as though I was affording them an external vantage point—an escape from the intensely involuted world in which they found themselves. Yet, though I tried to be as frank as I could about what I thought about apartheid without impeding my relations with them, they did not really trust me—some throughout my stay, others at its beginning. (Obviously what I said varied with their political position, but I tried to be as consistent as possible so that their gossip would not destroy my relations.) I was carefully watched by all the members of the community which I was studying (as well as by the Special Branch). Was I spending more time with the Afrikaners or the English speakers? The conservatives or the liberals? The Pentecostalists or the Anglicans? I was often warned about people I was interviewing. These warnings were not simply small-town gossip but a way in which the villagers were trying to convince me of their particular views. Persuasion, argument, dodging, and resistance were important undercurrents of my research there. Nearly all my informants aimed at some level to turn me into an apologist abroad for white South Africa. On a personal level, it was far more complicated, but generally I would argue that in attempting to persuade me of the validity of their views on apartheid, they sought transcending moral sustenance from me, an outsider, deemed, quite irresponsibly, to have the authority of an expert. The dynamics of the field situation revealed not only their moral ambivalence toward apartheid but also the way in which their "moral entrapment" led them to configure the outsider. Clearly it was not just the "good life" that led them to perpetuate apartheid, as many outsiders simplistically maintained, but also, perversely perhaps, the way in which their moral ambivalence often produced stubborn justifications for their position. It certainly points to the moral engagement sometimes demanded of the anthropologist and the consequent moral turbulence that can easily promote simplistic judgments, including those embedded in ethnographic description and interpretation.

The whites' witnessing my daughter, my wife, and me, however required by evangelical Christianity, can also be seen in terms of the persuasion demanded by their moral ambivalence. This is not the place to discuss the relationship between the two except to note their mutual displacement. Evangelical Christianity gave them certainty—the security of the Word, the promise of salvation, and an escape from moral, political, and other pressures that besieged them. It provided them with a transcending, if not transcendent, perspective which radically changed their relationship to their—crumbling—world. (Most of the villagers involved in the revivalist movement were what I [1985:210 and passim] have called the middling middle classes: those whites—English and Afrikaans speakers—who had no international connections to turn to in case of a bloodbath [a constant fear], no skills that could easily be transported to other countries, and insufficient wealth [if they could in fact export it] that would allow them to live independently. They were literally trapped in South Africa.) In many respects their evangelical Christianity resonated allegorically with the political situation in which they found themselves. Think only of the evangelicals' focus on the apocalypse, salvation, the Second Coming of Christ (in their understanding a deus-ex-machina figure), forgiveness of past sins, and a future orientation (Crapanzano 2000).

I found myself an inadvertent player in this allegory and a central figure of the evangelicals' proselytizing. Somehow—I have never figured out exactly how—my conversion, the conversion of my family, outsiders as we were, would validate their spiritual (their otherworldly) stance and their political (their this-worldly) one. It was certainly clear that they put greater effort in trying to convert us than they did other villagers. In fact, as I was to learn, a group of women prayed for our salvation at a prayer meeting one morning, and Jesus instructed them to form three teams, each of which would be responsible for the conversion of one of us. As the fates, as God, the gods, would have it, ignorant of the meeting, I called one of the women who was responsible for my conversion for an appointment some twenty minutes after she returned home from the meeting. Their prayers had been heard. I had had a very interesting interview the week before with her—let me call her Pam—who was a Baptist and one of the leaders in the revivalist movement. I met her that afternoon. Before I could start the interview, Pam said, "Vincent, you've asked me a lot of questions. May I ask you one?" I agreed, and she asked me if I had been reborn. I said no, and she began to witness me—a witnessing that lasted more than four hours. I recorded it, but I have never dared listen to my recording. I do remember that I was caught between a barrage of questions about my spiritual life, my life in general, interrupted by quotations from the Bible, their explication with regard to my life, and prayers which I felt obliged to say *and* intense, embarrassing erotic feeling about Pam. She was in her late twenties, quite attractive, dressed like a Berkeley hippie from the sixties, who slid to the floor as she witnessed me, pressing her crotch against one of the legs of a coffee table. I never converted, though when I returned home, my wife asked me what was wrong. I had lost all color.

I have described this meeting in some detail, as I will return to it in my discussion of the dynamics of the field encounter. I have also been witnessed several times in my work with American Christian fundamentalists. They took different tacks. In one instance, a Mexican American evangelical bullied me, refusing to answer any of my questions because I could not possibly understand his answers until I was reborn. He tried to catch me up by angering me. (Certainly I was angered in other field situations that affected my research both positively and negatively. Anger, as Aristotle (1941:995–997 [Nic. Eth. Bk IV, Ch 5]] understood, can have a rhetorical function.) As I worked primarily with professors and master's students at Bible seminaries, mainly in Los Angeles, I adopted—we adopted—collegial relations, which precluded proselytizing, but underlying their patient answers to my questions was the certainty, I am sure, that I, an intellectual from New York, had been brought to them by Jesus. The book I was researching was simply his ploy. I found their knowing patience a burden. I used to joke that I was probably the only person in Los Angeles who looked forward to traffic jams as I drove from interview to interview. It gave me the time to come down.

I was reticent, non-confrontational, and hesitant to speak a language in which Jesus and the Bible predominated. I would like to say that my reticence was simply a way of avoiding being witnessed, but as secular as I am—I have had no religious training—I was moved by an awesome respect, a spiritual etiquette, that I found troubling. My first interviews were very difficult because I simply did not know the vocabulary of conservative evangelicalism. My knowledge of Protestantism was academic. I had studied the Reformation, read

Luther, Calvin, and, of course, Weber and Troeltsch. I had even studied the philosophy of history with Paul Tillich, whose "godless theology" was anathema to the evangelicals. None of this prepared me for my meetings. Even after I had achieved some mastery of their language, I found it difficult to challenge them, however delicately, in their idiom. I felt constrained by it, hypocritical.

I do remember one meeting, however, in which I offered a critique of evangelical Christianity in its own idiom. I was interviewing an elderly professor of New Testament theology who had just completed an enormous commentary on Revelation. He was a gentle, understanding man, warm but not particularly charismatic, who had had to cancel our first appointment nearly a year earlier because of an emergency heart operation. I could not help thinking that his confrontation with death had given him a wider perspective than most of his colleagues. I told him that one thing that troubled me about evangelical Christianity was its focus on Christ's Second Coming. It seemed to ignore His first coming and His message of love. The professor was startled by my observation. He remained silent for an inordinately long time. The room darkened for me; he suddenly seemed frail and very old—vulnerable. I regretted my question and was sure that I had hurt him deeply. Finally he spoke. "I've never thought of that. You may be right. I'll have to think about it." The room brightened; the professor lost his frailty, his vulnerability, and became a man of wisdom, spiritual wisdom (see Crapanzano 2006). Not only was I relieved by his answer but I felt open to him, as I believe he felt open to me. I have had a few similar experiences in the field, and far more in ordinary life. We may refer to them in Gadamer's terms as a blurring or blending of horizons, but Gadamer does not speak of the emotional impact of such moments. We may also speak of them in terms of a collapse of interlocutory distance.

.   .   .

I have touched on only a few modes of encounter in fieldwork, but I believe they are indicative of the rich texture of field experience and of some of the most important problems it poses. Obviously, there are many other emotional experiences beside being humiliated, tested, watched, persuaded, witnessed, prayed over, angered, morally engaged or entrapped, and caught within a seemingly shared subjectivity. These would include being sympathetic, loved, spurned, despised, mistrusted, feared, seduced, adopted, afraid, elated, euphoric, and saddened. They are all common experiences, and that is perhaps the most important characteristic of fieldwork: everydayness—the quotidian in the exotic.

But this everydayness has at once to be guarded, experienced as it is, and yet, if only through reflection, defamiliarized. As fieldwork progresses, the balance between the two changes. At first, at least in exotic sites, the weight is on the unfamiliar, but with time the unfamiliar becomes familiar. *And* from an anthropological perspective, this familiarity, as necessary as it is ethnographically, is not without its dangers, ethnographically, for we risk losing track of what was once salient. Personally, I have found it far more difficult to render the familiar unfamiliar and yet maintain its familiarity than to render the unfamiliar familiar and yet maintain its unfamiliarity.

We have to take into account the trajectory of fieldwork and recognize our ever-shifting perspectives and the artifice of what I have called an editorial vantage point, an orientation that is at once outside—supported not only by our research but by other pertinent, and perhaps not so pertinent, episodes in our biographies, including our training and our relationships with our mentors and colleagues—and inside—sustained by the demands of the task we have set ourselves and those made by the people we study. Embedded, as we are, in the field situation, and removed, as we are, from it, we find any perspective unstable. Throughout our fieldwork, we are constantly negotiating our respective identities and our understanding of the situation in which we find ourselves. In *Tuhami* (1980) I focused on the way Tuhami and I negotiated the field experience over months: what was relevant, how it was expressed, who we each were and how we related to each other. As I reviewed the course of our exchanges, it became clear that our understanding of what we were doing shifted, at times dramatically, as when I decided to take a more active, therapeutic role and Tuhami, to whose desire I believed I was responding, acquiesced.

Such dramatic shifts need not, of course, be initiated by the anthropologist, as my encounter with Pam demonstrates. Against my will—my conscious will at least—Pam converted our research encounter, in which I was more or less in control, into a proselytizing one in which she—under the auspices of Jesus, as she would have understood it—was in control. I was, of course, caught by surprise and trapped by my desire to maintain good relations with her and the rest of her community and perhaps by curiosity, or even temptation. Pam had broken the idiosyncratic interview conventions that we had negotiated. (My use of "we" does not necessarily imply equal weight in these negotiations.) What rendered Pam's reformulation of our relationship unusual was her directness. In my experience, most shifts are less dramatic and far less self-conscious.

I would like to draw attention to another mode of dramatically breaking conventions, one which, I believe, will enable us to better understand the power of Pam's abrupt reformulation of our encounter—our relationship. You may recall that I mentioned Qandish, one of the Moroccan curers who liked to display the power of his exorcisms, you-better-believe-it style, not only to his followers but, quite consciously, to me as well. Qandish, one of the most brilliant men I have ever met, never allowed our encounters to become conventional (except, perhaps, in their unconventionality). I never knew what to expect. At one meeting, he would not say a word; he would simply tickle me or gently beat me with a switch he sometimes carried. At another he would be so talkative that I could never get in a question. On these occasions what he said sometimes made perfect sense and at other times no sense whatsoever. At still another time he would answer my questions with what seemed to me to be irrelevances, but when I went over my notes, I discovered that he actually had answered nearly all my questions but not directly after I had asked them. Qandish was very much a trickster, and he used his tricks not only in our encounters but in his cures. He achieved his cures, I believe, by creating a semantic vertigo in his patients, thereby heightening their suggestibility. When they had reached a level of hyper-suggestibility, he would issue instructions with full clarity. Though I never succumbed to his suggestions, I was dizzied in some of our meetings. I have noted similar, though less dramatic, techniques among other curers, shamans, an eccentric white South African Anglican priest, noted for his dramatic cures of alcoholics, and political protesters who, in the style of Vergès or Sandero Luminoso, exploited the unexpected and the non-conventional.

But to return to Pam—in a way her Jesus played in her witnessing a role not dissimilar to that of the anthropologist's mentor in the ethnographic encounter. They both give at least the illusion of authorizing the interventions we perform. In a number of papers (e.g., Crapanzano 1992:72, 88–90), I have argued that negotiations of interpersonal relations and their relevant context, indeed any negotiation, makes reference to what I have called the Third. It is a function whose functionality is stable but whose definition is unstable, except in the most conventional encounters, since it shifts with the witting or usually unwitting appeals to it by all the parties to the encounter. I have suggested that this Third serves a meta-pragmatic function by authorizing various pragmatic or indexical maneuvers, which define the encounter, its relevant context, its personnel, its modes of communication, how that communication is to be taken, the appropriate etiquette, and thereby fitting interpretive strategies and their transgressive possibility. I have argued further that this function is conceptualized in terms of the law, grammar, or convention and embodied in authoritative figures like gods, totems, fathers, and even experts and their iconic materializations (images, statues, fetishes, masks, and actors who are identified with them in one way or another). I cannot do justice to my argument here, but I do want to make one important point: sometimes, particularly in explicit or even implicit hierarchical situations, the Third may be embodied—for the time being—in one of the parties to the encounter. The anthropologist? The informant? In complex encounters that have not yet become fully conventionalized through habit or repetition, like the ethnographic, the Third appealed to may be outside the encounter. Examples would be Pam's God or my mentor. In authorizing a particular framing of the situation and the conduct that follows therefrom, they may clash with each other. (Perhaps that is why I found my erotic desires so disturbing. They were not authorized.) In any case, I do not want to pit whoever my mentor was—I'm not even sure I ever had one—against God, giving our encounter a dramatically transcendent dimension it never had.

·   ·   ·

Thus far I have assumed that anthropological research is conducted, or assumed to be conducted, in ordinary times, but it can also be carried out in exceptional ones: after an earthquake, life-threatening inundations, fires, epidemics, polluting explosions, and—ever more common today—warfare, terrorism, and street violence. Though I have never done research in such exceptional circumstances, except in South Africa, I have worked with many people who have experienced and suffered from violence. Fear was an ever-present undertone of my meetings with white South Africans who talked about current riots, violent protests, and ("necessary") police brutality and near-obsessively about the likelihood of a bloodbath when the "blacks" would finally rise up en masse. (I myself witnessed riots in Cape Town; I saw how a peaceful protest was nearly turned into a violent riot by the way the military police—their name tags removed—used ferocious dogs to threaten the protesters; and I had rocks thrown at my car as I drove past a "colored" hamlet on my way home one afternoon.) I often served as an external vantage point for whites, particularly when they speculated about their violent future, as, paradoxically, they tried to draw me into their own perspective. They were trapped, and I often felt ensnared by them. This was especially true when I told them how rocks had been thrown at me. Not only did they take what seemed to me to be vicarious pleasure in my experience, but they looked at it as a sort of initiation. "Now you know what our life is like," one man said and went on to describe how he had nearly been killed when this had happened to him. Our entrapment seemed to mirror one dimension of the larger political situation. Violence seemed the only way to break out. Needless to say, I was deeply disturbed—angered—by this feeling. At the end of a day's work I would collapse on my bed, fall into a syncope, and awake twenty or thirty minutes later in time for dinner. The effect of this situation lasted for some time, until I had finished writing *Waiting*, my book on white South Africans. Did writing serve as an exorcism?

These effects were, of course, in no way comparable to those experiences of anthropologists who, like Christopher Taylor, found themselves in the midst of violence. Taylor was doing fieldwork in Rwanda in 1994 when genocidal war broke out. He wrote:

> It has taken me several years to move beyond the grief, the anger, and the bewilderment that I felt looking back on Rwanda when once again I set foot on American soil returning to the cocoon of ignorant security and complacency that most of the country and elsewhere in the West call "peace" and take as our God-given right. Yet how often our peace seems predicated on someone else's misery. (Taylor 1999:181)

Taylor was writing before September 11, 2001, and the wars in Iraq and Afghanistan, but his point is well taken even in these more turbulent times. Detecting anger—ironic anger—in his words, I wonder if he or anyone else who lived through such times can ever move beyond. It is perhaps less a question of buried traumata than the clarity of remembered violence that persists.

It is not just the actual experience of violence that has its effect on us but also descriptions of the violence that our informants have suffered. This is particularly true when they relive the experience as they tell it. For the last several years I have been working with the Harkis, those Algerians who sided with the French during the Algerian war of independence, most of whom were slaughtered immediately after the war by the Algerian population at large. The survivors were finally brought to France, where some of them were incarcerated in camps for as long as sixteen years. Listening to their stories and those of their children has been deeply disturbing, not only in terms of their descriptions of what they underwent but also in their attempt to recruit me as a political advocate. I resent their efforts to manipulate me as I empathize with them. I feel at times helpless as they relive their experiences, for there is nothing I can do to alleviate their pain. I have found that they resent emotional expressions of sympathy, as they express themselves emotionally, if only because my sympathy challenges their possession of those emotions and experiences around which many of them have constructed, if not their identity, then a partial identity. The paradoxical situation in which I find myself increases my sense of helplessness before them and all the emotions that stem from that helplessness. As I have not witnessed what they describe, my imagination is less constrained by reality. As the Greek tragedians knew, the power of unseen violence is far more effective than its depiction onstage. I have come to believe that as our explanations of violence have never been satisfactory, all we can do is describe it and its effects. This of course is harrowing.

My aim in attempting to delineate some aspects of the dynamic anatomy—or, better, physiology—of the field situation has been to call attention to the complex internal and external plays of power and desire that constitute that situation. I have focused on the internal in this chapter, but it should be recognized that the internal is encompassed by the external—that is, by the way in which anthropological research is framed and thereby situated within a particular historical moment. Among other things, we have to give critical recognition to the way in which such taken-for-granted practices and their glosses as "research" and "fieldwork" as well as their subject matter constitute themselves and are constituted in and through larger institutional structures, the etiquette those institutions demand, the emotions they condone or censure, the interpretive strategies they encourage or discourage, and the transgressions they permit and forbid. These institutional structures not only determine (within limits, to be sure, if only because of the contingent and the foibles of human freedom) the practices and their glosses and evaluations but are evoked, performed, and confirmed by these practices, glosses, and evaluations. They found a stratum of unwitting responsiveness which at this particular historical moment we situate in the human psyche and the "unconscious." The mini-dramas of fieldwork are pragmatically and, more important, meta-pragmatically constitutive. In their particularity, in the absence of fixed conventions, in the struggle to establish such conventions, to permit meaningful communication and yet to preserve the uniqueness of the ethnographic encounter, these mini-dramas are disturbing insofar as they challenge the taken-for-granted and its naturalization.

The danger is that we might lose sight of the complexity of field research, ignore the challenges it poses, and succumb to one authoritative position or another—that is, to accept uncritically whatever the fashionable ideological or theoretical paradigm is. That paradigm may afford understanding, at least an illusion of understanding. I certainly do not want to deny the possibility of understanding. It may facilitate the denial of the artifice of our position, its instability, its frailty, its situational particularity, and its contingency, promoting a social and cultural complacency that, in my view, sabotages the anthropological mission and the moral as well as the intellectual turbulence it must produce to be itself.

References

Aristotle. 1941. "Nicomachean Ethics." In R. McKeon, ed., *The Basic Works of Aristotle*, 935–1112. New York: Random House.

Bachnick, J. M. 1986. "Native Perspective of Distance and Anthropological Perspectives of Culture." *Anthropological Quarterly* 60:25–34.

Brecht, B. 1982. *Brecht on Theater: The Development of an Aesthetic*. New York: Hill and Wang.

Crapanzano, V. 1980. *Tuhami: Portrait of a Moroccan*. Chicago: University of Chicago Press.

———. 1985. *Waiting: The Whites of South Africa*. New York: Random House.

———. 1990. "Afterword." In M. Manganaro, ed., *Modernist Anthropology: From Fieldwork to Text*, 300–308. Princeton, NJ: Princeton University Press.

———. 1992. *Hermes' Dilemma and Hamlet's Desire: On the Epistemology of Interpretation*. Cambridge, MA: Harvard University Press.

———. 1994. "Kevin: On the Transfer of Emotion." *American Anthropologist* 96 (4): 866–885.

———. 2000. *Serving the Word: Literalism in America from the Pulpit to the Bench*. New York: New Press.

———. 2004. *Imaginative Horizons: An Essay in Literary Philosophical Anthropology*. Chicago: University of Chicago Press.

———. 2006. "The Scene." *Theoretical Anthropology* 6 (4): 27–45.

Danforth, L. 1989. *Firewalking and Religious Healing: The Anastenaria of Greece and the American Firewalking Movement*. Princeton, NJ: Princeton University Press.

Derrida, J. 1976. *Of Grammatology*. Trans. Gayatri Spivak. Baltimore: Johns Hopkins University Press.

Devereux, G. 1967. *From Anxiety to Method in the Behavioral Sciences*. The Hague: Mouton.

———. 1969. *Reality and Dream: Psychotherapy of a Plains Indian*. New York: New York University Press.

Ewing, K. P. 1987. "Clinical Psychoanalysis as an Ethnographic Tool." *Ethos* 15 (1): 16–33.

Gadamer, Hans-Georg. 1975. *Truth and Method*. New York: Crossroad.

Geertz, C. 1968. *Islam Observed: Religious Development in Morocco and Indonesia*. New Haven, CT: Yale University Press.

Heidegger, M. 1967. *Being and Time*. Trans. J. Macquarrie and E. Robinson. Oxford: Blackwell.

Kracke, W. 1987. "Encounters with Other Cultures: Psychological and Epistemological Aspects." *Ethos* 15 (1): 58–82.

Lévi-Strauss, C. 1984. *Tristes Tropiques*. Trans. J. and D. Weightman. New York: Atheneum.

Milbank, J. 1990. *Theology and Social Theory: Beyond Secular Reason*. Oxford: Blackwell.

Parin, P., F. Morgenthaler, and G. Parin-Matthèy. 1966. *Les blancs pensent trop: 13 entretiens psychanalytiques avec les Dogon*. Paris: Payot.

———. 1971. *Fürchte deine Nächsten wie dich selbst: Psychoanalyse und Gesellschaft am Modell der Agni in Westafrika*. Frankfurt am Main: Suhrkamp.

Plato. 1987. *Phaedrus*. Trans. R. Hackforth. Cambridge: Cambridge University Press.

Robbins, Joel. 2006. "Anthropology and Theology: An Awkward Relationship?" *Anthropological Quarterly* 79 (2): 285–294.

Rosenberg, D. V. 1990. "Language in the Discourse of the Emotions." In C. Lutz and L. Abu-Lughod, eds., *Language and the Politics of Emotion*, 162–185. Cambridge: Cambridge University Press.

Shklovsky, V. 1992. "Art as Technique." In H. Adams, ed., *Critical Theory since Plato*, 751–759. Rev. ed., Fort Worth: Harcourt Brace Jovanovich.

Taylor, C. C. 1999. *Sacrifice as Terror: The Rwandan Genocide of 1994*. New York: Oxford University Press.

Traimond, Bernard. 2008. *L'anthropologie à l'époque de l'enregistreur de paroles*. Bordeaux: William Blake and Co./Art and Arts.

Wengle, J. L. 1988. *Ethnographers in the Field: The Psychology of Research*. Tuscaloosa: University of Alabama Press.

3 Disorientation, Dissonance, and Altered Perception in the Field

James Davies

Empiricism must neither admit into its constructions any element that is not directly experienced, nor exclude from them any element that is directly experienced.

William James

THE CONDITIONS OF FIELDWORK, wherever this work may occur and whatever these conditions may constitute, are invariably different from those we enjoy or endure in our most customary surroundings. As we progressively adapt to the unfamiliar context of the field, the conventional structures that directed our lives increasingly exert by their growing distance a more remote influence. Once these familiar bindings are somewhat loosened, not only are new aspects of our emotional and imaginal lives freed for expression, but our practical and emotional adjustment to the novel site often produces new personal affects that are not immediately familiar to us. Our slow integration into the field, in other words, by either loosening existing ties or forcing new adaptations, commonly generates *new states and ways of being* significant to the work we undertake.[1]

While such reflections will interest the psychologist concerned with processes of human adaptation, when considered in the context of anthropology they become immediately relevant to the realm of methodology. For in a discipline where immersion in the field is essential to the generation of our disciplinary knowledge, we must enquire how far the human consequences of such immersion affect these very processes of production. And it is precisely this enquiry which I shall undertake in this current chapter.

By broaching this consideration we at once confront many difficult questions. Firstly, if the sum total of each fieldworker's different history, personal ability, and prior experience of cultural difference renders his or her field experience somewhat idiosyncratic, is a study aiming to identify general field experiences (albeit within wide parameters) in any way possible? Furthermore, if such commonalities can be discovered, in what way can they be said to count as data relevant to anthropological understanding?

While exploring such questions would doubtless require a study far more comprehensive than current space allows, this will not discourage my attempt to advance at least some preliminary propositions. These will follow from my analysis of one "anomalous" field experience, which, aside from its evident particularity, I shall argue contains many affective experiences that are widely encountered in fieldwork. Insofar as we neglect these common features and thus negate their epistemological relevance, I shall conclude, our understanding of participant observation is to that extent impaired.

Immersion

To start, it is widely agreed that becoming immersed in the field is at the heart of anthropological enquiry, so much so that this process has attracted many names. To recall a few, Edward Evans-Pritchard (1973:4) long ago called it "adjustment transference"—the process of coming to live the symbolic and practical life of the people among whom one conducts research, insofar as it is possible to do so. It was implied in Clifford Geertz's (1973) concept of "social arrival"; one arrives through gradually assimilating a state of mind and a set of behaviours congruent with those of the hosts. Glen Bowman (1999) more recently referred to it as "altering"—namely, the process of embodying new ways of perceiving and responding to the distinctive events of another community. And finally, Kirsten Hastrup (1995) spoke of "incorporation"—one learns culture through a process of gradual familiarisation in practice.

While these authors might differ in their views about the nature of what the fieldworker apprehends (i.e., a distinct "other" or an "intersubjective" and/or "co-created" space), and while there is disagreement about the means of apprehension (through participation, embodiment, or more distanced observation), there is an identifiable consensus on at least two points: firstly, that immersion is never total or immediate but always an approximation that transpires gradually; and secondly, that one's adaptation to, or emerging relationship with, the studied community, invariably involves some sort of ethical, cognitive, or emotional transformation, no matter how perfunctory or short-lived. In other words, fieldwork affects the very instrument, the anthropologist, through which data is gathered and represented—a fact obliging a serious phenomenology of the subjective conditions of the field.

The Case Study

To illustrate the potential of this argument I would like to provide a case study concerning one anthropologist's experience during fieldwork in Nepal. I shall then tease out three themes for extended discussion.

> I had been living in the village for some time; over my weeks there I had integrated well into the community, so much so that on occasion my concept of home often felt shadowy, oddly inaccessible. This sense that I was moving within myself, almost unimpeded, from a known cultural space (home) into this unfamiliar terrain, was at times strong, almost ominous—I think now in retrospect that it was this sense which made me fertile for the experience that followed.
>
> It was on the night of a day spent visiting a local Hindu burial ground that I awoke to a sudden and startling feeling of disorientation. Describing this feeling now, I would say that it was as if I stood in a no-man's-land between two locations—the one I had left behind and the one I was slowly entering. From the position of that threshold I felt a terrible doubt concerning not merely the intellectual but the experiential status of my own sociocultural world, a doubt which threw me into a disturbing panic. The more I gazed at home from this new position, the more fabricated and accidental it appeared. I felt as if I were looking at my own world through the wrong end of a telescope—how little, insignificant, arbitrary it looked, how vain in all its claims of certainty and correctness. In proportion to the growing sense of estrangement my panic grew, and soon I found myself slightly trembling. I think it was at the peak of my distress that I realised I must do something decisive. I remember almost instinctively grasping my rucksack and emptying its contents out onto the floor, groping for objects of familiarity—objects, no matter how mundane, that might bring familiar associations with them. Along with this I fought hard to conjure recognisable images of my friends and family, of places, memories of my fiancée, etc. I remember sitting on my bed and repeating my name over and over, for example. This all happened very spontaneously, and after a while, and to my relief, these activities started to have a soothing effect. It is only in retrospect that I realised that these odd manoeuvres served to counter my disorientation. These apparently simple acts, and these simple objects around me, seemed to reaffirm the authority of my usual reality and thus to pull me back from the intensity of that threshold from where everything was doubted.

The first question I would like to pose is whether anything that occurred to this researcher can inform us about fieldwork more widely. Here we enter the controversy about whether we can generalise from individual experience—a question that occupied our informant for some time after his leaving the field: was his experience a prototypical happening peculiar to himself, or rather a more personalised (if not intensified) version of something more generally encountered? One way to address this question is to set down his experience within the context of other fieldwork accounts, with the aim of discerning any comparable features. This I shall now do with respect to three salient aspects of his account—firstly, his experience of disorientation; secondly, the manner in which he managed his disorientation; and finally, his altered perception in the field which among other things made him doubt the authority and meaning of home.

It is well known that early anthropologists warned of the disintegrating effects of fieldwork. Evans-Pritchard (1973) spoke of the "bewilderment and despair" that often attends the initial phase of integration, while Margaret Mead (1959) warned the fieldworker not to drown in the powerful sea of new impressions. Similarly, Hortense Powdermaker (1966), while asserting that the pendulum swing of "moving in and moving out of cultures" is essential for anthropological knowing, cautioned that when on the swing away, one could suffer debilitating isolation and on the swing towards, one could lose one's identity and sense of orientation—as she felt happened to her in the Lesu dance. Other authors have elaborated more graphically on the difficulties of immersion. Dorinne Kondo, in her study of the fieldworker's self, stated: "Though participation and rapport are highly laudable goals for the anthropologist in the field, in my case participation to the point of identification led also to a disturbing disorientation, and uncertainty as to which role I was playing"; she experienced this disorientation as "a sense of vertigo, and as a fear of Otherness—in the self" (Kondo 1984:79 in Hastrup 1995:158). Paul Rabinow, reflecting on his fieldwork experience in Morocco, felt his immersion as a series of incremental movements (Rabinow 1977:154). Some moves towards understanding happened imperceptibly and effortlessly. Others occurred with his full awareness, and were experienced as a kind of "rupture." Rabinow speaks of one such rupture when his informant became offended by Rabinow's desire to be alone—Rabinow's sudden understanding of the gulf between them made him experience the feeling "of being on the edge of an abyss and a rush of vertigo" (Rabinow 1977:114).

In the case study set down above we observe an experience of disorientation quite similar to those just described. What seems to separate all these experiences, in other words, is not their differing content but the different factors that generated them: for one it was a sudden awareness of the Other's fundamental difference; for another it was being overwhelmed by this difference to the extent that her normal sense of self became shadowy and unreal; for yet another it was the assimilation of this difference, the partial conversion, so to speak, to the temper and tone of the new phenomenal world. All these instances of disorientation were experienced as though one's centre of gravity had become unanchored from its "moorings"—these moorings being the internalised cultural values, habits, cognitive and emotional dispositions and proclivities that we embody during our socialisation, and that are thus endowed with an aura of factuality and permanence—moorings which thus habitually order and orient our lives in ways that stabilise us emotionally and intellectually. So far as such moorings help order the flux and flow of unruly experience, disorientation describes the partial or sudden collapse of them before the overwhelming presence of difference, a collapse allowing a sea of new impressions to sweep away, no matter how momentarily, the stability that the moorings afforded.

Along with the disorientation that can visit the fieldworker, we should not be surprised to find evidence of spontaneous attempts to manage it. In the case of our informant, his disorientation, we recall, was tempered by his unplanned use of familiar objects and memories to assert his habitual identity, to "bring him back," so to speak, from that awful threshold where the authority of his customary life was doubted. It is in this sense that defensive/reparative manoeuvres were used to assert the existing structures of his internal life. Such attempts to assert steadiness in times of disintegration I shall call *strategies of withdrawal*—strategies employed to mitigate the disorientation which can often attend any radical re-orientation to unfamiliar instrumental and symbolic worlds.

Strategies of Withdrawal

That fieldworkers have always sought solace from disorienting conditions is clear from reading personal fieldwork accounts. Describing her emotional reactions to her fieldwork experience in Africa, for example, Elenore Bowen stated, "It was only in the privacy of my hut that I could be my real self. Publicly, I lived in the midst of a noisy and alien life. If I wanted familiar music, I had to sing it to myself. If I wanted counsel from my own people, I had to turn to books. I could escape my cultural isolation only by being alone for a while every day with my books and my thoughts. It was one means of hanging on to myself, of regaining my balance, of keeping my purpose in being out there before me" (Bowen 1954:162).

Another illustration of withdrawal is found in Rosalie Wax's wartime study of Japanese Americans, which documents the considerable anxiety she felt during the first phase of fieldwork. She says, "At the conclusion of the first month of work I had obtained very little data, and I was discouraged, bewildered and obsessed by a sense of failure." It seemed that her motives were under question by the Japanese Americans whom she had come to study. In trying to maintain her identity as an "observer of sociological phenomena" in the face of her hosts' resistance, she eventually reached a point of crisis during which she spent "days alternately crying or writing letters to relatives and academic friends" (Wax 1957:67). Finally she succumbed to an urge to eat voraciously and in three months gained thirty pounds.

Robert Winthrop's study of graduate fieldworkers found that in times of stress they unknowingly used many coping devices—one of which, as in Wax's case, was to turn to the consumption of comfort foods. Another was to spend more time than necessary dictating into tape recorders or typing up field notes; a further strategy involved seeking out places of privacy even if this meant leaving the field site for periods to access local communication systems.

In Paul Rabinow's case, he endured times of difficulty by contemplating the loving *communitas* to which he would return (Rabinow 1977:148). Margaret Mead consoled herself with her relentless occupation of writing home. Rosemary Firth found relief in writing in her diary, which she called "a lifeline, or a checking point to measure changes in myself. . . . Mine was used as an emotional outlet for an individual subjected to disorientating changes in his personal and social world" (Firth 1972:15 in Wengle 1988:24). In all these cases, these reparative strategies offered varying degrees of emotional respite. And while the objects used to manage and mitigate disorientation were various, the expressions of disorientation prompting this usage share common features.

So far we have identified only those strategies of withdrawal which make use of material objects (diaries, letters, books, familiar foods, etc.). These are easier to identify than what we might call "non-material strategies," which can include "cognitive" forms of withdrawal. Cognitive strategies, for instance, are the kinds of intellectual tricks we play on ourselves to help steady the self, but because of the non-material forms they take they are more difficult to recognise. However, no matter how comparatively veiled they may be, they can also, like the more conspicuous strategies, offer stabilising antidotes to disorientation. Take, for instance, the common device of believing precipitously that we have grasped the other's worldview, that in "very little time" we have surprisingly "cracked the code." Often these claims of early epiphany are accepted without due recognition that moments of premature knowing, when viewed in the light of the anxiety that "not-knowing" can evoke, may be less early epiphanies than in fact timely remedies: formulations hastily contrived to either mitigate the anxiety of being subject to a context that we do not fully understand or ward off the disorientation that truly giving ourselves over to difference can evoke. In cases where such formulations are used defensively it is clear that they spring from the wrong impulse—i.e., the need to steady the self. Furthermore, by being used to fend off painful disorientation they can quickly come to perform a self-protective function and thus become hard to disavow, impairing the ability to advance new theoretical formulations in the light of fresh observations.

Whether our strategies of withdrawal are employed via cognitive, material, or imaginal means, they are always of methodological significance insofar as they influence the nature of our contact with the community studied and the degree to which we are able to relate, reach out, and fully immerse ourselves. And as the nature of our contact *with* the community largely determines what we can *know* about the community (e.g., detachment and immersion each reveal different kinds of facts), anything influencing this process of contact must fall within the realm of our methodological concerns.

This more radical empirical take on withdrawal strategies has not been acknowledged in the numerous criticisms of early anthropological detachment. Commentators such as Clifford Geertz were prone to locate the source of anthropologists' distancing in their servility to modernist method and theory, and from this standpoint thereby overlooked the psychological motives for detachment. Unlike most anthropologists today, many early anthropologists could not familiarise themselves with the world they were about to enter by the previous study of existing ethnography—a lack of preparation possibly making their initial encounters more psychologically difficult.

Furthermore, unlike later researchers, our forebears did not have ready access to modern devices of withdrawal—their immersion could not be tempered by a trip to the local town with its Internet and phone connections, nor could it be eased by the knowledge during difficult times that in a couple of days they could always be flying home. These reflections might ask us to modify our current understanding of the infamous veranda,[2] which, rather than simply expressing a modernist penchant, might also have served unbeknownst to the users as a reparative or stabilising fieldwork device.

Be that as it may, what concerns us is not that anthropologists perform such strategies in the field, and that these strategies are various and change over time, but that they are often performed *spontaneously, without either the full recognition of the fieldworker or a full appreciation of their methodological implications*—as was the case with our informant who could not make sense of his actions till he was long out of the field. While exercising withdrawal, as Michael Jackson (1989) has rightly said, can doubtless bolster the self in testing periods, further questions arise as to whether withdrawal, if applied unwittingly or excessively, can inhibit the flow of immersion essential to familiarisation and anthropological knowing. After all, sustained withdrawal is the very antithesis of sustained immersion, both antitheses colouring how and what can be empirically known. It is only by making explicit the why, how, and implications of withdrawal that fieldworkers will be better equipped not only to monitor and modify their experiential processes when in the field but also to understand the methodological sacrifices and benefits that any applied modifications may entail.

Mourning and Loss

When considering our opening case study in the light of these reflections, notwithstanding its remaining specificity, our informant's disorientation and withdrawal no longer appear quite so anomalous. With this said, I would now like to analyse the third theme of his account, a theme which we will also notice has its documented precedents. The theme we shall consider is his momentary doubt and repudiation of home as "vain in all its claims of certainty and correctness." This included his viewing the associated activities of home, such as his academic and routine pursuits, as at that point also uncharacteristically devoid of meaning and worth.

Many fieldwork accounts contain similar confessions of doubt erupting during fieldwork—especially concerning the work one is doing. John Wengle, who raised this point, quotes Malinowski's confession in his diary that in difficult times he was prone to view "the life of natives as utterly devoid of interest or importance, something as remote from [me] as the life of a dog" (Malinowski 1967:167, cited in Wengle 1988:xix). Here Malinowski articulated a moment of uncharacteristic repugnance for the endeavour of social research. Lévi-Strauss, an anthropologist of comparable dedication, also succumbed to bouts of futility when in Amazonia. In *Tristes Tropiques* he generalised this sense in the following terms: "As he practices his profession the anthropologist is consumed by doubts: has he really abandoned his native setting, his friends, and his way of life, spent such considerable amounts of money and energy, and endangered his health for the sole purpose of making his presence acceptable to a score or two of miserable creatures doomed to early extinction" (Lévi-Strauss 1963:167). A similar misgiving also pierced Hortense Powdermaker's dedication at the beginning of her fieldwork among the Lesu; she stated: "Why am I here, I asked myself repeatedly . . . what am I doing at the edge of the world. . . . There seemed to be no adequate reason: anthropology, curiosity, career—all seemed totally unimportant" (Powdermaker 1966:53).

The frequency with which these visitations occur should give us pause for thought. While we could certainly advance many hypotheses as to their arrival, I would like for a moment to consider these occurrences in the light of the anthropologist Walter Sangree's reflections. He suggested that the loss of friends, of family, and of clear identity markers can activate in fieldworkers certain feelings typically experienced by people undergoing processes of separation or bereavement—to illustrate his thesis he cites aspects of mourning, such as depression, longing, and preoccupation in fantasy with what has been lost, as also operative in the fieldworker. One integral feature of mourning which Sangree underplays, however, is the emergence of ambivalence towards the lost object or objects. For instance, we can all recall those young lovers whose unbending admiration for the beloved is only broken once the tie has been cut. It is as if with such severance the beautiful veil that once draped the imperfect reality is suddenly torn off. With the underside now exposed, a reevaluation (often critical) of the lost person begins. This birth of disenchantment was early identified by Freud, and later by psychologists such as John Bowlby, as integral to the process of separation—the emerging criticism being thought to encourage the detachment necessary for reattachment to a new person or "object" of regard. To put it differently, the emerging criticism helps to free the individual to pursue new connections, affiliations, and identifications.

If the mourning analogy holds any currency, then the disenchantment with and criticism of home and its associated activities that immersion can entail might help us better understand not only Malinowski's, Lévi-Strauss', and Powdermaker's temporary doubt towards what they were doing but also what appeared to them to be their irrational anger towards the scene into which they were integrating—a scene, it must be remembered, that called them from the comfort and security of familiar pursuits. Furthermore, another point, which Sangree overlooks, is that separation anxiety occurs both in the face of absence or loss and in the face of overwhelming presence.[3] Overwhelming presence in this sense creates a de facto sense of absence. But what is this absence? Jackson (1998) in his *Minima Ethnographica* suggests that it is the profound sense that one is inadequate to this confrontation, that one is unable to bear it or to know what to make of it. Here another level of complexity is added to the experience of mourning. Certainly mourning can issue from the loss of familiar persons and routines, but it can also arise from a prospective alteration to what the confrontation demands: "I don't want to do this," such a species of mourning declares.[4] Jackson writes:

> It is not a matter of mourning something absent but of cringing in the shadow of an incomprehensible presence. You see this clearly in the New Guinea high-landers' reactions . . . [to their first contact with whites]. People go into mourning, though it is not the ancestral dead they mourn but the living people who were absent and have returned. The experience is too much to take. Staggered by the technological mastery that the strangers have at their command, people feel they have lost control over their own destiny. But this sense of loss is born of an unbearable discovery: the world is infinitely vaster and far more complex than one thought (Jackson 1998:117–118).

All culture contact (whether for the contacting or the contacted) evokes both a retrograde imagining—the attempt to retrieve something lost—and a projective imagining—the sense that one must enter this new world and acquire what is needed to survive within it. Here the person or fieldworker is confronted with something which necessitates a response. In this case loss becomes a secondary effect, a consequence of there being something before you—too much to assimilate and transcend.

Such retrograde and prospective experiences mark many occasions of first contact, and can rejoin anthropologists at the point when they return home. This may happen insofar as fieldwork, through forcing new adaptations and changes to ourselves, alters us in ways that make our reintegration somewhat bumpy. Again the biographical literature is replete with descriptions concerning the difficulties of reintegration, of returning to a mould which one no longer seems to fit. Paul Rabinow, upon his return to New York, found the city and his friends that were once so familiar now impenetrable to him: "The maze of slightly blurred nuance, that feeling of barely grasped meanings which had been my constant companion in Morocco overtook me once again. But now I was home" (Rabinow 1977:148). Giovanna Bacchiddu's return was also marked by intense displacement; she says, "I did not know who I was, where I was, in what language I was organising my confused thoughts. . . . I felt I had lost myself in a world that did not belong to me, and I was unable to find my old self" (Bacchiddu 2004:5). William Borchert, who had lived for many years in China, analysed his difficulty of reintegration as one of "reinvesting his previous relationships and identity with a sense of reality, given the radical change in identity he had undergone" (Kracke 1987:59).

For the returning anthropologist, once-taken-for-granted aspects of home can appear to be mere "situational adjustment"—that is, less natural facts than familiar facts (Meintel 1973:52). It seems that familiarisation with an additional yet equally viable set of cultural dispositions inevitably challenges previous conceptions of self and, by implication, the social world which sponsored them (Meintel 1973:53). Robert Bellah emphasises the same point in the following words:

> In legend the hero returns home and lives happily ever after. In [anthropology] . . . the hero returns to an even deeper doubt about the very meaning and existence of home than he had before he set out. Perhaps that tells us that the journeys we know we must go farther and deeper than any that have gone before. (Bellah, quoted in Rabinow 1977:xiii)

The conflict between self and environment, which may be experienced when first entering the field or, as we have seen, when returning home, let me call here *dissonance*. Dissonance occurs when external and internal conditions and structures no longer accord. Of course, dissonance may be experienced as uncomfortable, liberating, vexing, etc., depending upon the conditions to which one is adjusting—a fact, as an aside, which modern tourist companies know only too well. By seeking to re-create or improve the conditions of home abroad, they do all they can to banish (uncomfortable) dissonance from their clients' experience: Of new experiences, only the "improved" or pleasant ones are preferred—those fostered by being served, waited on, massaged, smiled at, danced for, catered for, and so on. They also aspire to provide familiar foods, room furnishings, and media, in their effort to expunge any stray incursions of foreignness which can place uncomfortable demands upon the visitor. In short, these companies *circumscribe* experience—we think here of tour buses, cordoned beaches, secured hotels, and tour guides who parry raw confrontations of culture with their picturesque and "entertaining" renditions. By vetting experience, they can prevent (deflect) the emergence of difficult dissonance between internalised disposition and external circumstance. Resorts thus ensure that geographical traveling and psychological journeying are not coterminous—or if they are, that the first at least does not beget any uncomfortable species of the latter. All these devices make good economic sense to companies. By keeping things light, they ensure a continued demand.

This purification of unpalatable experience is not possible for anthropologists. They reside in the field unprotected and subject to whatever chance thrusts upon them. Their dissonance is not managed by a corporate other, but by their private and spontaneous selves. They alone are responsible for regulating immersion, or the speed with which they incorporate new modes of perception. And whatever the distance traversed to reach the field, the same dilemma confronts them—for as soon as concepts of "home" and "field" are understood in psychological rather than geographical terms, "home" and "field" become wherever one experiences them to be, irrespective of their physical location. Home is the psychologically habitual, but what is habitual can be easily dislodged as the customary and supporting social conditions are removed.

If I have so far spoken of immersion only in terms of its management (withdrawal) and two of its possible effects (disorientation and loss), let me now briefly consider the process of altered perception that accompanies familiarisation—a process which, while helping to diminish dissonance in the field, can set up the conditions for reverse dissonance at reintegration. To concretise these claims, let us turn to an extract from Kirsten Hastrup's (1995) *A Passage to Anthropology*—which expertly captures the change in perception to which I am abstractly referring.

Perception

To paraphrase her, as part of her participant observation she assumed the role of milkmaid and shepherdess, tending thirty cows. Becoming established in her new identity, she soon came to know her flock very well. Some cows were nice, others friendly, but there was one cow in particular that always annoyed her—once this cow occasioned a sprained thumb, which, as she said, was very inconvenient for a milkmaid. She felt there was a mutual dislike between them:

> After six months I left the farm to go elsewhere, but also to return six months later. On my return I immediately found my old place in the cowshed and went from cow to cow to recall their names. In front of my old enemy I sensed the

well-known feeling of anger and murmured: "So there you still are, you silly old beast." Next morning, when the farmer and I went into the cowshed to do the morning milking, the beast was lying dead on the floor, for no apparent reason, I was deeply shocked, because I knew that in previous times such occurrences had brought witches to the stake.

The point of this tale is not only to show how the cow recognised me as "of the Icelandic world" so full of magic and witchcraft, but that even I, the anthropologist disguised as a milkmaid, was prepared to take responsibility for the death of the cow. I had internalised an experiential space where time was another and where the usual patterns of causality were suspended. While undoubtedly in some sense a space of my own creation, the experience was real— and of the kind that makes ethnographers doubt self-evidences.

My own implicit allegation of witchcraft (as against myself) was not a question of belief, and far less of superstition. It was an expression of my experiencing a distinct reality of which I was temporarily part, and which once and for all taught me that we cannot separate materiality and meaning. They are simultaneities in the world in which we live, and as such they write themselves onto the ethnographer who temporarily shares the world of others. (Hastrup 1995:18–19)

A further example of such "internalisation of experiential space," and how this incorporation affects one's perceptual field, was offered by the following researcher upon return from fieldwork in the tsunami-struck region of eastern Sri Lanka. He had been living in the area for some months when he had the following dream:

I was standing alone upon a beautiful beach, looking out across the sandy expanse, when there in the far distance I noticed a solitary figure. I remained motionless as it approached nearer and nearer till at last he stood about two feet from me. He was an old monk swathed in the most beautiful golden shawl. For some time he remained motionless, staring at me with an intoxicating serenity. I stood completely captivated till at once his face contorted into an expression of horrid dread—pointing to something right behind me he suddenly cried "look out"! At this I woke with a start, swirled on my bed to find there at my window a dark figure trying to clamber into my room. Instinctively I shouted out (I can't remember what), but something obviously sufficient to frighten the startled figure away.

What is significant about this fieldworker's dream was the imprint it left upon him while still in the field. As he told me, "I would usually submit an event like this to relentless rational scrutiny, but there in the deeps of Sri Lanka, surrounded by my Buddhist hosts, I could not help believe, as they undoubtedly believed, that I had been somehow warned." As with Hastrup's experience of the cow's death, this young researcher in spite of his usual scepticism adopted his hosts' interpretation of the event. The environment itself coaxed our unbeliever into a consideration of portents, their reality, and their worth. "It was only once I had returned home," he later reported, "that my scepticism returned, and so I reviewed the event with a noncommittal, and perhaps less enjoyable, nonchalance."

In both situations the conditions of the field had a profound impact upon the anthropologist's perceptual apparatus. In both, incredulity capitulated to unintended belief, and in both this shift was conditional upon each of them having first reached a substantial degree of immersion. The perceptual shift made each of them consider possibilities they would not usually have entertained, and yet both felt that this shift was nevertheless advantageous, as it endowed them with what they experienced as a deeper experiential appreciation for their hosts' worldview.[5]

Many theories of personality are based on the idea that our behaviours and attitudes are changed as a result of changing perception (Sanders 2006:22), theories which thus implicitly privilege the mind over the body. With fieldwork it seems the causal arrow is reversed, or at least can point in both directions: while new perceptions can alter our affective and somatic states, sincere embodiment of a novel world of meanings and practices can also alter our total perceptual apparatus, stimulating new experiences and concomitant coping devices pertinent to the work we do. In this sense I extend Michael Lambek's (1998) insights about the incommensurability of mind/body distinctions, distinctions which remain universally distinguishable in thought but whose particular usage is revealed only through analysing specific cultural practices. When we analyse the particular cultural practice of fieldwork we notice that it involves a process by which perception alters soma and soma alters perception. This two-way process, which can result in changes to both mind and body, could thus be considered as transpiring within the mid-stage of a trinity of stages integral to anthropological work—being situated between first contact, on the one hand, and the act of sociocultural representation on the other.

Let me now summarise in diagrammatical, and thus in the most schematic, language the various points I have advanced concerning this mid-stage of fieldwork:

Familiar Internal Structures
(Existing and embodied values, habits, cognitive and emotional dispositions, and proclivities)

First Contact and Dissonance
(Placing familiar internal structures under strain—creating occasional disorientation due to the dissonance between external and internal conditions)

Reactions to Strain, Dissonance, and/or Disorientation
Can Produce:

⇓

Withdrawal	Oscillation	Complete Immersion	Mourning	Altered Perception
⇓	⇓	⇓	⇓	⇓
In extreme cases withdrawal, while stemming disorientation, can compromise the immersion essential for anthropological knowing. Withdrawal strategies can use material and non-material means.	Anthropologists must be aware of their internal responses to the conditions of the field and be able to monitor these responses to better navigate the balance between participation and observation.	Complete immersion causes difficulty in reaching the observatory pole of fieldwork. It is to be balanced by periods of detachment, but not to the extent that the participatory pole is alternatively compromised.	Mourning allows us to partially separate from existing "objects" and form new connections, identifications, and affiliations. But it also may set up difficult responses to the research activity— loss of interest, meaning, or inspiration.	This phenomenon, while allowing deeper apprehension of the others' worldview, can also set up reverse dissonance upon the return home (which in turn may have implications for writing up—in what way do the psychological consequences of returning somehow leave their imprint upon the written account?).

Textbook discussions of participant observation often pass only cursorily over the anthropologist's emotions in the field—and say little or nothing about associated issues of intense experiences and their bearing upon methods. This omission is regrettable, for immersion, as we know, often evokes powerful subjective reactions which can either enable or inhibit the understanding that it aims to generate. Insofar as this is true, charting these reactions can contribute to the task of further understanding the processes of anthropological knowledge construction. If we accept this claim, we must also embrace the many difficult problems it raises. The first concerns how far psychology can assist our understanding, bearing in mind that our psychologies always presuppose concepts of the person which are to some extent situational. How might we appropriate insights from systems for which there remains a varied, and some would say warranted, scepticism? Furthermore, if we do interpret field experiences in terms of a favoured psychology, is there a danger that when in the field we will create ourselves in its image rather than in the image of the person embodied by our hosts? It is certain that we should never go so far. Fieldwork, we believe, is not only a subjective confession. Yet on the other hand, we intuit that to some extent good fieldwork is a psychological achievement—and thus can presumably benefit from a selected application of psychological concepts. Perhaps such concepts should be approached with caution, played with rather than slavishly adopted, but above all considered sparingly (i.e., before entering the field or during times of necessity)—an approach that would safeguard against, at the very least, our becoming more interested in our internal responses than in the scene at hand.

Another problem is that of specificity. If the conditions of the field are unique to each fieldworker, then so too is that fieldworker's "reality-as-experienced"; as mentioned earlier, the sum total of each individual's personal history, ability, and prior experience of cultural difference will undoubtedly affect that person's perceptions in the moment. This observation problematises our final question: can any insights gathered by such a phenomenology inform our general methodology? Or should we attain our knowledge from anecdotal accounts that enlighten students informally? Indeed, there is no substitute for reading personalised accounts—these contain nuances and singularities that any systematic study would be hard-pressed to accommodate. And yet such informal reading does suggest that certain experiences follow identifiable contours, and so from the particular case we tease out insights of more general pertinence. This I have attempted to illustrate by way of discussing four persistent correlates of fieldwork (disorientation, withdrawal, doubt, and altered perception), suggesting that these are not isolated happenings, but within wide parameters visit fieldwork with regularity. In fact, many of the experiences usually collated under the generic "culture shock" often contain some or all of the correlates discussed above. Where this paper goes beyond classic acknowledgements of culture shock is by identifying those aspects of the experience unconsidered in previous work, such as dissonance, altered perception, and the tendency to withdraw, and by further tracing their methodological implications. That we could identify a number of other common experiences evoked by immersion in the field—others which will also have their attendant methodological implications—should less serve to overwhelm researchers than to inspire a deeper appreciation of the relevance of these phenomena for the continued development of fieldwork methodology.

In the end, this chapter must be viewed as a preliminary attempt to delineate certain responses that regularly attend processes of immersion. These responses, it must be said, are by no means universally experienced (only commonly experienced—especially among new researchers), and are by no means exhaustively described above (we may all think of responses that I have excluded). But these caveats do not forbid us from regarding these experiences as more or less general phenomena, occurring in what we have called the "spaces between," the spaces I have considered here being those between "person and environment" and between "first contact and writing up." The emotional responses that these relations can evoke (e.g., dissonance, disorientation, altered perception, reverse dissonance) are made methodologically relevant if only we depart from the traditional empirical scheme and employ a radical empirical epistemology—an approach by which their particular pertinence may be brought into fuller relief.

References

Bacchiddu, G. 2004. "Stepping between Different Worlds: Reflection before, during, and after Fieldwork." *Anthropology Matters Journal* 6 (2): 1–9.

Bowen, E. S. 1954. *Return to Laughter*. New York: Harper and Brothers.

Bowman, G. 1999. "Radical Empiricism: Anthropological Fieldwork after Psychoanalysis and the *Année Sociologique*." In M. L. Angerer and H. Krips, eds., *Freud and Culture Now*, 79–107. Vienna: Viennese Bohlau Verlag.

Evans-Pritchard, E. E. 1973. "Some Reminiscences and Reflections on Fieldwork." *Journal of the Anthropological Society of Oxford* 4:1–12.

Geertz, C. 1973. *The Interpretation of Cultures*. New York: Basic Books.

Hastrup. K. 1995. *A Passage to Anthropology: Between Experience and Theory*. London: Routledge.

Jackson, M. 1989. *Paths towards a Clearing*. Bloomington and Indianapolis: Indiana University Press.

———. 1998. *Minima Ethnographica: Intersubjectivity and the Anthropological Project*. Chicago: University of Chicago Press.

Kracke, W. 1987. "Encounter with Other Cultures." *Ethos* 15 (1): 58–81.

Lambek, M. 1998. "Body and Mind in Mind, Body and Mind in Body." In M. Lambek and A. Strathern, eds., *Bodies and Persons: Comparative Perspectives from Africa and Melanesia*, 33–49. Cambridge: Cambridge University Press.

Lévi-Strauss, C. 1963. *Tristes Tropiques*. New York: Atheneum. (Orig. pub. in French in 1955.)

Mead, M. 1959. *An Anthropologist at Work: Writings of Ruth Benedict*. Boston: Houghton Mifflin.

Meintel, D. 1973. "Strangers, Homecomers, and Ordinary Men." *Anthropological Quarterly* 46:47–58.

Powdermaker, H. 1966. *Stranger and Friend: The Way of the Anthropologist*. New York: Norton.

Rabinow, P. 1977. *Reflections of Fieldwork in Morocco*. Berkeley: University of California Press.

Sanders, P. 2006. *The Person-Centred Counselling Primer*. London: PCCS Books.

Wax, R. H. 1957. "Twelve Years Later: An Analysis of Field Experience." *American Journal of Sociology* 63 (2): 133–142.

Wengle, J. 1988. *Ethnographers in the Field: The Psychology of Research*. Tuscaloosa: University of Alabama Press.

Winthrop, R. 1969. "An Inward Focus: A Consideration of Psychological Stress in Field-work. In F. Henry and S. Saberwal, eds., *Stress and Response in Fieldwork*. Boston: Irvington Pub.

Notes

1. Seen from this perspective, fieldwork is both "liminal" and "structural"—liminal because we are somewhat called out of our bounded worlds, structural because we are asked "to participate" in the conditions of the new. In Ghassan Hage's terms, we "vacillate" between these modalities, subject not only to what vacillation evokes within us but also to where it deposits us. It is in this sense that all fieldwork entails both geographical journeying and journeying of a psychological kind.

2. The veranda was the place from which some early anthropologists were accused of conducting fieldwork. In short, informants were called to the anthropologists' veranda, where the former would deliver knowledge of anthropological relevance. By this method the anthropologist avoided entering the community itself. Whether this

practice actually occurred is a moot point. Even so, the term "the veranda" is now used to metaphorically denote those anthropologists who would conduct their enquiries from afar.

3. For this insight I am indebted to Michael Jackson (in this volume), who suggests that while separation, anxiety, and the mourning that this might induce can take the form of the type described above, in many other cases it is the face of presence that is difficult.

4. Michael Jackson extrapolates from the following example to the experience of fieldworkers: "There is some intriguing film footage by Bob Connolly and Robin Anderson of Papua New Guinea highlanders' first encounters with whites. These films capture the stricken faces and extreme grief of those confronted. This display of loss seems to derive from the sense that the world which was taken as the world is no longer the world, it is simply a part of this other world inhabited by other people who have guns which can kill, and all this stuff which they lug around, and this power to command other people to do their bidding. And I feel that this for me resonates much more with my experience. With fieldwork you are up against something that you can't comprehend or control and it is a little like the paranoia that finds its routes in this experience—if I can't control it is there something there that is preventing me from controlling it or is trying to control me . . ." (Personal communication, Harvard University, 2007).

5. The question as to how such perceptual shifts affect our understanding in the field is one that is bypassed in much anthropology. Do such shifts present opportunities for deeper immersion and understanding, or are they irrelevant to learning in the field, especially if viewed as a cognitive process? Furthermore, in what way might reverse perceptual shifts when we return home render researchers unfaithful to what the first perceptual shift revealed? If writing-up is a ritual or rite by which reverse dissonance may be diminished, from which perceptual standpoint is the field data interpreted and written about? How much is lost via this ritual reassertion of the anthropologist's self? In the case of our dreamer, his "rational" self?

4 Using Emotion as a Form of Knowledge in a Psychiatric Fieldwork Setting

Francine Lorimer

THIS CHAPTER IS WRITTEN AS AN EXPERIMENT for two audiences: a psychoanalytic audience and an anthropological one. It presents a case of countertransference that I experienced while doing fieldwork at a Danish psychiatric hospital, and it contributes to the discussion in anthropology of whether a psychoanalytically learned mode of knowledge can provide useful information within a context of anthropological fieldwork. The fieldwork, conducted for one year in 2004–05 and made possible by a research grant from the Danish Social Science Foundation (SSF), involved researching patients' experiences of treatments for depression in a psychiatric ward that specialized in depression, which I will call Ward 4.[1] This was my second fieldwork stint. My first fieldwork was in 1993–94 and focused on Southeast Cape York Kuku-Yalanji Australian indigenous people's struggles with cultural identity in a time of rapid change. This essay is not about fieldwork among Kuku-Yalanji, but I mention my first fieldwork experience in order to compare my fieldwork methodology then with the methodology I used while in the psychiatric hospital. The contexts were very different: my first fieldwork experience was towards a Ph.D. in anthropology; my second was conducted while I was doing psychoanalytic training at the C. G. Jung Institute, in Zurich. While I have always worked within a tradition of reflexive critical thinking, the nature of this reflexivity has changed radically as a result of my interest in psychoanalysis. This change has taken place primarily because of the different way I have come to use my emotions as a tool for understanding.

The question I raise here for a psychoanalytic audience is this: To what extent can analysis of the countertransference I experienced with a person who suffered from major depression shed some light on the mechanisms of that person's depression as an ongoing self-perpetuating disorder? The question for an anthropological audience is this: To what extent can my emotional response to an informant be considered a reliable description of that informant's life, by comparison with a description of his or her personal or national history, for example, or his or her social networks? Finally, a question for both: Does an approach to researching depression that is both emotionally and socially engaged change the way we think about the illness?

These questions bring together quite different analytic traditions. Psychoanalysts use the emotions they feel in a session with a client in a different way than anthropologists use their emotions in the field. And anthropologists move beyond the protected one-on-one relationship that psychoanalysts rely on to do good analytical work. Necessarily then, the methodological hybrid that I am describing here does not belong properly within either discipline as it is classically defined. Nevertheless, the present volume is a space of playing with possibilities in order to take emotions more seriously as an important component of an engaged anthropology. My approach to depression through analyzing my countertransference leads me to suggest that ongoing social relationships with co-patients outside the hospital setting can stimulate ongoing patterns of intersubjectivity that arise out of depression and in turn perpetuate the depression. Such a perspective hopefully adds to our understanding of how people with mental illness are constantly re-creating viable lives within and in terms of the revolving-door system of contemporary mental health care.

There is a long tradition in anthropology of exploring the value of psychoanalytic techniques for fieldwork, including the relevance of countertransference for the anthropological project. Among the many early anthropologists who were excited about the relationship between anthropology and psychoanalysis, one of the most groundbreaking was the psychoanalyst and anthropologist George Devereux. Devereux (1978) argued that the two disciplines have different analytical aims and therefore they need different methodologies—one for understanding the individual, another for understanding the group. Nevertheless, Devereux himself relied on countertransference in his interviews with informants (cf. Devereux 1951) and engaged in some creative theorizing about the relationship between mental illness and culture, such as the notion that shamans in traditional societies would be considered psychotic in Western societies. More recently, Vincent Crapanzano (cf. 1980, 1994), Luhrmann (1994), and others, such as Waud and Herdt (1987), Ewing (2006), Stein (2000), and

Grolnick (1987), have explored the relevance of countertransference for how we interpret ethnographic encounters. Through theoretical discussions and ethnographic descriptions, they show us that countertransference can give us a knowledge of people that is different from the knowledge we initially think we have arrived at. To take one ethnographic example, Robben (2006) compares his favorable impression (and amnesia as to what was actually said) following interviews with Argentinian generals who had perpetrated torture with his subsequent analysis of the interviews on tape. It was only when reviewing on tape what actually happened that he became aware of how he was being inveigled by the generals into conducting the interviews in a way that would protect them. Comparing his responses on tape with his actual feeling state after the interviews provided him with a way of identifying and learning from his countertransference.

These authors have made use of a technique that was developed in psychoanalysis to get around unconscious blocks in clients. Psychoanalysts acknowledge the explicit meaning of what is said, but if they feel a strong sensation in their body or emotion, they include this sensation as data that might indicate the presence of unconscious tensions in the client. The potential for inaccurate interpretation of bodily responses is clear, and psychoanalysts spend hours evaluating the source of the responses, so that they do not allow a misinterpretation to skew their capacity for empathy, understanding, and holding. When countertransference is applied as a technique in fieldwork, the potential for ethnocentric misunderstandings is obvious.[2] As Davies discusses in his introduction to this volume, and as I have discussed elsewhere (Lorimer 2004), emotional responses during fieldwork can often indicate our own frustrations as we struggle to be empowered in an unfamiliar setting (cf. Overing 2006).[3] Emotional responses are a vital and central aspect of the fieldwork experience, and they are also central to understanding, but they are seldom straightforward. Countertransference is a tool for exploring the multidimensionality of emotional responses. When an anthropologist is doing fieldwork in a psychiatric hospital, where the emotions of the population are the object of attention, it becomes almost absurd to deny the presence of emotions in the anthropologist.

The anthropologist Sue Estroff (1981) acknowledged the centrality of emotions in her pioneering fieldwork among people with schizophrenia in an outpatient program, and it is to her credit that she attempted to be as candid as possible about her own emotional struggles when doing this work. I was also doing fieldwork with people receiving psychiatric treatment. In this situation, countertransference takes on an added importance. Sometimes the cognitive meaning of an action is impenetrable not just to anthropologists but to informants themselves. In such cases, a psychoanalyst would say that our only way forward is to pay attention to how we feel. As anthropologists, can we do that in good faith? And how do we achieve this? If we acknowledge the inevitable self-interest in our feeling response to a situation, how seriously can we take such a phenomenon as anthropologists? This chapter defines countertransference as a feeling mode of knowing and critically explores the extent to which this mode of knowing can complement empirical and interpretive understanding for anthropologists working in psychiatric settings.

Fieldwork in a Psychiatric Hospital

I begin by elaborating a little on the differences between doing fieldwork in Southeast Cape York and doing fieldwork in Ward 4. It is relevant to compare the two fieldwork sites as a way of introducing what it was like to do fieldwork in a psychiatric hospital. There was an important similarity in the two fields: in neither could I gain the information that I wanted simply by doing interviews. Thus, in both contexts I faced a challenge of having to be creative in the ways I learned about how people thought. Peter Sutton (1978) has written well about the frustrating realization as a novice anthropologist in Cape York that his Cape Keerweer informants were not telling him the information he wanted so much as acting the role that fitted the occasion or, at the very most, speaking obliquely about political relationships using a language that Sutton was at first quite deaf to. Others have described a similar learning curve (Brady 1990).

With a sensation that I was feeling my way in the dark, I relied heavily during that first fieldwork experience on empirical documentation: I noted everything I saw and heard in as much detail as I could manage, believing that by doing so I could let the lived events of local politics and conflicts around cultural identity issues speak for themselves (Lorimer 2002). I was hungry at the time for some kind of certainty, establishing who said what, when, and where, and hoping that the more reflexive "why" questions and the more critical issues of interpretation and personal and professional bias could be discussed later in relation to the empirical facts. In other words, I was relying on the kind of methodology that produces an empirically grounded ethnography—rich in detail, gathered largely by watching and listening—which could be digested later in a wide variety of ways. I did not use my bodily state as a tool for learning until after I had left the field.

And once I did, the emotion that I reflected on most in my writing was anxiety. It was quite clear to me even during fieldwork that my body was usually in a state of intense anxiety as I tried to negotiate all the demands being placed on me by my ever-widening network of relationships in the field, as well as by my own two-year-old son, in a heroic and fruitless effort to maintain my personal dignity.

When I look back on it, I can see some similarities between the fieldworker I was then and the informant that I came to know during my fieldwork at Ward 4, and will soon introduce.[4] Ironically enough, however, I myself no longer suffered from anxiety while doing my fieldwork at Ward 4. Anxiety is a critical component of depression. It might seem at first strange, then, that I was not even more affected by anxiety in my second fieldwork site than in my first. There are many ways of making sense of this. From a purely empirical perspective, anxiety was present at acute levels in both social fields. In the Kuku-Yalanji setting it was not named, but the stresses of postcolonial life in Aboriginal Australia existed here, as in other Aboriginal societies, and was multiply present in everyday life. In the hospital setting, anxiety and depression were central too, but anxiety was named and contained within a well-structured system. In some ways, then, the anxiety existing in a psychiatric hospital was easier to address than the unstated, untreated real anxieties associated with racism, inequality, and social marginalization that Aboriginal people contend with on a daily basis. With regard to my own state, I had become more familiar with anxiety as part of my own self-experience and perhaps was no longer as uncomfortable when I felt its presence. I was also working with psychoanalysts, who had developed ways of addressing anxiety and in the process reducing its power. So, while my Danish informants were in the grip of anxiety as part of their depression, I could witness it, even witness how it felt in me, and allow it, as William James put it, to be part of my radical empirical approach to fieldwork. The difference in my emotional state during my second fieldwork, then, was related to the radical change in my methodological approach, and it is therefore relevant to describe in more detail why and how my approach to fieldwork had changed.

Countertransference as a Fieldwork Method

I have always had a parallel interest in psychology, and it was a natural development in my life that while continuing to teach anthropology, I began training as an analyst. I chose a Jungian approach, but any other psychoanalytic tradition would just as surely have led me to the theme of countertransference. As a result, I developed a greater awareness of my emotional responsiveness to other people, as well as an increased ability to reflect on my emotions rather than be led by them. I have also discovered that I am no longer able to leave my awareness of my emotional state out of daily life. This change in my personal way of relating has sometimes proved annoying; these days I find it impossible to just separate my head from my body, as I used to be able to do, and be analytical. So my new style of fieldwork was partly related to the personal changes I experienced during my own analysis.

When I lived with Kuku-Yalanji, I approached my fieldwork with a brain like a recording device, getting it all down on paper the next day. During my fieldwork in the hospital, I tended to just sit with people, talk with them, and then spend the afternoon on my own, walking or cooking for my family, absorbing how I had felt when with that person, and trying to find a way of relating to those feelings. I also met on a weekly basis with a Jungian supervisor and again with an analyst. During these meetings, I talked about the people I was getting to know in Ward 4, so that I could understand how their condition was perceived by the analyst and also be aware of my own emotional response to them. I still had fieldwork-related anxieties, but they were far less acute than they had been in my first fieldwork experience. They were not so much about my relationships in the field but more about whether I was actually doing anthropological fieldwork. For example, I asked myself: "Is it all right to spend so much time absorbing my feelings about a person rather than taking copious notes about their movements and words?" I did take notes, but they were nothing like the ones I had taken in Cape York. And yet fieldwork in Ward 4 was just as exhausting as it had been in Cape York! I was quite aware that I was working just as hard, but in a different way.

When I reflect on the reasons for this exhaustion, I believe it was because I was engaged in a project of a specific kind of understanding: I was learning less about forms of knowledge or social practices, and more about a group of people's mode of self-experience and how this self-experience transformed during and following the time of their hospitalization. Through countertransference—being in touch with my own self-experience—I strived to grasp what it meant to have a depressed experience of self, and, as patients received treatment, how their depressed self-experience transformed in a way that led them out of severe depression into a state of hope. An analysis of countertransference is vital for such research to the extent that it allows for a grasp of what people mean when they say they have been genuinely heard, they feel connected to a friend, they have found God, or they are confident about the authority of medicine. To this extent, countertransference gives us some personal grasp of the self, which we can draw on for an empathic grasp of human experience. It is important because self-experience of depression and of healing involve a combination of conscious and unconscious responses that take place at a physical and feeling level. Without countertransference, it is difficult to assess the impact of these responses on a life.

An approach to the self that seems to come close to the transformative nature of self-experience during times of psychic disturbance and treatment programs is that of Jenkins (2004), who asserts that self-experiences of people who have psychotic episodes cannot be understood just in terms of political differences, culturally shared notions of personhood, or social stigma. It involves a basic reconstruction of how the self is experienced that comes about as one goes through cumulative moments of social or clinical responses to who one is—in other words, as one lives an understanding of oneself while engaged in inter-subjective relationships:

> I would suggest that, when we speak of subjectivity we actually mean to invoke the notion of intersubjectivity. . . . The idea of intersubjectivity has been formulated in deliberate contrast to the logic of subject and object through entry into the interactive zone of lived experience in which the self is processually, dynamically, and multiply constituted. (Jenkins 2004:47)

Jenkins' understanding of the self comes from the knowledge she has gained of the fluidity of self among people with schizophrenia. She employs a phenomenological approach taken from European psychiatry to argue that shifts in the self in schizophrenia are an indication of the dynamic nature of the self in all people. To set the grounds for an anthropological approach that is open to all selves as ever changing, Jenkins suggests a view of subjectivity as something that is constantly in the process of becoming in relation to others. She argues that the self may be fluid in people who have schizophrenia, but it is also fluid in people who are working in hospitals, treating those with schizophrenia. Self-experience is more or less fluid in everyone. That is why patients' self-experience can become transformed when they are active in the social life around them, and why depression can be "caught" by nurses in psychiatric hospitals.

It seems that the fluidity of self is a tool and a boon just as much as it is a curse. At an experiential level, it is the object and subject of treatment in a psychiatric hospital. Everyone in such an environment is aware of the uncertainty of what is at stake, and all are striving to deal with "what matters" (Kleinman 2006). Because countertransference brings together one's own self-experience with another's self-experience at a feeling level, it can help the ethnographic project of understanding what is actually taking place. Through countertransference, I came to understand depression not as a clinical state but more as a sense of emptiness, and I came to understand improved mental health—when it happened at the hospital—as linked with feeling connected with others, or possibly nature, or God, or a mental health professional, which led to an experience of feeling genuinely known by them, and ultimately feeling connected with self.

Countertransference, then, is valuable in that it contributes to a different way of knowing. Because it enables reflection on feelings, it allows us as ethnographers to be emotionally involved without that emotion coming to define us. It also allows us to visit different self-experiences without adopting them for ourselves. It is a tricky business because self-experience is such a powerful and primitive human experience. For this reason, Jungians refer to fairy tales of enchantment to convey the experience of becoming caught in another person's self-experience. If we follow what happens to the hero of the fairy tale, we can get some clues as to how to protect ourselves from such enchantment, or how to slowly find our way past it. At some level, then, being aware of my countertransference responses allowed me to preserve my own personal integrity in an environment where personal integrity was perpetually in jeopardy. Psychiatric anthropologists have written about the struggles of patients to maintain their sense of self while in institutionalized care (cf. Estroff 1981; Rhodes 1991; Biehl 2005; van Dongen 1988, 2002, 2004; Desjarlais 1997). It is also a challenge for the anthropologist. It strikes me now that this is why I needed to spend much time doing nothing.

I have described this process because I think it is important to identify what it means to say that emotions are a tool in fieldwork. During the fieldwork with Kuku-Yalanji, emotions were a by-product of a fascinating and life-changing experience, but I did not use my emotions as a tool for learning until after the event, when I reflected on what I had learned. This was not because countertransference was not relevant for the experience; it was simply because I was not self-reflective enough at the time to be able to become aware of and reflect on my countertransference, except in cases where I met resistance that I couldn't understand (cf. Lorimer 2004). By contrast, at Ward 4, my emotional response was of critical importance at the moment of doing fieldwork in order to find out what I needed to know. I could not afford to ignore my emotional state because I had to be aware of whether a mood was brought on by the person I was speaking with or was more obviously connected with an aspect of my own life. Thus I came to accept that all the downtime and speaking with analysts was necessary in order for me to be clear about the nature of my own emotional state, so that I could learn with as much clarity as possible about the people I was working with.

In fact, it has not historically been the case that anthropologists have used a psychoanalytically oriented approach when doing fieldwork in psychiatric institutions. Anthropologists have often followed in Estroff's footsteps and reflected on how they felt when doing fieldwork, but the fieldwork itself consisted of ways of continuing the more traditional empirical tradition of documenting objectifiable data, whether in the form of life histories and the politics of institutionalization (Estroff 1981; Desjarlais 1997), psychiatry as an institution (Barrett 1996; Rhodes 1991; Good 2003; Luhrmann 2000), culturalized narratives among people with psychosis (van Dongen 1988, 2002, 2004), the impact of culture on treatment of mental health (Young 1985; Kleinman 1988; Kirmayer and Robbins 1991; O'Nell 1996), or an experiential approach to psychiatric illness (Jenkins and Barrett 2004; Kleinman 2006; Larsen 2002).

The above approaches have sensitively documented client experiences of having a mental illness, being treated for this condition, and how they have come to define themselves and their lives, or they have looked at how people who treat mental illness have learned to conceptualize and respond to the condition. As such, anthropological fieldwork in psychiatric settings has great value as part of the anthropological humanistic tradition of documenting the politics and existential realities of social suffering. Critical to this approach is the tradition in anthropology of relying on empathy to come to know the other. The empathy an anthropologist feels is part of his or her desire to be in a real human relationship with some informants—one that will outlast fieldwork. It is a celebration of a genuine mutual understanding between anthropologists and the people they come to know, based on the anthropologist's struggles to grasp what informants really mean in their own terms. The empathy that a humanistic approach brings to mental illness has made clients' humanity, and their suffering as human beings, of central importance.

But what is the nature of a deep emotional connection that does not celebrate a transcendent human connection but rather stirs up confusion? What happens when a sad story given by an informant creates excitement in the field-worker, or when an exciting story given by an informant meets with nothing but boredom in the fieldworker? When doing fieldwork in a psychiatric setting, I often was surprised by the mismatches that happened at an emotional level between me and a patient. It is likely that anthropologists have these kinds of mismatch responses all the time but tend to dismiss them because they don't fit with their meaningful construction of fieldwork and their informants. Here is where I borrowed from psychoanalysis to take a different approach. I chose to see my mismatch emotional responses as forms of knowledge about people in mental distress; I treated them as countertransference reactions. By doing so, I accepted the psychoanalytic notion that mental illness is an expression of human suffering, that we are all capable of mental illness, and that mental ill-nesses are in some—by no means all—ways panhuman. Therefore, if I was able to digest my emotional reactions, I could glean at least some hunches about how people were suffering.

But this does not mean that I bypassed culture. By the very act of attend-ing to emotions, I was already in the domain of cultural understanding. In her study of schizophrenia, Jenkins points out that emotions are central to the self as a culturally constructed locus of agency when she discusses how "the study of schizophrenia illumines our understanding of culture and subjectivity more generally" (Jenkins 2004:52). In this same spirit, my approach assumed a flow of self into other, and vice versa. I came to grasp this intersubjective flow of selves by analyzing my countertransference. And then I had to also be aware of how difference played into the equation. To do this, I had to compare my counter-transference response with all the other details of my fieldwork interactions. It was only by exploring the relationship between countertransference and other modes of fieldwork research that I could arrive at a cultural understanding of what I observed.

This chapter will discuss the relevance of my countertransference responses to one individual, Caroline, and of how countertransference helped me grasp the role of the "milieu" in how she responded to the treatment regime for major depression. I will suggest that my transference response to her helped me grasp what took place in her social relationships. By combining an awareness of my countertransference with an awareness of what went wrong in her relation-ships, I was able to develop an understanding of why the time she spent in this excellent psychiatric ward helped her to recover in the short term, but not in the long term. I suggest that what I picked up on was an aspect of Caroline's illness that could not be treated by hospital techniques but that was in fact a central element of hospital culture; it was a mode of living that belonged to the subculture of patients. A certain way of relating between hospital users was sparked in the hospital by the conditions of hospital institutionalization and was kept alive by relationships between discharged patients as they left the space of the hospital. I explore this phenomenon by focusing on how one person with severe depression lived in and out of this subculture in a way that perpetuated these kinds of social relations because she was not able to define herself to others in a healthy way. I suggest that Caroline's relatedness with other discharged patients was carried on outside of the hospital in a way that eventually led to her re-hospitalization eight months later.

Impressions of Ward 4

Anthropologists have compared doing fieldwork in a psychiatric hospital to working in exotic places (cf. Estroff 1981:3), but to me such a comparison is problematic. As I have already suggested, mental illness is culturally meaningful, yet it is not simply a cultural system. Despite my belief that mental illness could not exist outside of a social context, I also take it as given that mental illness has its foundations in an embodied state and indicates a state of disjuncture within a self that can evidence certain predictable patterns.

Kuku-Yalanji Cape York is culturally remote from my own environment, and it took months for me to grasp what was really going on, yet I had no doubt that my Kuku-Yalanji informants were for the most part not mentally ill. This assumption was based on my experience of the nature of the rapports I established with people. Despite different beliefs, despite the ongoing tragic consequences of colonization,[5] despite different expectations of what was involved in a relationship, I could easily identify relationships that were based on a good rapport and those that were not. And when rapport was not good, it was clear to me that the people knew their own mind; they had just chosen to not share what was on their mind with me.

The experience of doing fieldwork in a hospital ward where people were being treated for serious emotional disturbance was quite different. People were culturally different from me: they were Danish; I was Australian American. Since I had already spent four years in Denmark, I was familiar with the cultural context of Denmark. I could recognize cultural differences between us, just as I could recognize cultural differences between myself and Kuku-Yalanji people. But it was not often as easy for me to establish a personal rapport with my Danish informants as with my Kuku-Yalanji informants. In moments of conflict with Kuku-Yalanji people, I was able to work through the different elements that contributed to the conflict. I could reflect on my own thoughts, realize to what extent they were conditioned by certain expectations, and gradually distance myself from these expectations so that I could attempt to come to grasp expectations that belonged to this local moral world (Kleinman 2006; Lorimer 2004).

But what kind of reflexivity was demanded in a field where people were confused about their own local moral worlds and their place within them? My response to this challenging situation was to change the logic of my reflexive style. No longer did I focus on describing actions and statements for analytical ends; now I began with my intuitive observations. Following time spent with an informant in Ward 4, I would mull over a feeling of being walled out, bruised by the rejection, or I would marvel at the extraordinary openness that someone showed in telling me stories that made them doubt the basic goodness of human nature, or I would feel a slipperiness and shiftiness and want to wash myself clean. I was alarmed by the sexualized cues I would sometimes register when sharing time with people who had suffered early sexual abuse, and by the difference between the maturity of another person's thoughts and the infant-like nature of his needs for succor.

The emotional expressions I was picking up on were natural human responses to intolerable living conditions at some point in these people's lives, but they were responses that eventually led to a meltdown in their ability to take care of themselves as adults in society. I tried to carve out the emotional landscape of each person as an aspect of their personal situation. In order to learn how they responded to treatment, I had to have some way of grasping why they needed treatment. But my emotional responsiveness went even further: I tried to give form to the feelings I registered in order to come to know them more clearly. To this end, I did not just identify a feeling; I allowed myself to flow with the feeling as a fantasy. I saw this meaning-making exercise as a way of imagining how I as a feeling human being was being invited to respond to the person. Thus sometimes I would have a desire to engulf a person with motherly warmth; sometimes I would feel deep wariness; sometimes I would feel obliged to become chummy with someone when I didn't want to; sometimes I had the uncomfortable feeling that someone wanted to creep into my skin and own me.

I did this as part of my approach to emotions as a tool for knowing. Many of the patients in the hospital seemed to have an unbalanced relationship with their emotions: either they were stuck in them in perpetuity, in the grip of some earlier trauma, or they seemed to have no relationship with their emotions whatsoever and did not want to talk about emotions at all. In their view, they were perfectly happy, but were just exhibiting all the physical symptoms of depression and were therefore in the hospital long enough for the medication to rectify the problem. I wanted to understand how, given the emotionally valenced nature of social relationships, patients who had some kind of disturbed relationship with their own emotions were living in relatedness to others. If they were able to live meaningfully in relatedness to others after they left the hospital, it was an indication to me that their condition had improved. If not, I was interested in why they had not entered into such relationships.

Caroline

I now describe Caroline, one of my main informants, how I came to know her, and how her life developed after she left the hospital. Caroline was a tall woman in her forties, with thick blond hair and a friendly, outgoing disposition. She played on a local soccer team, and got on superficially well with friends and neighbors, a few of whom she had known for many years. However, Caroline had had a series of difficulties in being able to hold down a job. An initial ten years of intense anxiety had developed into a debilitating depression, which had led to her first hospitalization and the breakdown of her marriage. Over the years, Caroline had come to rely on high levels of antidepressant medication. She was deeply sad about her situation, because she doubted whether it was still possible for her to have a fulfilling relationship with a man.

I came to know Caroline during the long, uncomfortable hours I spent sitting in the ward's lounge. There was a kind of rhythm to this lounge sitting. The room was where smoking took place, so there was no need to talk. Bodies moved in, sat down, smoked, stared at the television or out the window, and moved out again. Or, sometimes, there would be intense and important talk— about the staff, about whether or not it was fair that one should be forced to do physical exercise, about what had happened the night before that had surprised everyone, or small gossip about another patient, monitored by the speakers in such a way that either the talk was harmless or the people listening were harmless. Frequently a couple of people who had befriended each other would have a long heart-to-heart about their lives and significant others, and when there were many young people staying, the room was sometimes full of ribald joking and laughter. Ward 4 was a place where people were being treated for depression, but when they left, they frequently felt that they were leaving behind the kind of intense and blooming friendships usually reserved for a holiday cruise.

Caroline entered my life during one of these lounge afternoons. I had introduced myself as an anthropologist who was doing fieldwork on patient experiences of treatment for major depression. Caroline and another patient, Anders, were interested in my previous fieldwork with Aboriginal people and asked me to tell them about that. I found it interesting to talk with one group of informants about my work with another group of informants, and the irony that I was at this moment studying these two people's lives as I had once studied Kuku-Yalanji people's lives did not escape them. Caroline had some experience with anthropology, and during that same conversation she offered to be my "main informant." I laughed and did not take her seriously, as I think many anthropologists would not take seriously any stranger who at once offered to be a main informant. And yet, while many of the people I came to know in that lounge opened up their hearts and souls to me one week and left forever the next, Caroline put herself in my service. She did become one of my main informants about experiences of treatment for depression; she preferred to describe herself as my guinea pig.

The second day, we went for a walk around the hospital grounds. During this walk, she talked about her life and about the deep sorrow that she still felt about the breakup of her longest relationship. Life is not worth living, she told me, if it cannot be lived with the ones we love. My feelings during and after this walk were so vivid. A feeling of euphoria that I could not explain welled up in me as we moved together through the leafy hospital grounds and explored this newfound intimacy. I was having a strong countertransference reaction. And when I fantasized how my body wanted to respond to Caroline, I realized I wanted to tell her: "But life *is* worth living, just wait, I can show you that joy exists: you will feel it too."

I have already stated that countertransference is an important form of knowledge in psychoanalysis. But for psychoanalysts, countertransference is very much in the service of healing. It works like this: a client visits an analyst; he talks about his life, his problems, his worries, or the weather. The analyst feels something very distinctive, which does not have to do with anything that has been talked about. The analyst registers the feeling and does what the client has not done—makes a mental note of it. Thus, the analyst has made of her own body an instrument that registers an emotion that the client him- or herself is bodily playing out but without realizing it—in other words, unconsciously.

That feeling then becomes one of the hues in the shared relationship that the client and analyst will gradually deepen during the time they spend together. Metaphorically speaking, they create a shared work of art, and each emotion-laden event is another hue added to the co-created work during their shared time. Gradually, these hues can be identified and pointed out so that they become familiar instead of strange. A person becomes enculturated to emotions as they are experienced in this social field. Thus the emotions are no longer raw biological facts; they are interpreted, felt presences. They are culturalized; they are an aspect of narrative (Jenkins 2004:49). And when the emotions become more consciously experienced, they become less like viruses attacking the body and disabling it; the once hidden, raw, acute, formless emotions of the client are no longer so, and when this happens they lose their disabling force. Instead, ideally, the client has developed a medium for giving form to his or her emotions, and can even come to play with these emotions, build up the painting, so to speak, or use different colors.

The above is an idealized representation of a therapeutic relationship. Many people have experienced wounding so crippling that it is unrealistic to expect such a transformative encounter. Often when people are at the point where they require hospitalization, the only thing that helps is an intensive combination of therapies, including milieu therapy, physical therapy, group therapy, medication, and sometimes electroshock therapy. Nevertheless, no matter what state a person is in when in a hospital setting, an anthropologist or caregiver who uses emotions as a learning instrument will have some kind of countertransference response to the person, and from this response can learn about how he or she is suffering.

As I discussed above, we have been trained as anthropologists to be aware of emotions in the field; emotions are an integral part of culture shock, from which we learn about our own culturally located expectations of right behavior—it is the cornerstone of a reflexive approach. However, it is really within the framework of clinical psychoanalysis that the approach to emotion as a form of countertransference has been developed. As I have undergone my own Jungian psychoanalytic training, I have become used to discovering that emotions, while culturalized, while narratives, can also be so embodied that they are not available to our thinking selves. And in this embodied form, they can act in ways that are not consistent with our thinking selves. I have come to believe that we all experience anxiety when stressed, we all split thinking off from emotion as a way of surviving difficult living conditions—it is a survival mechanism.

Conversely, if an emotion is there, debating its presence is a waste of time; it's much better to accept it and ask: what does it tell me about what is going on? I might be wrong, of course; just because an emotion is patently there does not mean that the interpretation of it is necessarily accurate. It is in the discussion of an emotion, the teasing out of it, relating it to oneself, relating it to what is taking place in a person's life, that an emotion can become a tool for learning about something as massive and destructive as depression.

If I look at my initial reaction to Caroline, what I might guess at would be that I was picking up on her longing to be loved. But I don't think it was this straightforward. One tricky but important aspect of countertransference is that it tends to be strongest when people are not aware of their own feelings. The fact that I myself was feeling euphoric at the very moment when Caroline was telling me about the deep sadness in her life points me to another emotion, namely the feeling of power located in me. Perhaps I felt empowered because Caroline was not only confiding in me, but somehow laying in my hands the very core of her being. And yet I had to remind myself that I was having a conversation with a stranger who was in a hospital for treatment. When I pondered the moment later, I had the feeling that some kind of a pact was taking place. Countertransference knowledge can often be uncomfortable. It involves picking up on feelings that are unconscious for a reason: they are not nice to own. At the time, along with this feeling of euphoria, I was aware of disquiet. I did not understand why my response to Caroline was so strong. I mulled it over a lot, and talked about it for months with my supervisors and analyst friends. I was aware that Caroline suffered from some of the problems I had suffered in my life, and yet I did not experience my responses to her as an identification. The way that my emotions eventually came to make sense was through the fieldwork that I did with her after she left the hospital. I began to see the same expressions of euphoria in the attitudes of the people Caroline was getting to know as she entered into increasingly more involved relationships inside and then outside the hospital setting.

The psychiatrist who ran the ward sometimes spoke of it as a place where patients could enter playfully into social relationships for learning purposes. It was a place of play because one could get into the same kinds of scrapes as one did in "the real world," but here there was a doctor or a contact person available to help patients work out why budding, promising relationships frequently led to anger or withdrawal. Ideally, people learned something about themselves, and then could recognize when they fell into the same traps in relationships outside the hospital. But frequently people developed friendships that were so powerful that they lasted beyond the protected space of the hospital. This is what happened with Caroline. She befriended Emil, a handsome, highly intelligent but extremely shy Turkish man, who was quite a bit younger than Caroline, and who left the hospital before she did. I also became good friends with Emil, so I witnessed the relationship bud from both Caroline's and Emil's perspective, and I also spent time with them together. While Emil was still in the hospital, Caroline taught him to drive. She happened to live in the same suburb as he did. After Emil was discharged, Caroline told me that she checked on him regularly to make sure he was all right. One day, when Emil did not answer his phone, Caroline visited his apartment and knocked loudly on the door until he answered it. One aspect of mental illness that I came to be familiar with is that people often regulate their own medicine to suit their bodies and emotional states (cf. Estroff 1981; Harding et al. 1987; Whyte, van der Geest, and Hardon 2002). Emil was going through a difficult time adjusting to being at home again, and Caroline was worried that he might have taken too many sleeping pills. Emil was deeply touched that Caroline would do such a thing, and he came to trust her as a new and important friend. Because Emil did not have a car, Caroline helped him do the shopping necessary to get his apartment in order, and this became a major project they did together, even though Caroline's own apartment was in dire need of maintenance. When Emil felt down, he would say to Caroline: "Let's go for a walk along the sea," and Caroline was happy to oblige. Emil was happy because he was getting out of his apartment and making a friend, and Caroline was happy because Emil was happy. My intention is not to go into their lives, which I came to know well, in detail. Even though their identities are hidden, it is still a hurtful exercise. But there is some purpose in describing Caroline's return to the hospital, because it makes clear how the logic of emotions played itself out in such a way that a return to a state of depression for Caroline was a likely outcome.

I left in the summer of 2005, exactly at the end of my year's fieldwork. After a year in the States, I planned a visit back to Denmark. When I told Caroline by phone about my planned visit, the crisis had not yet happened. She offered to pick me up from the airport, even though the plane was to land early in the morning. However, a week later, closer to the time of the trip, I got another phone call; this time Caroline was in distress. We talked on the phone for a while. I learned that she was distressed about her relationship with Emil. By this time, she had even traveled overseas with Emil, overcoming her fear of flying to do so. Once, when Emil was visiting another European country for work, he had rung Caroline to tell her that he feared he was becoming depressed again, and Caroline had flown to be with him. Emil then did go into another depression. He began taking several oxazepam tablets a night, relying on Caroline and another person to furnish his supply when he ran out of his own prescriptions, and Caroline had begun to feel increasingly responsible for his welfare, even his life. She began to stay with Emil every day, all day long, watching television with him. When Emil told Caroline that he was worried that it was too much for her, she replied that she enjoyed being with him. Even so, Emil told me that he felt uncomfortable. He was worried that the two of them were involved in some pact in which they were reinforcing each other's sickness, but he did not know how to establish a different kind of life. Eventually, the pact fell apart when Emil asked Caroline to take some photos of him to put on a Web-based dating service. At this she finally said no. She told Emil that she could not bear to help him put his photo on a matchmaking service. At that time, she also wrote to me, saying, "I feel almost drunk from taking so many pills."

My own response to this crisis was bewilderment, because I was far from the event, but also I was amazed to see Caroline acting out of anger. I had never seen her act in this way and, quite frankly, it felt right. She was setting a limit to what she could do for someone else, even though—and perhaps in this case because—she cared so deeply for this person. But in getting in touch with her emotional self, she had quite literally lost that aspect of herself that she prized most—her reason. I later found out from Emil that soon after this event, Caroline had become very drunk and in this state unleashed a tirade at Emil. She abused him and vilified him, bringing up all the ways in which she now felt he had taken advantage of her. Emil was less hurt than alarmed, since Caroline had never acted this way before. He rang Jonas, an ex-lover of Caroline's who also struggled with mental illness, and one of her closest friends. Jonas called an ambulance. In hospital, it was found that Caroline's body was so toxic that she might easily have died had she not received emergency care.

When I heard about the crisis, I was left soberly reflecting on what it meant, in fact, for Caroline to get in touch with and be able to express her anger. It was such an explosive event that it seemed to have destroyed her relationship with her closest friend and almost killed her in the process. It seemed clear, though, what had happened: these two people, who had met in the hospital ward, had initially found the kind of human involvement that they both longed for in relationship with each other. However, perhaps because they were not lovers, the involvement eventually became strained and insupportable. Furthermore, even if they had been lovers, neither Caroline nor Emil was able once they had left the hospital to function properly in their daily lives. Caroline allowed herself to live for another so much that her own lifeline was almost snuffed out, and Emil was not stable enough to be able to perform his job well enough that he did not fear succumbing once more to depression. They therefore clung to each other for strength, initially with a feeling of euphoria but ultimately with a feeling that they were both drowning in each other's illness. The pact had to be broken, and it was done by both, in their own ways: Emil asked Caroline to put a photo of him on a dating Web site, and Caroline worked herself into such a state of fury that she completely alienated herself from her newfound friend.

The whole situation was in some ways a function of the revolving-door system of today's psychiatric treatment programs, in which patients in Denmark—who at least have the luxury of state-funded hospitalization—leave usually within three months of admission, due to funding pressures on hospital wards. The time in hospital is long enough to get relief from the debilitating effects of major depression, but not long enough to build up new living habits, despite the valiant efforts of the ward's staff. While there is an outpatient counseling system, many people do not attend it, and its effects are often not enough for people who have needed hospitalization. However, even within a revolving-door system, there is some value to becoming aware of the emotional dynamics of the kinds of relationships people become involved in after they leave the hospital, and to understanding the condition of depression as having to do with social relatedness as much as with biochemical imbalance.

I elaborate on Caroline's depression as a disorder of relatedness not by explaining it in terms of her early childhood, which I could easily do, but by focusing on the ways in which she was caught up in ongoing spirals of destructive relationships in the present. I look now at the response of Emil's and Caroline's other close friends after her outburst and return to the hospital. I tell the events from Emil's perspective.

Once Caroline had been hospitalized, Emil met with Jonas and Caroline's other ex-lover, Erik, who lived outside of Copenhagen but often visited, and they all debriefed, going over all the events that led up to the crisis. They then began talking about how Caroline had acted towards each of them. Emil told me later that he was shocked that Caroline had said things to him which he thought reflected her special care for him, when, it turned out, she was also saying the same things to her other close friends. And then Erik and Jonas discovered that Caroline had been two-timing them for a while some years back. Emil told me that he had lost a lot of respect for Caroline after the realizations he made about her. Caroline herself told me that when one of these friends next visited her, he had spat in her face. Incidents with other people in Caroline's life had also caused painful ill will towards her. This is how things stood when I returned to Denmark. I soon received a call from another woman patient I had also come to know during my fieldwork, who was ringing from Ward 4 to let me know that Caroline wanted me to visit her there.

When I met up with Caroline, I felt many conflicted emotions myself. I was in Denmark for only a few days and had not planned to return to the hospital, so I hadn't informed staff that I would be visiting, yet I felt obliged to go if Caroline wanted me to visit her. Also, I was not sure what it would be like to meet up with Caroline after her re-hospitalization. As it turned out, she and I had a warm reunion. We drove to an idyllic Danish restaurant to have some lunch. The restaurant sat across the road from where we had once spent a memorable day with Emil and Jonas, exploring a river. But these were very different times. I was now living overseas, the life that Caroline had built since leaving Ward 4 had fallen apart—again—and all her friends and close kin had expressed their disgust with her. Caroline told me the story, in all its excruciating detail, with a calm voice. I listened and was amazed at how open and honest she was about it. She told me that she had started to have many dreams. The one she remembered most clearly was that she had been caught with her pants down. I thought of the conspiratorial and revelatory meeting of her men friends and ex-lovers after her hospitalization.

A common countertransference around people who have major depression is that one feels drained of energy or very tired. But I did not feel drained as I sat listening to my dear, suffering friend. I felt intensely sad for her, angry at all the people to whom she was close, who seemed to be punishing her because they were seeing a different side of her. And I was so happy to be with her again. When I was with Caroline, I felt alive.

My feelings of aliveness brought back the emotion of euphoria I had felt during that first walk on the hospital grounds with Caroline. I also was clear now that this euphoria was connected with some kind of unstated agreement that I become empowered through her. I reflected on what had taken place immediately after that first walk. As the walk was finishing, I had suggested that she find a circle of friends in the hospital itself and meet informally with them. We were approaching the entrance door to the ward when she had replied,

"Yes, let's you and I do that right now!" I had felt a little taken aback at the immediacy of Caroline's wish. But since she was keen and I was doing field-work, we organized a group meeting later on that day, which eventually became a routine arrangement for six patients who were in the process of becoming discharged. We did this in the following way: Caroline and I were sitting in the hospital lounge, when Caroline told two patients we were with: "Francine is going to run a therapy group. Francine, tell them about it." Although I felt extremely uncomfortable at suddenly being put on the spot and represented as a "therapist," I nevertheless tried to act like an organizer, since I had been precipitously placed in that role. I suggested that it might be worthwhile for a few people to meet together outside the hospital either just before or after their discharge, but that I would not act as a therapist because I wasn't qualified yet. I would be an anthropologist, who would listen to their discussions about their experiences of treatment. People seemed surprisingly keen about the idea, and I felt a little like a schoolgirl setting up a secret club. There was a conspiratorial, anti-establishment feeling to the meeting, and I felt uncomfortable as I watched two nurses walk past the room and observe us through the glass walls. When I reflected on why the meeting had this atmosphere, I wondered whether it was because it provided a way that patients could maintain a network of structured contacts with each other once they had left the hospital. I wondered whether people were striving for some way of strengthening themselves as *social* actors towards a future when they would no longer be in the hospital. They were per-haps striving to retrieve their moral status as adult social beings, while at the same time keeping me as a kind of token therapeutic guide. We did meet for several months in each other's homes, and then the group fell apart because of disagreements between the participants.

My point in describing the above event is to give some indication of how much Caroline energized me. I think that she was very keen to make something happen, to generate an event, to transform a hospital condition into a more so-cially real event, but she could not do this herself. She needed someone else to act on her behalf. So she made me the leader. She empowered me to act towards a goal that, in an ideal world, she should have been realizing. Her idea actually pro-vided me with the closest circle of informants I ever had during my fieldwork at the hospital, whose personalities, families, and worlds I came to know with much more richness than I would have known if I had just visited them one on one.

I saw that as long as Emil was not in a depression, being around Caro-line had the same empowering effect on him, as their friendship bloomed.

Emil had been withdrawn and glum when I had first met him two months into my hospital fieldwork, but as his friendship with Caroline developed, he became engaged and enthusiastic, full of energy and humor. Emil told me that Caroline was deeply understanding of him, and it made him feel special to be with her. Only once, before the crisis that landed Caroline back in hospital and brought about the revelatory meeting between Emil, Erik, and Jonas, did I see Emil falter. This was when the three of us went to an evening talk given by Jonas, Caroline's still-close friend, about what it was like to recover from schizophrenia. Jonas told his audience that when he had been ill, Caroline had devoted herself to him, done everything to help him into wellness, and had even taught him how to drive. I saw Emil's jaw drop—Caroline was now teaching Emil how to drive.

Even when Caroline did not inspire life and love in people, she admired them and helped them. She told me that years ago when she first visited a psychiatrist, after some months she realized that she was listening to the psychiatrist's worries more than he was listening to hers. She told me with mild scorn: "I became his therapist." She allowed hospital staff to record therapeutic hours with her for their ongoing studies. And she had become my main informant, as she had volunteered to do when we first met. I even began to notice that she was increasingly playing the role of my therapist. The more that I visited her, the more I noticed I would want to talk about myself. I could see it happening and would remark on it to Caroline and reflect on it in my analysis. It was like a strong undercurrent, against which I had little power. Something was confusing me when I was with her, so that my aim to listen to her became overridden by a compulsion to talk about myself. To use a rather mixed movie image, it was as if my radar was being scrambled by strong rays coming from her radar, which acted like an invisibility cloak. She was making herself invisible by focusing all the attention on me.

This experience helped me to understand the effect that Caroline had on other people without being aware of it herself. It was as if when people were around her, they were given some kind of personal freedom to become empowered. For Jonas, this was being able to live, love, and drive; for Emil, this was being able to get around to do all his chores and also being able to shine in front of another's admiring gaze. For professionals, this might be a way for them to get on with their personal careers. For me, Caroline was helping me professionally by being my informant and allowing me hours of her time, and she was also encouraging me to express all my feelings to her. The irony is that

Caroline herself did not seem to be growing, thriving, or feeling empowered as a result of any of these relationships.

Over months of spending time with Caroline, I realized that she had a negative attitude towards feelings, which she regarded as base. When I asked why she never expressed anger, she told me: "If I did that, I would lose all control of myself." She felt that her own desires dragged her into ignoble ways of relating to people, so she acted like a hero who rode above her own feelings and simply allowed herself to be the fire that fanned other people's glory, success, empowerment. I believe that she was what Heinz Kohut and others have described as narcissistically wounded, though she was the kind of wounded person who thrives by mirroring others rather than by being constantly mirrored (Kohut 1977; Jacoby 1999; Asper 1993). She was Echo to Narcissus. But the root problem was the same: for some reason, she was not comfortable with all those aspects about herself that could not be related to in a rational way. She related only to other people's feeling selves and took some vicarious pleasure in building these other selves up, but her own self remained withered and neglected behind the glass wall of her defenses. I could realize this because I had allowed myself to follow my feelings towards Caroline, and then through fieldwork I watched how Caroline related to others in ways that perpetuated her invisibility and powerlessness as she promoted their visibility and empowerment in whatever ways were appropriate to them. I discovered that Caroline had very strong sides—for example, she was clever, caring about others, had a strong moral disposition, and she could be very funny. These qualities made her likeable to almost everyone. Perhaps, however, her cleverness worked against her: she was so good at dissimulating her own emotional loneliness that people often did not realize it was there. Her eyes were reflector glasses. People didn't see her when they looked at her; they saw how good they looked in her eyes. And when they stopped looking good in her eyes, they spat at her.

Conclusion

This essay describes how my countertransference to Caroline helped me understand how she related socially with people she met in the hospital in such a way as to reinforce her state of depression outside of the hospital. If I had not registered the euphoria that arose in me when I first met Caroline, it would have been harder for me to understand what went wrong in the other relationships she developed. It would have been hard for me to see how her way of becoming close friends was based on an empowerment of their agency in a way that denied her own. But my relationship with Caroline was only one aspect of a field-work experience in which I observed people both in the hospital and outside of it. If I had not spent time with Caroline and her friends outside of the hospital, I would not have observed how social relationships could subtly promote personal suffering in such a way as to lead to eventual re-hospitalization. As an anthropologist, I could see the importance of depression as a social construct, and I could see how the position of being disempowered in a hospital setting spurred people to create their own counterculture, as Estroff noted. My psychoanalytic contribution was to explore what was going on between people in such a group, to understand how a state of depression could be unconsciously promoted socially between friends.

We need to be careful as anthropologists when researching depression. After all, depression is multidimensional: it is biochemical, it is related to traumatic or chaotic living conditions, and it can also be brought on by institutionalization itself (Barrett 1996). Sometimes depression is best described as a state of being cut off from emotions. However, emotions are always an important ingredient, and therefore countertransference, which takes emotional responsiveness into consideration, is one way towards understanding. In a sense, my countertransference response to Caroline existed separately from but alongside my conscious grasp of her as a social person. Luhrmann (chapter 9, this volume) suggests that there may be value in keeping the conceptions of mind and body separate for heuristic purposes. Despite the holistic approach within psychotherapy, a countertransference approach acknowledges that mind and body may not always be working synchronously. This chapter illustrates clear differences between Caroline's thoughts about herself and my bodily responsiveness to her, and if we lumped those two things together we would be unable to tease out the conflicts between them. We would be unable to appreciate, for example, that Caroline's defenses, while problematic, had their purpose. By this I mean that perhaps Caroline's tendency to identify wholly with her rationality and repress her own emotions enabled her to at least function socially in a minimal way.

It is necessary to separate mind and body in order to see how thought and feeling can coexist in their own unique ways in a person. And yet emotion does bridge mind and body, and as anthropologists we can see how this takes place socially. The psychiatric anthropologist Arthur Kleinman made the observation while working as a psychiatrist in China that the Chinese patient Mrs. Lin described herself as having neurasthenia rather than depression. She told

Kleinman that her problems would be solved if the physical symptoms she was suffering, such as dizziness, headaches, and fatigue, could be cured. And yet, even though she experienced her problems as physical, she broke down and sobbed when speaking with Kleinman about her life, admitting that she was unhappy (Kleinman 1988:6). The human relationship between Kleinman and Mrs. Lin activated something that went beyond formal conceptions of depression, whether East or West. Perhaps it is here that anthropological empathy can combine with a more psychoanalytic notion of countertransference. Nothing would have happened with Caroline if I had not begun with a feeling of empathy in the sense that we liked each other. Our relationship began by coming to know each other as people. It was only because I had this initial social connection with Caroline and other patients that I was able to identify emotions in my own body that went beyond human connection or liking, reflect on how these emotions might relate to her emotional state, and, finally, go on to explore, after her discharge, in what ways these emotions existed in her social relationships. By bringing my countertransference into the relationship, I could create an ethnographic account that was not only empirical but "radically empirical." In such a way, I attempted to deepen our appreciation of the human dimension of social relationships between people who have been hospitalized for major depression. By bringing the reader back to the human dimension of patients suffering from depression, I am once again writing within the humanistic anthropological approach to mental illness.

Furthermore, focusing on countertransference provides a way of resolving the limitations that come from medicalizing mental illness as somehow located in the individual. Depression becomes fundamentally relational: here, as relational, depression was not flat or expressionless but was more like a secret pact between two or more people, so to speak, which could feel very exciting, even euphoric. In order to do justice to depression as relationship, it was necessary to draw on psychoanalysis and consider emotions as defenses that, while unconscious, were as effective as the practiced, culturally relevant defenses I had once described among Kuku-Yalanji. Caroline could shield her true feelings from me only if I became blind to them by focusing on my own feelings when I was with her. It was in fact amazingly difficult for me, after I had gotten to know her well, to talk about anything except my own feelings. But intellectually I realized that this powerful tendency I noticed in me was connected to the powerful defenses within her. Even just being able to point these out might help her begin to recognize them in herself and eventually to want to break them down a little.

It makes me wonder whether depression may be more like a language than a chemical imbalance: it does not begin within an individual body but rather as a felt state between two bodies, and once it is established, it thrives on contact with others (Jenkins and Barrett 2004; Tronick 2007). Perhaps a value of anti-depressants is that these drugs affect our biochemistry so that the way that we are habituated to registering and responding to others becomes blunted, and this blunting then inhibits the intensification of the depression.

It is not a straightforward matter to use emotion as a tool for knowledge in fieldwork. Many times, anthropologists become emotional themselves when they speak of emotion. Is this because we feel a moral responsibility to be true to emotion, just as we feel a responsibility to be true to our informants? From my years of studying psychology and psychotherapy, I have learned that emotions can be just as deceptive as statistics. But they can help us tease out the multidimensional nature of human responses to difficult lives. The challenge is to be able to identify and work with emotions and see how they bring added dimension to all the other modes of human expression that we as anthropologists are accustomed to working with in the field.

References

Asper, K. 1993. *The Abandoned Child Within: On Losing and Regaining Self-Worth*. New York: Fromm International.

Barrett, R. 1996. *The Psychiatric Team and the Social Definition of Schizophrenia: An Anthropological Study of Persons and Illness*. Cambridge: Cambridge University Press.

Biehl, J. 2005. *Vita: Life in a Zone of Social Abandonment*. Berkeley: University of California Press.

Brady, M. 1990. "The Problem with Problematizing Research." *Australian Aboriginal Studies* 1:18–20.

Crapanzano, V. 1980. *Tuhami: Portrait of a Moroccan*. Chicago: University of Chicago Press.

———. 1994. "Kevin: On the Transfer of Emotions." *American Anthropologist* 96 (4): 866–885.

Desjarlais, R. 1997. *Shelter Blues: Sanity and Selfhood among the Homeless*. Philadelphia: University of Pennsylvania Press.

Devereux, G. 1951. "Reality and Dream: Psychotherapy of a Plains Indian." *American Anthropologist* 53 (4): 565–567.

———. 1978. *Ethnopsychoanalysis*. Berkeley: University of California Press.

Estroff, S. 1981. *Making It Crazy: An Ethnography of Psychiatric Clients in an American Community*. Berkeley: University of California Press.

Ewing, K. 2006. "Revealing and Concealing: Interpersonal Dynamics and the Negotiation of Identity in the Interview." *Ethos* 34 (1): 89–131.

Good, B. 2003. *Medicine, Rationality, and Experience: An Anthropological Perspective.* Cambridge: Cambridge University Press.

Grolnick, S. 1987. "Reflections on Psychoanalytic Subjectivity and Objectivity as Applied to Anthropology." *Ethos* 15 (1): 136–143.

Guggenbuhl-Craig, A. 1971. *Power in the Helping Professions.* New York: Spring.

Harding, C. M., G. W. Brooks, T. Ashikaga, J. S. Strauss, and A. Breier. 1987. "The Vermont Longitudinal Study of Patients with Severe Mental Illness." Parts 1 and 2. *American Journal of Psychiatry* 144: 718–726, 727–735.

Jacoby, M. 1999. *Individuation and Narcissism: The Psychology of Self in Jung and Kohut.* London: Routledge.

Jenkins, J. H. 2004. "Schizophrenia as a Paradigm Case for Understanding Fundamental Human Processes." In J. H. Jenkins and R. J. Barrett, eds., *Schizophrenia, Culture, and Subjectivity: The Edge of Experience*, 29–61. Cambridge Studies in Medical Anthropology. Cambridge: Cambridge University Press.

Jenkins, J. H., and R. J. Barrett, eds. 2004. *Schizophrenia, Culture, and Subjectivity: The Edge of Experience.* Cambridge Studies in Medical Anthropology. Cambridge: Cambridge University Press.

Kirmayer, L., and J. Robbins. 1991. *Current Concepts of Somatization: Research and Clinical Perspectives.* Washington, D.C.: American Psychiatric Press.

Kleinman, A. 1988. *Rethinking Psychiatry: From Cultural Category to Personal Experience.* New York: Free Press.

———. 2006. *What Really Matters: Living a Moral Life amidst Uncertainty and Danger.* New York: Oxford University Press.

Kohut, H. 1977. *The Restoration of the Self.* New York: International Universities Press.

Larsen, J. A. 2002. "Experiences with Early Intervention in Schizophrenia: An Ethnographic Study of Assertive Community Treatment in Denmark." Ph.D. diss., University of Sheffield, Department of Sociological Studies.

Lorimer, F. 2002. "'Ngayku bubu'/'My bit of dirt': Themes of Belonging, Difference, and Separation among Kuku-Yalanji of the Bloomfield Valley in Southeast Cape York, Australia." Ph.D. diss., Sydney University.

———. 2004. "Forståelse: Et socialt forhold." In K. Hastrup, ed., *Viden om Verden: En Grundbog I Antropologisk Analyse*, 53–69. Copenhagen: Hans Reitzels Forlag.

Luhrmann, T. M. 1994. "Psychological Anthropology as the Naturalist's Art." In M. Suárez-Orozco, G. Spindler, and L. Spindler, eds., *The Making of Psychological Anthropology II.* New York: Harcourt Brace College Publications, 60–79.

———. 2000. *Of Two Minds: The Growing Disorder in American Psychiatry.* New York: Alfred A. Knopf.

O'Nell, T. 1996. *Disciplined Hearts: History, Identity, and Depression in an American Indian Community*. Berkeley: University of California Press.

Overing, J. 2006. "The Backlash to Decolonizing Intellectuality." *Anthropology and Humanism* 31 (1): 11–40.

Rhodes, L. 1991. *Emptying Beds: The Work of an Emergency Psychiatric Unit*. Berkeley: University of California Press.

Robben, A. 2006. "Ethnographic Seduction, Transference, and Resistance in Dialogues about Terror and Violence in Argentina." In A. Robben and J. Sluka, eds., *Ethnographic Fieldwork: An Anthropological Reader*, 29–32. Oxford: Blackwell.

Scheper-Hughes, N. 1987. "Mental in Southie: Individual, Family, and Community Responses to Mental Illness in South Boston." *Culture, Medicine, and Psychiatry* 11 (1): 1–25.

Stein, H. 2000. "From Countertransference to Social Theory: A Study of Holocaust Thinking in U.S. Business Dress." *Ethos* 28 (3): 346–378.

Sutton, P. 1978. "Wik: Aboriginal Society, Territory, and Language at Cape Keerweer, Cape York Peninsula, Australia." Ph.D. diss., University of Queensland.

Tronick, E., ed. 2007. *The Neurobehavioral and Social-Emotional Development of Infants and Children*. New York: Norton.

van Dongen, E. 1988. "I Wish a Happy End: Hope in the Lives of Chronic Schizophrenic Patients." *Anthropology and Medicine* 5 (2): 169–192.

———. 2002. *Walking Stories: An Oddnography of Mad People's Work with Culture*. Amsterdam: Rozenberg.

———. 2004. *Worlds of Psychotic People: Wanderers, "Bricoleurs," and Strategists*. London: Routledge.

Waud, K., and G. Herdt. 1997. "Introduction: Interpretation in Psychoanalytic Anthropology." *Ethos* 15 (1): 3–7.

Whyte, S., S. van der Geest, and S. Hardon. 2002. "Women in Distress: Medicines for Control." In *Social Lives of Medicines*, 50–62. Cambridge: Cambridge University Press.

Young, A. 1985. *The Harmony of Illusions: Inventing Post-Traumatic Stress Disorder*. Princeton, NJ: Princeton University Press.

Notes

1. The term "patient" can itself carry stigma. When I use the term, it is solely as an identifier of their hospital status. When referring to someone receiving psychotherapy, I use the term "client."

2. See Lucas and Barrett (1995), "Interpreting Culture and Psychopathology: Primitivist Themes in Cross-cultural Debate," *Culture, Medicine, and Psychiatry* 19:287–326, for a historical review of scholarship about how research on the mental health of culturally different populations has affected contemporary research.

3. Guggenbuhl-Craig (1971) notes the same unacknowledged striving for power among psychotherapists.

4. For purposes of confidentiality, I have disguised the identities of the hospital and the informants discussed here.

5. For a critical historical review of psychocultural studies and a discussion of how global processes have affected new studies in the field, see Conerly Casey and Robert Edgerton, eds. (2005), Introduction to *A Companion to Psychological Anthropology: Modernity and Psychocultural Change*, 1–14 (Malden, MA, and Oxford, UK: Blackwell).

II   Political Emotions in the Field

5 Hating Israel in the Field

On Ethnography and Political Emotions*

Ghassan Hage

IN JANUARY 2006 I began researching the "political emotions" generated by the Arab-Israeli conflict and the particular way these were experienced by Muslim immigrants in the West. From my previous fieldwork I have come to see that these emotions, particularly as they were intensified by what was often perceived as Western bias in favour of Israel, played a central role in limiting the way Muslim immigrants to the West identified with the countries they have migrated to.

Since 9/11 there has been a growing awareness among at least some political leaders, as reflected in their political speeches, of how important this question is among not just Arab immigrants but all Muslim immigrants in the West—and indeed all Muslims. While none of the politicians formulated it this way, the implication of this reality was nevertheless clear: how a Western nation's foreign policy towards Israel is evaluated by its Muslim immigrants is important in shaping their sense of belonging or lack of belonging to that nation—that is, their social integration. This was brought home to me even more starkly at an earlier stage when I was examining how to conduct this research in a manageable way. I carried out a preliminary survey—with, I hasten to say, no scientific pretensions whatsoever but with a revealing outcome nonetheless. I made a point of asking one face-to-face question to between twenty and thirty Lebanese-born Muslims in France, England, Australia, and the United States. It went something like this: You are often complaining that

* Material in this chapter was adapted from "Hating Israel in the Field" by Ghassan Hage, which appeared in 2009 in *Anthropological Theory* 9 (1): 59 79.

your government doesn't do enough to counter anti-Muslim stereotypes and discrimination, and that your government is too pro-Israeli. If, hypothetically, the government says to you: "OK . . . look . . . I can't do both things at the same time. You have to choose one or the other: either I stop anti-Muslim racism or I stop being pro-Israeli. Which one would you choose?" From the one hundred or so people I asked, only a handful (eight, exactly, as they were unusual enough to remember) said that stopping local anti-Muslim racism was more important to them. As I chatted with some of these people, it was also clear that they saw Western bias towards Israel as a global extension of anti-Muslim racism rather than as a separate issue. This not only brought home to me the affective centrality and primacy of the Palestinian question to what must be a substantial proportion of Lebanese Muslim immigrants, but it also highlighted the larger question of the transnational dimension of political self-constitution among them. It is this phenomenon in particular, which I am linking directly to what I call political emotions, that I am now examining ethnographically.

During the first couple of months, I had begun working on Arab-Muslim modes of imagining the Euro-Zionist settlement of Palestine and the ensuing conflicts, as expressed in political statements, songs, films, art, and poetry. I also examined how the emotions expressed in these media have changed historically. Finally, I began reading theoretical literature on emotions to reflect on key questions related to my research, such as: What are political emotions? Are there such things as emotions that are sui generis political, or are there merely emotions in general that we end up investing in various spheres of social life, the sphere of politics being one among many?

The core diasporic population I was working with were Shi'a Muslims from South Lebanon living in France, the United States, and Australia. As with my previous transnational work (Hage 2005, 2006), I began in the villages in Lebanon and moved outward towards the global migratory locations. My first visit to Lebanon in relation to this project was in March 2006. It was then that, through a mutual friend, I was introduced to Ali. He invited me to his house in a village near Nabatiyyeh, where I met his wife and his two children and a couple of neighbours. We talked about the possibility of my living for a few months nearby in a house which belonged to one of his relatives who was then in Canada. I also made plans to visit Ali's village again in August.

What happened after my return to Australia was totally unexpected. In July, just as I began my work with the South Lebanese diaspora in Sydney, the Hezbollah fighters infiltrated the Lebanese-Israeli border, kidnapping two Israeli soldiers and killing others. From the information that is now available to us, it is clear that Israel used this incident to launch a strike on its own behalf but also on behalf of other Western and conservative Arab nations. This strike was obviously a long time in preparation and was clearly a response to what was perceived, by Israel, the United States, a number of Arab regimes, and some Lebanese factions, as the growing Islamic/radical/Iranian threat in the region. Thus begun Israel's now infamously ferocious (I am still emotional enough about it to say barbarian) bombardment of Lebanon that destroyed its only-just-rebuilt infrastructure, flattened many Shi'a residential areas, killed more than a thousand civilians, and left behind in agricultural areas and villages thousands of unexploded cluster bombs that continued to explode and kill and maim civilians well after a cease-fire was agreed upon.

Very quickly during and following the bombardment, my "research landscape" disappeared. It did so physically. The village where I was preparing to do my fieldwork was destroyed. Ali died along with his two children when an Israeli missile hit his car. I was told that only his wife survived, but she had lost an arm and a leg. I never got to meet her again. The scene among the South Lebanese Shi'a in Sydney became one of generalised mourning as one family after the other began "losing" members in Lebanon. There was, needless to say, an overwhelming feeling of anger and hatred towards Israel—and I wholeheartedly shared this anger and hatred.

In the first part of this chapter, I will reflect on the nature of my anti-Israeli hatred and anger in an auto-ethnographic mode. I want to scrutinise it insofar as it represents a "political emotion" that I shared with my informants. I will show how by reflecting on my own political emotions I began refining my analytical conception of what these emotions entail.

In the second part, I will reflect on the emotional dimension of participant observation. Although it was clear that by sharing certain emotions with my informants I was getting closer to them, it was equally clear that the very nature of participant observation required me to distance myself from those emotions. I want to examine the nature of the emotional ambivalence generated by this posture, and will argue that this ambivalence generates its very own set of emotions that are specific to ethnographic practice. Borrowing from Spinoza, I will call this ethnography-specific emotion "ethnographic vacillation" and will argue that a degree of awareness of it is a crucial part of ethnographic research.

Talking about Anthropologists' Emotions in the Field

Before proceeding, however, some preliminary reflections seem to me necessary. Talking about anthropologists' emotions in the field necessarily brings
out personal dimensions specific to each anthropologist. This is true even
when concentrating on emotions that have to do more with the social, political, or structural location of the anthropologist in general than with his or her
specific biography. As many who have worked on emotions have noted, they
are always located at the intersection of the individual and the collective, the
personal and the public, the psychological and the social (Lutz and White 1986;
Milton and Svašek 2005). While this is certainly no reason to stop talking about
the anthropologists' emotions, it is enough reason to make one reflect critically
about what it means to do so.

Firstly, there is a way in which such talk lives up to the joke about the postmodern anthropologist who told his informant: "But enough about you—let's
talk about me." Clearly, the way anthropology as a discipline has turned on
itself to examine its social and historical conditions of possibility, its weaknesses and strengths, has been an important and enlightening endeavour. But
as many have already argued, the reflexive turn has generated its own problems. This is especially so where reflexivity has become a substitute rather than
a complement to what is by far the discipline's most important achievement:
instilling in ourselves and in our readers the desire and the capacity to *know
otherness seriously*. Yes, Malinowski was naïve in not noticing the colonial conditions of possibility on which he built his whole enterprise. But does that do
anything to diminish what is by far his most important achievement, which
was to lay the groundwork for a rigorous and systematic method by which one
can act out the "desire to know otherness seriously"? Drowning oneself in a sea
of self-reflexivity is hardly more "anti-colonial," for instance, than that desire
to *seriously* reach out for otherness. Contrary to this seriousness today, both
the "hatred" and the "respect" and "tolerance" of otherness are made out to
be a frivolously facile endeavour. This is done by effectively either effacing or
simplifying the very otherness of the other that is particularly difficult to comprehend, their radical alterity. In such an environment, the seriousness that is
part of the anthropological desire to know otherness acquires a particular not
only intellectual but also political importance. I have often shown in my work
on Australian multiculturalism (Hage 2000, 2003) how those who "love" some
category of otherness and those who "hate" it share in common the fact of not
having much to do with the others they profess to love or hate. This is certainly

the case with respect to the Western relation to Muslims with which some of my work is concerned. Knowing seriously what is particularly and radically other about Muslims is certainly important in an era when people are divided between those who "love" and those who "hate" Muslims, all doing their loving and hating with equal ease. How can one know anything and have such reductionist emotions towards it as "love" or "hate"? It was and still is the strength of anthropology to go way beyond such simplistic and often politically driven sentiments to capture the complexity and ambivalence of feelings that the encounter with otherness brings about.

Talking about the emotions of the anthropologist does not necessarily go against such an analytical endeavour, though it can. This is where one needs to be critically reflexive about analysing the anthropologists' emotions. Psychoanalysis has shown us that we are in many ways "other," or, as Julia Kristeva has put it, "strangers," to ourselves (1991). In this sense, if reflecting on our emotions is a reflection on the "strangeness" or otherness contained within us, reflections on the emotions of the anthropologist can only enhance the general anthropological project of deepening our knowledge of cultural otherness in all its manifestations. If this is not kept in mind, talking about emotions still carries with it the danger of making "knowing the self" a substitute for knowing otherness.

Related to this issue is the kind of emotions one chooses to talk about. There is obviously a limit to the kind of emotions that one wants to talk about and that one finds it useful to talk about. It would hardly be a revelation to say that there are certain emotions that the anthropologist experiences that he or she would find shameful to talk about. And, of course, there is nothing that says that the more shameful an emotion is, the more it is good to talk about it. This goes for more than the obvious case of sexual feelings.

For example, I have attended many conferences at which anthropologists make a virtue of the need to avoid projecting colonial relations of power into the fieldwork situation, such as the classical "avoiding to racialise and inferiorise informants." Not many anthropologists, on the other hand, like to talk about the opposite process of being inferiorised by your informants. Although there are a number of classical texts in which male anthropologists refer to being humiliated by their male informants, particularly through a questioning of their sexual prowess, not many seem to dig into this tradition these days. It makes one appear far grander, more superior, and more noble (and one might even add "Western") to talk about the heroic effort one is undertaking to stop humiliating others than to talk about the effort involved in dealing with others who are humiliating you.

My core "problem" with the males in the Lebanese villages where I do my fieldwork was not about how they judged my sexuality, although there were definite insinuations in this direction; it was more about how they judged my very profession as an anthropologist. After interacting with them long enough for them to know what I spent my days doing in the village, they all came to realise that I am a "talker"—someone who spends most of his time "talking." Of course, it is not that rural Lebanese men don't enjoy talking: they love talking and boasting about themselves and their achievements (see Gilsenan 1996). But there is talking and there is talking. And it was clear that I liked the wrong kind of talking, which was more about how people *felt* concerning this and that issue. This was the kind of talking that women indulge in. To be classified a "talker," a "*hakwaji,*" was to be feminised. The ultimate humiliation came when I went to see a relatively big landowner whom I had been wanting people to introduce me to for some time. He politely listened to me for five or ten minutes as I was telling him what I wanted to do. But when his wife came in with the coffee, he stood up and said to her: "See what he wants . . . he wants to talk." I wasn't sure which was more humiliating: what he said or the plain fact that he actually trusted leaving me alone with his young wife, something that no man does with a male stranger.

I mention all this not because it is this kind of humiliation that I want to examine here but because this feeling of humiliation is only the tip of that enormous iceberg of "emotional field experiences" that are not pleasurable to talk about. I also mention it because such an experience makes one weary of the idea that talking about anything is necessarily good. It adds another dimension to the sociological analysis of "what talking means" (Bourdieu 1982).

One last preliminary critical reflection: when we decide to talk and write about our emotions, don't we, in the name of combatting the dominance of a specific kind of Western rationality that neglects the role of emotions, simply work to subject and reduce emotions to rationalistic interpretations, regardless of whether the aim is to "explain" or to "understand" them? If we are to really undermine the primacy of rationality over emotions, ought we not find ways of feeling how we talk rather than talking about how we feel? Or should we not be searching for a poetic language that accompanies and carries our feelings rather than a language that aims to ossify them and re-present them—in short, a language that has an intrinsic relation of capture (Deleuze and Guattari 1977) with them?

As I have already pointed out, I don't think that any of the above negates the importance of examining and reflecting on the emotions generated in the process of fieldwork. Rather, by keeping these issues in sight, I hope it will help me, and the reader, to avoid certain pitfalls and to recognise certain limitations.

Between the Personal and the Political 1:
Hating Israel in Palestine

Writing to a primarily Western readership, and with an Arab name that invites a specific kind of political presumptions, stereotypes, and imaginaries, requires an autobiographical clarification: hating Israel is not a "natural" or "primordial" sentiment that I have grown up with. Quite the contrary. In my conservative Christian Lebanese environment, it was far more common to idealise Israel and Israelis as people who have managed to create a bastion of Western civilization and modernity despite being surrounded by fundamentally "agro" and backward Muslim hordes. This was a fantasy that many, though by no means all, Christian Lebanese shared. I did. Though politics was only a marginal preoccupation for me, I grew up to be an unreflexively pro-Israeli person throughout my early and late teenage years in Lebanon. It was only when I left Lebanon and was midway through my undergraduate study in Australia in the late seventies that I slowly turned into an "anti-Israeli." This was part of my general transformation into a "leftie" via a deep immersion in Marxist literature—a common enough transformation at the time.

At that stage, however, mine was a very intellectual anti-Israel-ism based on associating Israel and Zionism with Western colonialism and imperialism in the Middle East. Such anti-Israel-ism did not have, to me at least, the "affective" component (smash-the-"Zionist-entity" type). Despite my new political leanings, I continued to associate emotional anti-Zionism with the "backward Arab masses" that, in a slightly racist and classist way, I was still eager to distinguish myself from. Nevertheless, having been through the beginning of the civil war in Lebanon, and having experienced the Palestinians as "aggressors" wanting to take over Lebanon and Israel as a "saviour" and a "model," to end up perceiving the latter as "oppressors" and the Palestinians as "oppressed" took quite a shift in my worldview and the nature of my political attachments.

Later my emotions about Palestine deepened. I began a far more intensive reading of Middle Eastern literature, history, and social science. I also became more aware of the nature of Palestinian lives under occupation, especially after visiting Israel and the West Bank. Furthermore, I began reading Arab literature on the Palestinian question in Arabic, a language I had grown to reject at my French school. "Reading Palestine" in Arabic added an unquestionable layer of emotionality that the English and French languages did not provide. This is probably because there is some structural complicity between my earliest and therefore deepest emotional structure and the structure of the Arabic language, both being foundational elements in the making of my subjectivity.

Paradoxically, this deepening of my feelings towards the Palestinian question came at the same time as I began, under the influence of Bourdieu, to critically reflect on the nature of my initial intellectual leftism and the facile way it invited me to fuse political and social scientific pursuits. Bourdieu, after Weber, refers to this "leftism" as a "proletaroid" intellectual culture. He is critical of it as an intellectual position which gives precedence to political interests over social scientific interests. Instead, he argues for the autonomy of the intellectual field and holds that good politics does not necessarily produce good social science. He is also critical of this leftism as an ineffective political position. He argues in *Distinction* (1984) that it is the structural location of "intellectuals" as the dominated fraction of the dominant class that makes them more disposed, through a process of affective homology, to show solidarity with the dominated and oppressed peoples of the world. I took this reflexive critique on board, and by the time I was getting more affectively enmeshed with the Palestinian question, I no longer simplistically believed that being pro-Palestinian gave me better access to "the truth." Perhaps this detachment was facilitated by the fact that French, and even more so, English, were my analytical languages and my emotions towards the Palestinian question were, as mentioned above, more enmeshed in the Arabic language.

From another, very different biographical perspective, I have often felt that my sensitivity towards what I perceive to be situations of "quasi-total social domination" was structured by the kind of power my father exercised within the family realm. When I was growing up, my father, an army officer, wielded absolute and undisputed power in the household. He was not a physically violent person, but he was a classic case of a benevolent dictator who could not tolerate anyone challenging his power: he allowed us to do many things, but nothing could happen if it was not "allowed." And when something was not allowed it was always a non-negotiable edict that descended top-down upon us. Even late in our teenage years, there was no room for autonomy over the self and for its correlate: negotiation between sovereign autonomous wills. My father did not know what negotiation meant. He made decisions. And those on the receiving end were left with little choice: it was either obeying or secretly disobeying. This is what I mean by a situation of total social domination. It did not mean that those subjected to power were totally dominated. It meant more that those in power aspired to such total domination.

But what was even more objectionable in my eyes about my father's mode of wielding power was that when my two sisters and I were found to be doing something without his consent, it was my father who affected to have been "hurt"; his assumption was always that it was *we* who had "broken his trust" and behaved unjustly. This has made me particularly sensitive to the subtle and unsubtle ways in which those who wield excessive power exercise it and the plethora of capricious, vacuous, and self-serving sentiments of "hurt," "pain," and "sense of being misunderstood," etc. in which such power is couched. In turn, I have always clearly seen how those ultimately narcissistic sentiments cannot even be "felt" but for the relations of power that underlie them, no matter how well hidden these relations are from those concerned.

I have no doubt that it is this "patriarchal" experience which has predisposed me to empathise with those subjected to similarly structured forms of power and domination. This is why it has always been the "power and domination aspect" of the Palestinian-Israeli conflict, far more than some historical sense of injustice concerning the colonization of Palestinian land, that activates my anger. While I am sympathetic to the "they've stolen the land" discourse, I am nonetheless far more affected by the overwhelming power and capacity for domination that Israel vividly and daily displays when relating to the Palestinians, and that continuously aims at negating the possibility of even an inkling of Palestinian sovereignty. Good Palestinians are simply those who accept being powerless, and they can achieve "peace" by simply accepting Israel's proposals: again, no room for negotiations here. I am equally affected, if not more so, by the narcissistic and self-indulgent sentiments of "hurt"—"we are the victims," "they don't recognise our right to exist"—that accompany this formidable display of power and that to me feel very much like my father's self-indulgent "hurt."

While the elements discussed above were all present in the feelings of anger and hatred towards Israel that I experienced in the aftermath of the savage bombing of Lebanon, there was certainly another dimension which intensified both the anger and the hatred and which was not present in my identification with the Palestinians as victims of domination. A short presentation of my embryonic theorisation of political, and particularly national, emotions will help me analyse this in a useful auto-ethnographic way.

Political/National Emotions

When I began conceiving of "political emotions," my ideas were partly driven by what I felt was a somewhat obvious and yet neglected dimension in the analysis of the Arab-Israeli conflict: for the Arabs (and to a certain degree, all Muslims) and for the Israelis, Palestine and Israel are highly charged emotional entities. In my earliest fieldwork notebook, where I began noting the way people spoke of Palestine, I scribbled this convoluted, all-encompassing sentence: "The nation as an anthropomorphically imagined affective political entity." I was trying to capture in one sentence the analytically common conception of the nation as "imagined community," and the equally common fact that the nation is anthropomorphised. I was also trying to capture the fact that not only is the nation "anthropomorphically imagined" but there has always been an emotional dimension to this imagining: if "Israel is seething" and "Palestine is weeping" and I am a person identifying with either of these two nations, I will feel that I am seething or weeping too. This makes the experience of national identification more than just an imagining. We can call it emotive imagining, noting, however, that this means bending the meaning of a strict conception of imagining as something on the order of the image. Nonetheless, this was good enough to convey, in ways pointed to by Vamik Volkan (1997), that the identification with such "emotive imaginaries" was such that people felt that their whole mode of and capacity for self-constitution were directly related to the existence and well-being of such "anthropomorphically imagined affective entities": how they were perceived to be "faring" ("well," "weak," "fragile," "frightened," "angry," "nervous," etc.) shaped how the self was faring. Sudhir Kakar, in his account of Hindu-Muslim conflict in India, has given a wonderfully nuanced analysis of how this we-feeling fluctuates with the tempo and intensity of a confrontation (1996).

I constructed the basic elements of this conception of national/political emotions by putting together three anthropologico-philosophical accounts of the constitution of the emotional self: Spinoza's conception of humans as "joy"-seekers, Lacan's positing of a formative phase in human development in which the self seeks to overcome a sense of fragmentation, as developed in his analysis of the mirror stage, and Pierre Bourdieu's notion of *illusio*, which denotes a self that invests itself emotionally and libidinally in what is likely to make life meaningful.

In reading Spinoza, I have always seen him to offer the starting point for an understanding either of "political emotions" or, at least, of what is a political dimension in emotions. This is because his conception of "the affects" was specifically linked to power, which is central for any useful definition of the political. Spinoza's basic emotions, joy and sadness, were affects denoting changes in one's capacity to act and think efficiently—that is, at least as I see it, one's power over one's environment, or what Spinoza also refers to as one's state of perfection.

In conceiving specifically of the emotions that are derived from national identification, my starting point was Spinoza's Postulates P12 and P19 in the *Ethics* (2000), respectively, "The mind as far as it can, strives to imagine those things that increase or aid the body's power of acting" and "He who imagines that what he loves is destroyed will be saddened; but he who imagines it to be preserved will rejoice." In this sense, I was trying to examine what it means when that imagined object of love is a nation. One crucial "function" of the imagined nation is precisely to boost our "sense of perfection," our self-perceived conception of our capacities (Gatens and Lloyd 1999). As I have often shown in my work on nationalism, whether in Australia or in Lebanon, nationalist identification always involves taking what are considered the "best" capacities and qualities of individual members of the collective and making them the capacities and qualities of the collective. This allows all the individuals who identify with the collective to see "its capacities and qualities" as theirs. The nationalist as an individual might be a technological nullity but s/he is still capable of saying, "We've sent a rocket to Mars." S/he might not know how to swim, but s/he can still say, "We are better swimmers than most nations." That is, the "I" by imagining itself through the national "we" can acquire powers it cannot dream of having by simply imagining itself as an individual "I." Power here is through the acquisition of potentials: it is not that the nationalist who is uneducated becomes educated merely by identifying with a nation of educated people. Rather, the uneducated acquire power by thinking that they have *the potential* to be educated even if they are not so. This is part of what Nietzsche (1968) usefully calls "sense of power," a concept I found myself deploying along with Spinoza, and which is not about how much power one actually has but about what power one thinks one can potentially muster. It is precisely this "sense of power" that is at stake in national identification and that makes nations worthy of affective attachment: you attack me as a national or you attack my nation, you are not simply attacking who I am but who I fantasise I can be.

Pierre Bourdieu's notion of *habitus*, denoting the capacity of the body to efficiently act in a specific sociocultural milieu, is clearly inspired by Spinoza's conception of "perfection." Indeed, Bourdieu, in later works, argues that every *habitus* is endowed with a *conatus*, a Spinozan term denoting the tendency of things to "persevere in their own being." Bourdieu, however, does not explicitly locate emotions in relation to the *habitus* as much as in relation to what he calls the "*illusio*," which denotes the way we invest and attach ourselves to those elements of the social world that give our lives a meaning, whether it is our job, our personal relations, our reputation, our hobbies, or our ideals: whatever we pursue that makes our lives worth living for us. Bourdieu links *illusio* with a social libido because the way we invest ourselves in the social world is not only intellectual but libidinal (2000:164–165). He emphasises that in investing ourselves in the world, our whole being is on the line, so to speak. When someone offers a heated plea in defense of their nation, in support of the environment, or for the right to carry a weapon, we say that they are emotional because "it means a lot to them." In a sense, Bourdieu is emphasising the dialectical way in which this process of meaningfulness works: what means a lot to us is precisely what gives our lives meaning; we give it meaningfulness, and it gives our lives meaningfulness in return. At stake is the very viability of our life: that is why we get emotional about it. Looking at nationalism as a particular *illusio* allows us to capture the way nationalists invest their very being in their nation. Not everyone is a nationalist to the same degree, of course, but there is no nationalism, and no national emotions, without an investment in the nation as something that gives our lives a meaning.

Lacan's mirror stage adds an important dimension to this perspective (1977). If Bourdieu's *illusio* allows us to better capture the emotional nature of our social investments, and if Spinoza emphasizes the relation between emotions and one's power over one's environment, Lacan allows us to think about the relation between emotions and our power of self-constitution that is our power over the self. The two are of course related: our sense of power over ourselves is affected by our sense of power over our environment, and as we have seen with Bourdieu, by giving meaning to things outside of us we give meaning to ourselves. For Lacan, the individual "I" is structured very early in life by a feeling of fragmentation (a sense of being "all over the place," so to speak) and by the setting of an ideal non-fragmented and wholesome image of the self that we strive to become (the mirror image). My "self" as a subject begins to take shape insofar as it can constitute itself against this tendency towards fragmentation. An often used popular metaphor, which must denote the way this sense of fragmentation and the struggle against it are experienced in an everyday context, is the exclamation "Pull yourself together."

Using such a perspective, I found it useful to think about part of our emotions as deriving from the various degrees and modes with which we succeed—or do not succeed—in "pulling ourselves together" and at least give ourselves the appearance of a certain wholeness, coherence, and togetherness. These kinds of emotions are not simply about how much we "pull ourselves together" but the extent of anxiety with which we encounter our sense of fragmentation and struggle to overcome it. Some are more relaxed than others about feeling "not together," so to speak. One type of shame, for example, can be conceived as a result of a public exposure of our struggling-to-keep-ourselves-together at a moment that we wanted to keep private to ourselves. Or, to take another example: I have often noted that racism works in such a way that it actually aims to "shatter" those who are subjected to it. How much it can shatter the racialised subject will depend on the social and cultural resources that this subject has available to it in its effort to reconstitute itself, to "pull itself together." We can even say that the racists themselves try to "pull themselves together" through the act of being racist. Intuitively, I find it useful to think that the emotions experienced by both racists and those subjected to racism derive from these processes of self-constitution. Finding ways to capture this ethnographically has been one of the most interesting challenges of my research so far. The shattering effect of racism can sometimes be so extreme that the shattering of the symbolic self has an effect on the physical body. Some indigenous people subject to historical, intense racism, have difficulty keeping their very body together and appear to be physically disjointed.

One of the most useful aspects of this conception of emotions is that it accounts best for the way the nationalist's experience of the fragmentation of the nation and his or her constant struggle for "nationalist cohesion" and "national unity" can be seen to articulate with the struggle for personal cohesion. Lacan, or rather this fragment of Lacan that I am sure I have by now entirely reworked, deformed, and reinterpreted for my own purposes, offers us a productive way of explaining how nationalist emotions emerge at the point where the struggle for personal self-constitution and sovereignty over the self becomes articulated as the struggle for national self-constitution and national sovereignty.

These then are the perspectives that I fused and took as my starting point in developing a working theory of political emotions that I can activate ethnographically: political emotions are those emotions related to our sense of power over ourselves and our environment as we pursue those goals, ideals, and activities that give our life meaning. Let me now go back to the anti-Israeli emotions of anger and hatred that I experienced during and in the aftermath of the bombing of Lebanon.

Between the Personal and the Political 2:
Hating Israel in Lebanon

As I pointed out in concluding the section before last, besides some similarities, my anger towards Israel when the bombing of Lebanon began was more intense than the anger I experience when Israel engages in its daily attacks on Palestinians. This clearly had to do with two things: my own national identification with Lebanon as the land of my birth and my professional identification with South Lebanon and the South Lebanese which made them far less abstract entities to me than Palestine and the Palestinians are. The way these elements combined can be seen in this e-mail I sent to my friend and colleague Michael Jackson, who had been to Lebanon a few years back when I held a visiting position at the American University of Beirut and who e-mailed from Harvard to ask me "what I thought about the war" and "how I felt":

> I'm really too disgusted to talk about the war. The village where I do my field-work has been destroyed. A family I know has suffered massively, the father and two girls have died, literally disintegrated, and the mother has lost an arm and a leg . . . I just find the whole experience of a technologically over-equipped brutal state rampaging with impunity the way Israel did just, well . . . unspeakable. As Abbas said [Abbas el-Zein, a friend who had published an op-ed piece in the *New York Times*], it took those of us who have experienced the civil war a good ten years to convince ourselves that the war has ended. So, to have this monstrous destruction just as we thought we have left the war behind is very painful.

Here was instinctively listed first the anger derived from the effect of the bombing on specific South Lebanese people that I had come to know through fieldwork (as opposed to the abstract Palestinians that I encounter in my imagination when relating to Palestinian events), second, the anger that came from my national emotions—the way the ups and downs of "Lebanon" are experienced as my own ups and downs (and this in ways that are clearly different from the way I relate to Palestine), and finally, the anger rooted in what also makes me angry about the Palestinian situation: Israel's capacity to deploy its superior military power unchecked; what always appears as its sense of impunity—the hovering shadow of my father once again. Because I had already begun to intellectually reflect on emotions as the situation evolved, I also began to take notes about my own feelings throughout the bombing and its aftermath. Thinking about my attachment to Lebanon and my attachment to my informants helped me refine both my analytical conception of "political emotions" and my ideas about the significance of emotions in the field.

In the midst of Israel's bombing, I was in a coffee shop near the University of Sydney talking to another Lebanese Australian academic about the situation. We were both up in arms against the "Dear Israel, please take your time" approach adopted by some Western and Arab governments. We believed then, and it has become obvious now, that they were all hoping that the Israelis would quickly decimate Hezbollah and reduce Iranian influence on Israel's northern border and throughout the region. During the conversation, it crossed our minds that there was something racist in the way we felt the bombing as *so much more* objectionable than what the Palestinians endure on a daily basis. It was as if we were saying to Israel: "How can you do to us Lebanese what you do to Palestinians? Don't you realize we are . . . well . . . Lebanese!" I thought this simply meant that we were *more* affected by what was happening in Lebanon than by what happens in Palestine. Yet, as I further reflected on this, it became clear to me that the anger I was experiencing because of the Lebanese bombing was not that easily comparable to the anger triggered by the Palestinian situation that the two could be quantitatively compared in more-or-less terms. It was a different kind of anger. "Nothing strange about this," I have in my notebook. "I am experiencing this situation more personally rather than politically. Every bomb is experienced as an attack on my very being." This differentiation between personal and political was theoretically paradoxical because, as I have explained above, the emotions derived from a fusion between one's sense of well-being and the well-being of certain political entities such as the nation was at the core of what I was trying to theorise as "political emotions." Yet here I was, thinking that the emotions I was experiencing relating to Lebanon were more "personal" than the emotions I experience in relating to the Palestinian situation. This made me very quickly rethink the opposition I had initially created between personal and political emotions. Later in the evening I added a further note: "The way I am differentiating between the personal and the political is silly. Surely, all emotions are personal. The question is not whether they are personal or not but in *what way* they are personal?" This allowed me to think about the importance of the relations between the various elements that I have combined to define political emotions: the attachments that give our lives meaningfulness, the power over our environment, and the power over ourselves. To understand how political emotions differ from each other, we need to understand the various ways in which each of these elements combines with the others in specific situations. So, our political emotions derive from the way that certain collectivities we identify with operate as an *illusio*, something that gives our life meaning and something with which we imagine and reinforce the coherence of our personal identity. But the affective importance of each of these processes does not have to be the same for all such collectivities. One can speak of an important difference, for example, between an "identification with" and an "identification through." To identify *with* a nation keeps the nation at a certain distance from oneself, making it more an "object" of identification. To "identify *through*" is a far more intense kind of identification that does not allow for any separation. This, I feel, directs me towards a good explanation of the difference between my "Lebanese" and my "Palestinian" anger. I think that in the case of my relation to Palestine and Lebanon, I can easily say that I identify through Lebanon far more than I identify with it, and the reverse can be said about Palestine. There is more of Lacan and Spinoza than of Bourdieu in this identification, so to speak. This allows me a certain affective distance from Palestine that I do not have in relation to Lebanon. Thinking through the ramifications of this differential mode of identification can give us important insights in the way immigrants end up identifying with their host nation, if they ever do so: what are the conditions which lead one to identify with a nation and the conditions that transform this identification *with* to an identification *through*, or vice versa?

Political Emotions, Ethnography, and Power

In the above, I have shown some of the analytical and conceptual insights that grew out of my critical reflections on the biographical basis of my own political emotions in the field. In the remaining part of this chapter, I want to expose some further issues that emerged from a more specific reflection on my emotions as they interacted with the emotions of my informants within the context of participant observation.

As I began working with the South Lebanese in Sydney, it was clear that the feeling of anger that I shared with them allowed me to get closer to people on a one-to-one basis, as it created a common ground for personal interaction. It also gave me a participatory access to the mood that prevailed among them collectively. This "emotional participation" was further deepened when I organised to have the people who had lost close relatives interviewed, and began working on what I called "transnational mourning." The following e-mail, written by my research assistant, who was interviewing the Shi'a women to whom I had no direct access, reflects the intensity of the emotions at the time:

> Dear Ghassan, I finished the interview with X this morning. It was very sad and emotionally draining. I need to tell you this. I stopped the car and cried for quite a while on my way back home.

Initially, I thought that anything that contributed to the intensification of my emotions served a good research purpose. In my anger, I began to notice that Israel was getting more and more abstract in my mind. I was increasingly imagining it as an "evil person." In a process similar to that described by Kakar (1996), the Israelis that I know and have friendly relations with receded in my mind. I did not want to think of particular Israelis. They complicated the emotional picture. I just wanted to think of "Israel," which was easier to be angry with and to hate. Part of me was engaging in this quite consciously in a kind of "strategic abstraction." I had convinced myself that, given the nature of their personal loss, I could not possibly be as angry and upset as my informants. So I believed that anything that made me "sadder" and "angrier" towards Israel allowed me to acquire an experience closer to theirs. Yet, in the very process of doing so, I began to gradually notice something rather strange: my informants seemed less emotional about Israel than I was.

Their expressions of anger and hatred were certainly there, but they seemed always less intense than mine were. I could see that this was partly because their loss was personal before being political and that to think of Israel as you are mourning your father or mother was in some ways to demean and depersonalise the loss. Nonetheless, even when reflecting on the political dimensions of this loss, they seemed less emotional about it. The interview below most explicitly shows this. All of the interviewees were asked to relate what they were doing when they heard that their relatives had been killed and how they reacted to the news. This interviewee had heard a rumour that his father had died and was anxiously waiting to hear more.

> My sister rang in the afternoon. She was crying . . . so she didn't need to say anything. I started crying too.
> I know this is difficult but can you tell me what were your thoughts as you received the call?

I was thinking of my father . . . what else could I have thought of?

Yes, of course. I hope you don't mind me asking but can you tell me more . . .
  what exactly were you thinking about your father?

What kind of question is this!?

Sorry. You don't have to answer of course. But it would help if you tried
  . . . There was nothing exact . . . my head was just crammed with memories
    of my father, his face . . . when he visited here . . . when I saw him in the
    village . . . how he used to grab my arm when I was a child . . .

(. . .)

What were you doing when your sister rang?

I was watching the news. I still remember that there was an Israeli man from
  Haifa talking about shelters . . . May God never give them shelter.

How do you describe your feelings about what Israel has done?

(sarcastic smile) . . . my feelings about Israel . . . I have no feelings about Israel.

Surely you must be angry . . .

I am angrier with the Australian government. It really hurts that they did not
  condemn Israel. Howard [the Australian prime minister] even stated that
  they were justified in doing this . . . I am also angry with myself for not
  having been with my parents.

But surely, you must feel something about Israel. They killed your father.

If you are to be angry with someone you must think they are human beings.
  If a car killed your father you get angry with the driver or with the car? If a
  snake bit you . . . do you get angry with the snake? No, you just try to kill it.
  The Israelis . . . you know . . . they kill us, that's what they have always done.
  We can't afford to let them make us angry. They want us to be angry. But we
  have stopped being angry a long time ago. It is a waste of time and energy.
  We just have to concentrate on making sure they can't kill us anymore.

I puzzled over this kind of reaction—not so much the link between the dehumanisation of Israel and the lack of anger towards it, which was interesting but
clear, but rather the idea that one "cannot afford" to be angry and the fact that
there was something genuinely non-angry in the response that treated Israel
as some kind of "business" that needs to be dealt with. However, things became clearer to me when a similar point was made a few days after. The Lebanese prime minister was shown on television addressing foreign diplomats
about the catastrophic consequences of the Israeli bombing, and he began to
cry. I got a bit emotional myself seeing him on the news. But to my surprise, all

the people in the room started mocking the prime minister, and one person in particular recited a verse from a well-known Arab poem written about the fall of Granada. In the poem the Muslim leader who was supposed to have failed in defending Granada from the invading Christian forces went to his mother crying and she said to him: "You cry like a woman for a land you did not know how to protect like a man." This was not said from a "macho," "men don't cry" perspective, or at least not just from that perspective, for the women participated in mocking the prime minister just as much as the men did.

As I reflected on the Granada poem, it dawned on me that the whole discourse was structured by the opposition between passivity and activity in the face of Israel. Crying was perceived as a result of the prime minister's inability to act, and thus represented the historical powerlessness of the Lebanese government. Indeed, one can say that historically, the shadow of Israel's successive military victories in the fifties and sixties and its overwhelming 1967 victory looms large over the way the conflict is imagined, and the general Arab emotional experience of conflict with Israel is structured around a passive "look what they've done to us." While part of the success of the PLO among Arabs came from its capacity to generate a certain sense of pride in the ability of Arabs to be active rather than passive, it was really Hezbollah that made the first-ever claim of an active resistance that has produced actual results: the liberation of South Lebanon from Israeli occupation. This psychological gain was real, and there is plenty of evidence in official and non-official discourse to prove that it was experienced as a gain both by the Arabs who celebrated it and by the Israelis who deplored it. And there is no doubt that in striking Lebanon the way it did, Israel aimed at destroying the "ethos" that gave rise to this sense of power. This is why, despite all the destruction of the 2006 war, Hezbollah and its supporters considered the war to be a victory. Hezbollah showed itself capable of continuing to send missiles across the Lebanese-Israeli border and "acting on" Israel regardless of how destructive the Israeli onslaught against it and its positions were. This symbolic idea that "we can do things to them" and not just "look what they have done to us" was crucial in understanding the aftermath of the war and the emotions generated by it.

As I was thinking all this, I experienced one of those rare, and very pleasant, intellectual moments when one's independent theoretical readings and ideas that were just "lying around" suddenly become alive and start to creatively interact with one's interpretations of empirical reality, each feeding from the other. This happened when, as if out of the blue, Greimas' (1987) reflections on anger, which I had read some time before, suddenly came to mind. Part of Greimas' exploration of anger relies on his theorisation of a relation within the self between a subject of state that is acted upon and a subject of doing that acts. This attracted my attention because it brought power into the equation, particularly the more subjective Nietzschean notion of "sense of power," which, as seen above, I had posited as crucial in understanding political emotions. Our emotions are not the same when we experience ourselves as capable of acting on what affects us rather than as condemned to have to just passively endure it. Spinoza points to this in postulate P58 of the *Ethics*: "Apart from the joy and desire which are passions, there are other affects of joy and desire which are related to us insofar as we act." More recently, but within this Spinozean lineage, Alphonso Lingis (1999) has also shown how the hurt we experience when someone does something to us is likely to swell within us if we are not capable of reciprocating by "doing something" in return.

The above explains quite well why my anger and hatred of Israel were greater than those of my informants. If there is a relation between the power to act and the intensity of anger, is not the intensity of my anger a reflection of my own inability to act or my inability to fully identify with those capable of acting? Thus I could now see that there is something in the nature of my anger which is, at least partly, a reflection of my position as an intellectual: someone who, by definition, is a passive person watching events unfold and having no capacity to practically bring about any change to them. This made me think of how often intellectuals unreflexively project their own emotions onto political actors that they are in sympathy with, thinking, on the basis of these sympathies, that there is no difference between the two. They forget that regardless of the degree of sympathy, the emotions of political actors are precisely those of actors and are likely to be different from what has to be recognised in their sociological specificity as intellectual emotions.

But this was not the only issue at hand in this particular case. My informants, though they are in Sydney, see themselves as actors not because they have a concrete capacity to act against Israel but because of their deep *identification* with Hezbollah, a force that they see as capable of making a riposte, capable of hitting back. That is, to use terminology developed above, because they not only identify with Hezbollah but through it, they imagine themselves through it to be hitting back. This is where I realised that a key issue in the emotional differences between myself and my informants was not just my position as an academic observer. It was also in the nature of my identification with Hezbollah. Despite the fact that I did experience a sense of pride in Hezbollah, its capacity to respond to and its ability to survive the Israeli onslaught, being of Christian Lebanese background, being an agnostic person and a secular leftist, remembering that the rise of Hezbollah in Lebanon was accompanied by the murder of many Shi'a-background communist intellectuals and activists during the dark history of the Lebanese civil war—all of this worked to limit my identification with the party. And it was this lack of identification which explains the difference between my sense of power and that of my informants and the corresponding anger that went with it. Emotional identification with the informants, even more so than cultural identification, is not simply a matter of either/or, or a quantitative matter that the anthropologist acquires with time. It is rather a far more complex process that requires continual critical reappraisal. In the case of political emotions, it is crucial to ground emotional identification in the existing relations of power, and in one's location within and to these relations.

On Ethnographic Vacillation

To argue, as I did above, that there are some fundamental differences between the emotional experiences of anthropologists and their informants even when the former manage to identify and empathise with the latter does not mean that the two cannot share similar emotional experiences. It is simply to note that there is a limit to how similar these experiences can be. Indeed, and notwithstanding the above, there is no doubt that I shared emotions of sadness as well as feelings of anger and hatred towards Israel with my informants. And there is equally no doubt that this allowed me to understand what they were going through much better than what a purely "cultural"— to the extent that one can think of the cultural as differentiated from the emotional—response would have allowed. However, if as I illustrated above, there is a need to problematise what I *did not* share with my informants, this does not mean that what I shared with them is free of problems. But to critically reflect on what it means for an anthropologist to share the emotions of the individuals and groups with whom he or she is working and yet maintain an analytical eye at what is being shared takes us to the more familiar terrain of the contradictions that are part of participant observation insofar as they apply to emotions. It is to these contradictions that I turn in the final part of this chapter.

Indeed, it seems that the classical tension that is inherent to participant observation is intensified when played out at the level of emotions. There is a good case to be made that as an ethnographer you have not achieved good participation if you cannot participate in the collective emotional ups and downs of the culture you are studying. However, sharing in the moods of a group of people seems to be a much deeper immersion than sharing habits and culture. So, there is a case to be made that once the anthropologists start not only *acting* the way their informants are acting but also *feeling* what their informants are feeling, they are no longer operating on that imaginary cultural borderline which allows the movement between participation and observation. It could be said that they have stopped being "observers" and have become mere "participants." However, a more productive way of seeing this is that the emotional borderline is deeper into the culture of the other than the cultural borderline is. Once you are sharing your informants' emotions and moods, you are operating from a space where what Bourdieu calls social gravity—the force that pulls you into a society—is much stronger. It does not mean that you cannot remove yourself for observational/analytical purposes from the society you are studying, but it takes much more effort—an effort that is in itself emotional.

This is especially so when we are talking about emotions such as political anger and hatred, whereby the tension between participation and observation is compounded with the tension between the political and the analytical. For one can legitimately ask the questions Is the anthropologist allowed to hate? and What are the analytical consequences of such political feelings?

As I have already mentioned, for a long time now I have taken on board Bourdieu's point that there is a fundamental difference between the logic of intellectual inquiry and the logic of politics. The latter requires one, by definition, to take a political stand. Consequently, it has to stop inquiring and asking critical questions and become more consumed with a defensive posture. It reaches the point where it has to say, Here is where I stand. If you are not with me, you are my enemy. Bourdieu argues that intellectual inquiry cannot operate with this friend/enemy logic, as it simply cannot allow itself to take a stand, for to take a stand means to stop inquiring critically. From this perspective, it is clear that the notion of hatred belongs to the discourse of enmity and politics and as such should have no place in anthropology.

Consequently, I was constantly, and at the same time when I was experiencing anger and hatred, trying to recover some sense of emotional detachment and objectivity in examining the conditions for the generation of these emotions. Nonetheless, I was still drawn towards the political and towards taking a stand against Israel in the war. For example, I was motivated enough to work on organising a public ceremony commemorating the dead in Sydney Town Hall to highlight what Israel had done. I thought it necessary that the mourning of such Lebanese Australians, insofar as they were Australian citizens, should not remain private and ought to be shared and understood by the rest of the Australian population.

It was in this sense, then, that I was constantly negotiating among not only two but three modes of participating in reality: the analytical, the emotional, and the political. And what was difficult was not the fact that three states co-existed within me but the fact that they were often in a state of "friction," and this state of friction generated another layer of emotions which were specific to the practice of ethnography and which were grounded in the ambivalence that is a necessary part of participant observation.

It is here that one can locate an important difference between the classi-cal conception of the tensions of participant observation and the tensions be-tween observation and "emotional participation." Though there is a sense in which the "being part of and not being part of" is the same at the level of emotions as it is often conceived by classical descriptions of culture-centred "participant observation," there is a new dimension that emerges when this is played out in the emotional domain. Culture-centred participant observation, with the anthropologist fluctuating between his or her own culture and the culture of the other, does not produce a third culture unique to ethnography. Partly because of the individualistic dimension of emotions, emotion-centred participant observation produces within the anthropologist a set of emotions that is specific to ethnography. In my fieldwork, I felt that the capacity to share certain emotional states with informants and then to repress such emotions for analytical purposes, at the same time, did not simply mean that sometimes I was emotional and sometimes I wasn't. Nor did it mean that sometimes I al-lowed myself to be emotional and sometimes I didn't—as if emotions can be controlled and mastered in such a rational manner. Rather, as I have argued, it meant that I was constantly negotiating between being both emotional and analytical. This was particularly difficult given that the aim was not to reduce emotions to analytical language but to "capture them" as emotions.

Such a situation reminded me of a case of domesticating a particular type of llama, analysed by the French naturalist Isodore Geoffroy Saint-Hilaire (1861), and that I have used analytically before. Hilaire explains how farmers in a mountainous region of the Andes came to notice the quality of this llama's wool and were, therefore, quite eager to domesticate it. The problem was that no sooner was it caught and brought in from the wild and domesticated than the quality of its wool deteriorated. Therefore the domesticators faced a rather complex question: how to maintain the llama in the wild so that the quality of its wool is preserved, and how, at the same time, to stop it from being in the wild in order to exploit it. This was the difficult dialectic: there was a need to bring the llama in and make it part of "civilisation," but at the same time it was worthy of being part of civilisation only insofar as it remained outside it. The technique developed by the farmers is what Saint-Hilaire called the "*sauvegarde de l'état sauvage*"—the safeguarding of the savage state. In a very important way, this is how anthropologists have to treat the emotional states that they share with their informants if they are to analyse them. On the one hand, emotions have to be brought in and subjected to the rational analytical order, but on the other, the very process of "bringing them in" from the emotional wilderness, so to speak, and reducing them to "analysable" data, makes them lose their analytical value, which lies in their specificity as emotions. It thus becomes imperative to find a way to subject emotions (i.e., the wild) to analysis (i.e., rational civilization) without having them lose their specificity as emotional "wilderness." Consequently, ethnographers have to continuously negotiate the terms under which emotions are subjected to "observation" and constantly "safeguard them in their savage state" in the very process through which they are experienced.

It is this ethnography-specific negotiation, which, as I have argued, is infused with its own specific emotions, that I want to call ethnographic vacillation, borrowing from Spinoza's notion of a "vacillating *conatus*." Vacillation for Spinoza is the product of contradictory striving for joy. Basically, vacillation occurs because we do not always know what we want and because we often want contradictory things. Using Bourdieu's notion of *illusio*, we can say that vacillation is when we have contradictory *illusios*, when there are many incompatible things giving meaning to our lives and we find ourselves pursuing them despite their incompatibility. What is important, though, is that vacillation is not just a movement between various states of being; rather, it is a state of being in itself. This is why it captures the state of being that is produced by the ethnographic navigation between the analytical and the participatory so well. For the anthropologist, it is fundamental to share both the anthropological *illusio* and the *illusio* of belonging to the culture being studied. It is not a case of simply participating in one reality at one time and then another reality at another time. It is the attempt to invest oneself in both social realities with their contradictory demands that creates the specificity of the ethnographic modality of being. Dealing with emotional states highlights the fact that ethnographic vacillation is not a regular movement. It is not like the famous image of the swing, used by some anthropologists to convey the idea of participant observation, for the swing symbolises a kind of predictable and rhythmic movement between the two cultures of participation and observation. Ethnographic vacillation is more like being a table tennis ball on the beach being drawn in and out by the waves, with the sandy beach representing the informants' culture and the water representing the cultural world of the anthropologist. The movement of the table tennis ball is unpredictable and chaotic, yet it is certain that sometimes it will go deeper into the sea and sometimes get closer to the sand. Sometimes it might even stay on the sand for relatively long periods of time, only to be swept by the waves again. Sometimes it will be drawn deep into the sea, only to be inevitably pushed back to the shore.

It is probably the case that when dealing with less-emotional dimensions of cultural life, ethnographers will have a bit more agency over where and for how long to be on the beach or in the sea, but nonetheless, a capacity to recognise and critically reflect on this vacillation is central to any ethnographic enterprise.

References

Bourdieu, P. 1982. *Ce que parler veut dire: L'economie des echanges linguistiques*. Paris: Fayard.

————. 1984. *Distinction: A Social Critique of the Judgement of Taste*. Cambridge, MA: Harvard University Press.

————. 2000. *Pascalian Meditations*. Cambridge: Polity Press.

Deleuze, G., and F. Guattari. 1977. *Anti-Oedipus: Capitalism and Schizophrenia*. New York: Viking.

Gatens, M., and G. Lloyd. 1999. *Collective Imaginings: Spinoza, Past and Present*. London: Routledge.

Saint-Hilaire, I. G. de. 1861. *Acclimatation et domestication des animaux utiles*. Paris: La Maison Rustique.

Gilsenan, M. 1996. *Lords of the Lebanese Marches: Violence and Narrative in an Arab Society*. Berkeley: University of California Press.

Greimas, A. J. 1987. "On Anger: A Lexical Semantic Study." In A. J. Greimas, ed., *On Meaning: Selected Writings in Semiotic Theory*, 148–164. London: Pinter.

Hage, G. 2000. *White Nation: Fantasies of White Supremacy in a Multicultural Society*. New York: Routledge.

————. 2003. *Against Paranoid Nationalism: Searching for Hope in a Shrinking Society.* Annandale, NSW: Pluto Press.

————. 2005. "A Not So Multi-Sited Ethnography of a Not So Imagined Community." *Anthropological Theory* 5:463–475.

————. 2006. "Migration and the Transformation of Male Sexuality." In J. Gagnon and S. Khalaf, eds., *Arab Sexuality,* 107–129. London: Al-Saqi Books.

Kristeva, J. 1991. *Strangers to Ourselves.* New York: Columbia University Press.

Lutz, C., and G. White. 1986. "The Anthropology of Emotions." *Annual Review of Anthropology* 15:405–436.

Milton, K., and M. Svašek, eds. 2005. *Mixed Emotions: Anthropological Studies of Feeling.* Oxford: Berg.

Nietzsche, F. 1968. *The Will to Power.* New York: Vintage.

Lacan, J. 1977. *Ecrits: A Selection.* New York: Norton.

Lingis, A. 1999. *Dangerous Emotions.* Berkeley: University of California Press.

Kakar, S. 1996. *The Colors of Violence: Cultural Identities, Religion, and Conflict.* Chicago: University of Chicago Press.

Spinoza, B. de. 2000. *Ethics.* Oxford: Oxford University Press.

Volkan, V. 1997. *Bloodlines: From Ethnic Pride to Ethnic Terrorism.* New York: Farrar, Straus, and Giroux.

6 Tian'anmen in Yunnan

Emotions in the Field during a Political Crisis

Elisabeth Hsu

THE METAPHOR "FIELD" OFFERS A CONVENIENT if not a partially misleading image of the site in which anthropologists work. It is misleading insofar as this geographical metaphor (suggesting the solidity of a set and settled physical domain) underplays the less predictable and controllable aspects and events of ethnographic research. While an emphasis on the field as a "clearly bounded space" suits a vision of fieldwork in which using systematic methods has its dominant place (codified methods, after all, are always best realised in so-called bounded and controlled settings), it not only elides the "unexpected" in ethnographic research but subtly discourages how experiencing the unexpected can have valuable heuristic significance. This chapter explores how unexpected events interrupted well-organised field research, and how these events, while hindering access to certain domains of fieldwork, nevertheless offered the opportunity to gain an anthropological understanding different from the usual that we are taught to garner in classes on conventional fieldwork methods.

I will explore this claim that fieldwork consists of a particular form of living rather than a set of methods through my experiences before and after the military crackdown on Tian'anmen on June 4, 1989, while I was doing ethnographic fieldwork in a college of traditional Chinese medicine (TCM). On the one hand, I discovered that I now have forgotten almost all of the events I had then recorded in a personal diary. On the other, I note that the interviews I had with young acupuncture teachers towards the end of my fieldwork, six months later, were unusually personal and moving. I shall ask whether the subdued but undeniable repression of the spring events in autumn 1989 meant that the silently existent pressure on the social body, which at that time was experienced by many locals, had also affected my individual body. I shall also ask whether this submersion of the individual into the body politic enhanced emotional closeness to my interviewees. On reflection, it appears that it was not the interview method which made possible these moving encounters but rather the shared daily experience of sitting silently in front of the TV in times of tension.

The military crackdown on Tian'anmen on June 4, 1989, was by far the most emotionally laden time of my ethnographic fieldwork from September 1988 to December 1989. At that time I was in the role of an undergraduate student learning TCM at the provincial TCM college in Kunming city, the capital of Yunnan province, in the southwest of the People's Republic of China (PRC). As I recently dug through my field notes, I found a typed document entitled "Voices from the Province on the Chinese Pro-Democracy Movement"—undated, with pseudonyms—recounting in diary form events over a two-month period. It is thirty-nine pages long and covers the time from May 3 to July 5, 1989.

This chapter does not aim to feed into the flood of literature on the political crisis surrounding June 4, 1989. It will not even recount the most basic "facts" of the event, which in its acute phase was most visible from Hu Yaobang's death on April 14 to the Tian'anmen massacre on June 4 (and its immediate aftermath). Nor will it attempt to tease out whether the crisis was political, social, or economic or whether it was an event that brought to an end serious tensions within the military (since, as we know by hindsight, the Dengist reforms were implemented at an unprecedented speed in the 1990s).

Rather, I will recount living through an emotionally highly charged shared experience that affected the body politic at large, where state became personal (Greenhouse et al. 2002; DeSoto and Dudwick 2000; Nordstrom and Robben 1996), but unlike Greenhouse and others I will highlight how the personal rapport between researcher and respondents was temporarily diminished but later enhanced, and how it accordingly led to more valuable personal exchanges than are likely to be elicited through usual fieldwork methods. Finally I will suggest that the degree to which the researcher is prepared to be affected as a person by the fieldwork experience, rather than sophisticated methodology, determines the quality of ethnographic research.

The student unrest began after the heart attack of Hu Yaobang, two weeks before the seventieth anniversary of the May 4 movement of 1919, the date when the Chinese demonstrated against the Treaty of Versailles after World

War I, which had guaranteed Japan special rights in Manchuria (Mitter 2004). Throughout the twentieth century, in republican and socialist times alike (1911–47 and 1949–today), May 4 stood for nationalism, revolutionary thought, gender equality, a simplified writing system, a literature in the vernacular that made literacy possible for the masses, and—in 1989—"For freedom and democracy"; or, rather, among my classmates in Yunnan: "Against corruption and nepotism" (Hsu 1999:154).

Some Preliminary Comments on the Document "Voices from the Province"

Said document is populated by about three dozen different people, who all have pseudonyms. Upon rereading it, I noted that I had no inkling of who more than two-thirds of the people I mention were, nor did most of these notes remind me of the incidents, the lunches, dinners, after-dinner outings, and discussions I referred to. Nor can I remember when and where I wrote this document—in China, Britain, or Switzerland? The use of pseudonyms suggests I was wary of its being found or confiscated and exposing friends who had made political jokes or talked to me about personal issues that a neighbour might take against them, a worry I know I had not merely in China. It concerns one of the most exciting times of fieldwork, and yet I forgot so many details. This forgetting is the first point I will explore in more detail below.

I also was surprised how freely I spoke to people, how many people I interacted with, how diverse opinions were, how every day was filled with events and discussions relating to the movement. Although this diary exclusively concerns multiple voices and viewpoints on the movement, these discussions went alongside conscientiously following a full programme of daily medical training, as my classroom notes, tutorial papers, clinical practice notebooks, and my published ethnography make clear (Hsu 1999:196–197). In contrast to Beijing, classes in Kunming, and particularly at the Yunnan TCM college, continued to be taught throughout the crisis months, except on May 17, 18, and 19 and on June 5 and 6 (Hsu 1999:154).

There was excitement in the air. Compared to my tourist friends and other foreign colleagues who lived in Kunming at the time, I barely mingled with the demonstrators, but indiscriminately talked about this political crisis with whoever would speak with me. This worried my teachers at the college. One of the voices in the diary commented: "Aren't you aware that you are talking to spies in everyday costume?!" My diary ends with this very voice explaining why it had denounced others: "If you are asked who took part in the demonstrations you cannot happen to have forgotten the names. The students are better off in such situations but I have to think about feeding a family." Without revealing by whom, my acquaintance told me that he had been asked whether on June 22 I had been present in the clinic. I had not. My diary tells me I had stayed in bed with malaise after a sleepless night. His wife commented: "You better be careful too and do not say anything." With this admonishment, the diary ends.

I had been engaging in conversation with whoever was willing to talk about the events and spent no time reflecting on how interactions with one person would affect my rapport with another one. Nor had I taken care to make sure that those in charge of my welfare (my tutors and, in particular, the administrator of foreign affairs) were well informed about my alibis. It was obvious that my extracurricular activities as a foreigner were carefully monitored, and in retrospect, I see that uncertainties might have been reduced if I had been a bit more thoughtful to drop here and there a remark that I was going out for supper with foreigners or to the cinema with Chinese students or on a bicycle ride on my own, and if I had made sure always to send apologies when I missed a class or a clinical practical. As the body politic went into crisis, the research environment changed. How it affected interpersonal and social relations will be the second theme I reflect on.

Thirdly, I am struck by the certainty with which I express in this diary a particular political viewpoint. I blamed the students for lack of perseverance, especially in the two weeks after the nationwide demonstrations in mid-May and on June 4, and I condemned all those who thereafter, in my words, "mouthed the Party line" when they expressed approval of the military action on these "bad elements" of society who, against repeated warnings, camped on Tian'anmen. This reproachful attitude towards students whom we considered meek was shared by several other foreigners in Kunming, one of them an English teacher who thereupon decided to read a Martin Luther King text in class, "to teach them perseverance." I was very vocal in expressing my distrust towards those who applied brute force in what was portrayed as a protective act of saving China from chaos, and also in making known my distaste for those who chose not to do so. I now ponder the arrogance of the English teacher and my totalising viewpoint. Evidently, the movement ignited different hopes and expectations in foreigners and Chinese. As one official commented: "The foreigners and Chinese look at the issue very differently." My Chinese friends were right to say my attitude reflected ignorance of how politics are done in China.

Finally, I still have vivid memories about some emotions during and after this time period, which have not been expressed in the diary, and I will attend to these briefly too. Before embarking two decades after the events on this reflexive retrospective enterprise, let me present snippets of them from the diary.

The Events

Despite its closeness to the college compound (a five-minute walk), I barely went to the main square, which was the meeting point of the demonstrators in May and early June. In this respect I differed from my tourist friends and other foreigners. This was because after considerable personal efforts, and also sacrifices, it finally had been possible for me to pursue my doctoral studies in social anthropology, and my main concern was that I would have to break off my fieldwork prematurely because foreigners in these situations are easily denounced as activists. In mid-May, when Gorbachev's visit to Beijing caused unprecedented media coverage of the movement and thereby gave it increased impetus, the mayor of the city of Zurich visited Kunming within the sister city exchange programme that had made Kunming my research site. On the evening of May 17, Yunnan's provincial governor hosted a banquet in his honour at the Golden Dragon Hotel, to which another exchange student and I were invited, but he did not appear in person on that evening. The mayor of Zurich, who had just been flown into China and occupied a suite on the top floor of the hotel, showed no concern over this. The food was delicious, the service delightful, and speech after speech reassured friendship. After dinner, we went onto the rooftop terrace to catch a breath of fresh air. The mayor's five children, all dressed in white, were playing there. What an idyllic sight on the Golden Dragon Hotel's seventeenth floor, while less than half a mile away students were swinging their banners and shouting in chorus: "Down with corruption! End to suppression!" I had often seen such scenes in the PRC, but in films about the decadence of Chang Kai-shek and the Kuomintang, and thus experienced the cliché of lived experience coming close to clichés.

> I was there on Thursday, the 18th May. It was overwhelming to sit on the top of the tribune of the main square and overlook the masses of thousands and thousands of people. And from this sea of people moving freely about in peace and discipline, a power emanated which was elating. Each work unit formed a group of demonstrators, each indicating its identity with a banner and shouting its slogans, none was the leader . . .

I was there again on Friday, the 19th May, sitting on the tribune and watching the masses. The air was mild and the atmosphere peaceful, and at the same time there was such a power emanating from these masses of people. I later joined the students of the College in the midst of the square, just for a brief moment. Structures of organisation had already taken form among them. One, who came from a richer province and appeared more mature than his classmates, with a voice and accent that came close to that of official language, had been chosen the School's representative. He did not feel at ease to see me in their ring, but the seventeen year old students who were my classmates and had decided to stay on the square overnight, were glad for some company. I nevertheless felt uncomfortable and left after only a short chat. Apparently, most foreigners had been removed from the crowd already.

After mid-night, at 1.30 am, Li Peng's speech, which announced the imposition of martial law in Beijing, was broadcast onto the main square. The people dispersed. Not a single policeman had to be called in. So I was told by eyewitnesses. The universities and schools on the outskirts of Kunming had sent minibuses and the demonstrators were offered free rides back to their dormitories, 10–15 kilometres away. They all quit the square, even those who had prepared to go on hunger strike. Only a handful chose to remain.

On Saturday, the weather had changed. It rained so heavily in the early morning that I could not cycle to the clinic until 10.30 am. On my way I had to cross the empty square. It seemed like a dream that it had been vibrating from thousands and thousands of people the evening before. Yet, they came back. On Saturday evening, I was told, there was more of a crowd than ever before. And more tension was now to be felt.

Talking about emotions in the field, the most important issue was my worry not to be considered an activist and sent out of the country. I was eager to finish my studies in acupuncture and complete my fieldwork as planned. In awareness of possible implications for their studies, some of my anthropologist colleagues from Taiwan did not once go to the square, but I was driven by curiosity and excitement. As seen from the above snippet, even students of the college at which I studied were wary of my presence already during the height of the legally tolerated demonstrations in mid-May. Once the demonstrations had been declared unlawful, on the night of May 19–20, my teachers were adamant that I should not return to the square. I took their advice seriously. I only cycled through the square on my way to and from work at the provincial hospital's acupuncture clinic, twice a day, but each time very slowly to catch a glance of what was going on. All one could see of the demonstrators was a lonely tent in the shade of which I thought I had caught the glimpse of a few hunger strikers.

June 4 was a peaceful, sunny, and quiet Sunday in Kunming, and the news did not reach me until late in the afternoon when I went to wash my clothes with others in the courtyard. Shock. I had just been introduced to an advanced technique of *qigong* meditation the day before. I could not concentrate. The massacre of the students in Beijing led to havoc among the foreigners. Many instantly left China. Others were told to leave, as for instance all students on a grant from the United States of America. This sharpened the situation and made it more precarious for the anthropologist wishing to stay. On June 5, we had classes in the morning at our college, although many students of other colleges were on strike again. For the afternoon, an appointment was scheduled in Kunming City Hospital's acupuncture clinic to discuss arrangements for my training in the following winter semester. The foreign affairs official (I call him Wang in what follows), who had scheduled it weeks in advance, was already there when I arrived. The senior doctor who would become my future tutor was late; in fact, he was a whole hour late. When he finally arrived, he was breathing heavily. He had been to the bank. It had been packed: "The stock market in Hong Kong crashed." This caused a flurry of chitchat. Everyone was discussing what had happened in Beijing; no one was certain about the future. Then, suddenly, the conversation was on me:

"What is she doing here?", the senior doctor suddenly asked Wang. "What did she come here for?"

"I don't really know either," was Wang's response. "Medicine is not her subject. She does not have the basic education for being a doctor."

"What are you saying?!," I interrupted Wang angrily, "I have been attending Chinese medicine classes for half a year, I have been to the Provincial Hospital's clinic for another semester, I am now here because . . .". I tried to explain to the senior doctor why I insisted on attending the clinic rather than sitting in class, while Wang simultaneously spoke to a group of young practitioners, subtly distorting my situation.

"She is a sociologist," he said. This was not true and not good. The Institute of the Social Sciences in Beijing, which was considered the brain of the movement, had just been accused of being counterrevolutionary.

"No, I told you earlier, I am not a sociologist. I am an anthropologist who is
interested in medical reasoning, and that is not the same!" I was boiling. I
had dared openly contradict the Communist party official in charge of me.
Wang did not answer my explosive protest. There was a short silence. Then
I excused myself and left.

In the end the foreigner would be made the scapegoat, I knew this, but how
inappropriate for a foreigner to explode as I did. I was angry at myself.
I headed for the bookstore to calm myself down. There were crowds in
the streets, impossible even to push a bike through. So, I returned to my
dormitory room. My friend Wei was waiting there in front of the locked
door. He had come to say good-bye. He thanked me for the German
lessons I had given him in my spare time and was gone. Two weeks earlier
I had jokingly suggested to my Chinese friends that in the light of how the
situation was developing they would not dare to know me anymore in a
few months time. I had not expected it to be so soon.

The problem is, once one person is suspicious of you, other people, even those
who do not suspect you, must for reasons of their own security of being stig-
matised, avoid contact with you. I was determined to stay. Idealistically, I
identified with the anthropologist who has gone native. I did not want to be
seen as one of the "foreign friends" and "visitors" who had already left China.
However, in this situation where the country was in the midst of a political
crisis, it was only too apparent how non-native I was. A consensus existed
among my hosts that foreigners should not witness what happens in crisis
situations. On Tuesday, June 27, according to this diary (my dates in diaries
are not always correct), my tutor Peng at the acupuncture clinic held me back
for a moment "to discuss politics," after all students had already left. I was
very surprised, and sat down opposite him.

"I want to tell you some facts," he said and paused.
"Relations between countries are similar to relations between people," he
continued. "You would not come to see me at my home, if you did not
approve the way I punish my children. For this reason, foreigners do not
come to China now."

Evidently, my presence was uncomfortable. Classes had terminated, but I continued to attend the acupuncture ward. Most foreigners were now gone, but
fieldwork went on, case after case, day after day.

The diary ends on July 5. The following day—here I speak from memory—the representative of the Zurich-Kunming exchange programme appeared in the doorway of my dormitory room, unannounced. I was sitting at the table, reading. He had a bunch of lotus flowers in his hands and a frown on his face. Death had been on our minds for over a month, and I instantly knew it had struck. Who was it? My closest friend from high school had died in a car crash. It reverberated to a death from a car accident I had experienced in my early childhood, and my parents, who knew this, offered to pay for my flight home to attend her funeral. The next day I was in Kunming airport, walked in a daze through the loud and humid heat of Hong Kong, bought a flowering ginger, with a scent that was to accompany me on the following daylong flight and disappear two days later into her grave.

"This is a tribute to friendship" and "We did not know you were such good friends" were remarks I received at the funeral. We were sitting behind the farmhouse she had rented, on fresh green grass, overlooking wheat fields glimmering calmly in the afternoon sun. It felt "unreal" and yet was "real," even if watching videos on the following days alone in front of the TV seemed "more real." I had almost daily during the previous two months watched the evening news on a small black-and-white TV in Kunming, together with the young acupuncture teachers at the college. We gathered there in silence, listened to the reporter speaking of mostly other news items, and dispersed after the news was over. I had not seen the crowd on Tian'anmen then as colourful, lively, active, and upfront as it was here. It was also a much more verbal, and culturally more aggressive crowd than I had imagined. Evidently, it had been more vividly present in my parents' living room, and worldwide in living rooms outside the PRC, than ever in Kunming. I now saw for the first time the Statue of Liberty towering over Tian'anmen square, which to my sensibilities was more a symbol of the American way of life than one which expressed the Kunming students' slogan "Down with corruption and nepotism." I was given piles of e-mail correspondences, personal accounts of People's Liberation Army soldiers shooting at civilians, military tanks rolling over students' tents, and I sieved through them to a degree that became sickening, all the more as I was mourning a death myself.

Three weeks later, I was back in Kunming. The students were gone, except for a few, and the young acupuncture teachers would no more silently gather in front of the television for the evening news. The family who welcomed me back most warmly was the *qigong* healer's, in particular, his wife and his mother, but he himself refused to teach me any further meditation techniques. I was not ready, he presumably implied, when commenting that my life was marked by disruption (Hsu 1999:48).

Retrospective Reflections

The fact that I forgot so many encounters mentioned in the diary remains unsettling. Twenty years is a long time, but this alone cannot explain my almost absolute forgetting. Psychoanalysts do have an explanation for it: one forgets what one needs to forget. But if this is the case, what was it that had me forget the details of these most exciting two months of fieldwork?

The first of the two months was a time of openness, fluidity, talk, tingling excitement, perhaps even of hope for impending change, even if a sense of the precarious situation getting out of hand and an apprehension about future retributions were never absent. There was no reason to want to forget this first of the two months. On the other hand, I had experienced this month primarily as a threat to my studies. I had given up a career in the natural sciences to pursue studies in social anthropology, I had had serious arguments with my father, had been excluded from important events in the family, had left my home country and lived in tight financial circumstances, all for my idée fixe to learn to practise Chinese medicine in Chinese with Chinese people. In order to theorise about it, it was crucial to me that I attain a certain practical competence (Hsu 2006). The democracy movement bore the danger of having me terminate my studies midway. My tutors and teachers too were intent on not stopping teaching, but for other reasons. Some had lived through many Maoist mass movements, and they were still scarred by what they had suffered. No doubt they were sympathetic to the cause of the students, even if it was an unspoken and barely perceptible support, but they did not believe in their means—demonstrations funded with monies from abroad. The classes, private tutorials, and practicals in the clinic continued without any innuendo of political issues. This cannot explain why the contents of my diary feel like they were almost entirely wiped out either.

Apart from the many deaths on Tian'anmen, there was one death I thereafter experienced that was worth forgetting. Or was it perhaps, more enduringly, the subdued but undeniable repression experienced during the months after my return to Kunming, while I was mourning that death, that was worth forgetting? Whereas previously people all too readily would talk about the latest events, everyone now evaded anything to do with the student unrest. In an introductory remark to the above diary I say: "In mid-September, when the universities started courses again, the repression became worse and in late December, when I left the country, the economic situation in the PRC had deteriorated so badly that none of my friends was not affected by it (reduced monthly salaries, reduced clientele for making business, badly reduced energy supplies etc.)." Not that I was affected by this hardship directly—my hosts ensured my welfare, fieldwork went on and was sometimes eventful and interesting, and my eagerness to learn had not yet been deadened entirely by daily routine. Rather, the silently existent pressure on the social body seems to have affected the individual body. The body politic was repressed, the individual body subdued.

This raises important questions about the extent to which shared life experiences affect our bodies in the field—to what extent do we consciously oust from memory events which the social body demands that we expel? In other words, does some part of us *choose* to forget, or do we forget as a consequence of imperceptibly submitting to the demands of the social body? Is forgetting in this sense a by-product of submission? While asking such questions about our informants' experience is a worthy anthropological exercise, it is also useful to ask them about the researcher's field experience: Are we as anthropologists also vulnerable to these pressures from the social body? Can we also forget by means of the submission to the social body that immersion obliges? This is to say, can immersion in certain instances arrest the capacity to recall or perceive events that the social body would rather we overlook or forget? When regarding my Tian'anmen experiences, the social body, to which my and my informants' bodies were subject, clearly left its mark. The methodological lesson to be learnt is that only through a more radically empirical reflexivity did I become aware of this subtle influence—that is, my forgetting was not a symptom of some personalised, neurotic conflict I was trying to avoid, but rather a symptom of submission to an intense social pressure to which I was unavoidably subjected.

The realisation of how significantly the social body affected my own individual body emerges from memory only as I now recall the release I experienced when I left the country. After flying to Guangdong and embarking in the evening on a boat, quietly gliding down the Pearl River delta, and arriving early in the morning in Hong Kong, I found myself in a stream of Chinese travellers being pushed through dusty, dirty, grey corridors, when suddenly two huge and heavy doors swung open and we were hit by bright sunlight beaming through forbiddingly transparent and shiny glass, surrounded by polished marble and glittering chrome. It was no doubt a calculated effect on the part of the Hong

Kong authorities, but no less real. I noted that I breathed differently, my chest widened, my posture straightened. So, here I was in "freedom and democracy."

Was it worth it? Did these emotions and their aftermath, which went to the bone of my experience and research and scarred me for life, produce an ethnography that reflects this? An author cannot tell. However, a fieldworker can reminisce on how they affected my rapport with key informants in the field, and with friends. The ethnography I published ten years later contains among the comments on methodology this statement: "In retrospect, it is apparent that semi-directed interviews are the method best suited to anthropological inquiry in a Chinese work unit" (Hsu 1999:133). The comment was not without foundation. I had tried out various fieldwork methods: oral question-and-answer sessions in groups of four to eight students, written questionnaires, interviews with individuals commenting on the results of those questionnaires, and others. I had no difficulties finding people to respond to the questions I had about their biography and personal experiences of studying Chinese medicine, but one of the main problems I encountered was that I felt the respondents tried to find out what I wanted to hear, then said it and had me write it down. By contrast, I had had an entirely different experience with the junior acupuncturists at the college during the semi-directed interviews about their experiences as students and teachers of acupuncture, about the science of acupuncture and its future, and other related themes. The interviews were personal (I was careful not to let them become intimate),[1] psychologically complex, and nuanced. Several resulted in a feeling almost of complicity when we later happened to bump into each other on the compound, although relations with none of the interviewees were ever deepened, as I left the field soon thereafter. However, on reflection, it was perhaps not so much the ethnographic method as the memory of the daily sessions in front of the TV during the two months of extreme uncertainty, where a group of us regularly gathered and dispersed without commenting on the events, that made possible the extremely revealing one-hour interviews six months later. They were lived-through moments in bodily closeness marked by mutual concern and emotional tact.

Was it worth it, two months of watching half an hour of the daily news together, to have eleven moving semi-structured interviews about teaching acupuncture many months later? It is obsolete to ask questions of this kind about anthropological fieldwork, let alone about life. The subject matter is too complex to be reduced to one aspect of existence only, to efficiency or to methodology. One may query the usefulness of relying on codified methods alone. What makes a fruitful personal encounter and mutual understanding across boundaries of class, culture, gender, age, is located in an entirely different sphere of human experience, which makes any "fieldwork method" look hopelessly superficial. Sometimes the application of methods that allow systematic and quantitative assessment can even be detrimental and cover up insights into the unexpected. Had I, for instance, decided to distribute questionnaires among the young staff of acupuncturists, with yes-no and multiple-choice options, I would have wasted the opportunity to learn about their lives, their education, their profession, their hopes, and China's history with the complexities they were prepared to reveal to me in conversation.

The ethnography I published contains tables with quantitative data, and even though the numbers of interviewees are very small and numerically insignificant, they represented the entire sample (of, for instance, eleven young acupuncture teachers). What matters is discursively related knowledge, thoughts, and emotions that often cannot be evoked in an article but require the space of a carefully crafted monograph. Numerical, quantitative information is not unimportant, but the kind of anthropology that matters to me makes use of it for anchoring or adding complexity to the themes and sometimes hidden concerns that cannot be elicited through calibrated experimentation, calculation, and method alone. An anthropologist draws on many more qualities of human existence.

One of those prime qualities is to let oneself be affected by the field. This goes beyond acknowledgement of the platitude "culture shock" experienced upon one's return. Rather, an anthropologist should know that fieldwork cannot be bracketed out of life. It may result in lasting changes in the fieldworker's life, if not fundamentally transform the fieldworker. Naturally, everyone will want to keep fieldwork to a certain extent under control, be busy with experimenting with this method here, that one there, but my experience has always been that the unelicited information is the most valuable. You may call it "serendipity," but one can also see in it a human quality of being prepared to let things take their course, even if anthropologists must be wary to let this happen sometimes only to a limited degree. As we internally allow ourselves to be affected by what happens to us, we open up the people we work with.

Does this mean anthropologists embarking on fieldwork projects will undermine previous achievements and lifelong relationships? Many Chinese-language students who had partners back home in Europe, Australia, or America split up with them or, at the very least, experienced a crisis. It was a topos at the Beijing

Language School in the early eighties, often mentioned as excuse for engaging in more or less ephemeral affairs, which occasionally resulted in lifelong cross-cultural marriages. It is not that this does not happen among anthropologists, but it is less of a topos. Nor is it entirely a taboo. The openness I speak of is a trademark of our profession, it has been discussed, it is reflected on. Nevertheless, I would hesitate to say it is part of our training. Life cannot be learnt; it can only be lived.

Not that all experiences during the acute phase of the pro-democracy movement in May and June had positive effects on my rapport with the people I worked with. After attending lectures in the classroom for one semester and pursuing my studies weekly three days in the classroom and three days in the clinic in the second semester, I worked six days a week daily in the acupuncture ward of the Kunming City Hospital in my third semester, but the rapports in that clinic remained flat and superficial. In contrast to the acupuncture ward in the provincial hospital, where student numbers often had outnumbered those of the patients, the senior doctor to whom the foreign affairs official Wang had introduced me saw many patients, daily around sixty. I still have stacks and stacks of notes on these two months of clinical work. However, I barely have written anything about this placement.

Conclusion

Anthropologically relevant knowledge is not out there to be discovered, even if it may feel so to the fieldworker. It is created—sometimes in tense moments, sometimes in heartfelt mutual interaction. It is in this sense that radical empiricism may help us insofar as it is concerned with these spaces between—between person and person, and person and event. For instance, an interview is over after an hour or so, a series of interviews after a week or a month, and yet the knowledge created in the interaction can have lasting consequences, not only for the fieldworker but also for the work we do. No, I'm not into navel gazing. A radical empirical reflexivity about emotions in the field, which seeks to translate emotions into anthropological insight, should prevent us from falling into that trap. A politically eventful field cannot leave a fieldworker unaffected; the body politic affects the individual body and thus how the researcher conducts research, even if it results in the escape out of the field and feelings of disappointment over an unaccomplished task. Nor can "private life" entirely be bracketed out of ethnographic fieldwork. The one death, a month after the many on Tian'anmen square, resulted in the simultaneity of a collapse in the body politic and the fieldworker's individual body. Perhaps it explains why many others who lived through these events have not forgotten as much as I did, perhaps not. At the time, I soldiered on. I did not contact my Cambridge supervisor while I was in Europe. If he had been Chinese, he would have advised against my returning to the field.[2] At least so I feared. I did not give up my studies in Chinese medicine nor my ethnographic fieldwork in 1989, and yet what happened then and thereafter, together with other circumstances, has had a long-lasting effect on my field research. During the decade between 1978 and 1989 I spent almost yearly at least one month in the PRC, but I have not returned for long-term fieldwork in the twenty years since.

References

DeSoto, H. G., and N. Dudwick. 2000. *Fieldwork Dilemmas: Anthropologists in Post-socialist States.* Madison: University of Wisconsin Press.

Freud, S. 1907. *Zur Psychopathologie des Alltagslebens: Über Vergessen, Versprechen, Vergreifen, Aberglaube, und Irrtum.* 2nd ed. Berlin: S. Karger.

Greenhouse, C. J. 2002. "Introduction: Altered States, Altered Lives." In C. J. Greenhouse, E. Mertz, and K. B. Warren, eds., *Ethnography in Unstable Places: Everyday Lives in Contexts of Dramatic Political Change,* 1–34. Durham, NC: Duke University Press.

Herzfeld, M. 2000. "Afterword: Intimations from an Uncertain Place." In H. G. De Soto and N. Dudwick, eds., *Fieldwork Dilemmas: Anthropologists in Postsocialist States,* 219–238. Madison: University of Wisconsin Press.

Hsu, E. 1999. *The Transmission of Chinese Medicine.* Cambridge: Cambridge University Press.

———. 2006. "Participant Experience: Learning to Be an Acupuncturist, and Not Becoming One." In G. de Neeve and M. Unnithan-Kumar, eds., *Critical Journeys: The Making of Anthropologists,* 149–163. Aldershot: Ashgate.

Mitter, R. 2004. *A Bitter Revolution: China's Struggle with the Modern World.* New York: Oxford University Press.

Nordstrom, C., and A. C. G. M. Robben, eds. 1995. *Fieldwork under Fire: Contemporary Studies of Violence and Survival.* Berkeley: University of California Press.

Pieke, F. 1995. "Accidental Anthropology: Witnessing the 1989 Chinese People's Movement." In C. Nordström and A. C. G. M. Robben, eds., *Fieldwork under Fire: Contemporary Studies of Violence and Survival,* 62–79. Berkeley: University of California Press.

———. 2000. "Serendipity: Reflections on Fieldwork in China." In P. Dresch, W. James, and D. Parkin, eds., *Anthropologists in the Wider World,* 129–150. Oxford, Eng.: Berghahn.

Notes

1. The distinction I make between personal and intimate conversations lies in the political entanglement they may produce. Ethnographic intimacy can be perceived as threatening in politically charged situations, as it may offer an antidote to "myths of the state" (Herzfeld 2000), but I did not wish to become co-opted into politics. I would argue that personal encounters can also provide a key to successful ethnography.

2. Should "Health and Safety" regulations have monitored a student in the field during a political crisis more closely? Certainly not. The months that were the most difficult to live through were the autumn months when the political situation of China was under control and the population quiet. "Health and Safety" would have responded to the turbulent months but not hindered students from doing research in those months that, on reflection, presumably had the most detrimental effect on my long-term research engagement with the PRC.

7 Emotional Engagements

Acknowledgement, Advocacy, and Direct Action

Lindsay Smith and Arthur Kleinman

ANTHROPOLOGISTS HAVE HISTORICALLY BEEN, almost by definition, "engaged intellectuals." Our position in the field, our production of knowledge from the ground up, our methodological imperative to live day in and day out among our research subjects for the entire duration of our studies have given our discipline a unique history of engagement among the social sciences. In an anthropological sense, engagement has often emerged from the particular relationship of intimacy with a group of people that the ethnographer develops in her time in the field. As such, anthropological engagement is not necessarily or exclusively the ethical choice of public intellectuals to align themselves with causes and struggles quite distant from the academy. Rather, for anthropologists engagement may be, and oftentimes is, born out of proximity, as the inevitable result of a long-lasting process of active involvement and witnessing—what we call "participant observation." Whether or not, as anthropologists, we choose to become "public intellectuals" in the French tradition, whether or not we choose to share our expertise in a language accessible to a general audience, whether or not we find our informants' struggles sympathetic or repugnant, at the very core of our discipline is the inescapable intersubjective experience of ethnographic fieldwork. It is that experience that engages us, for it never allows us to imagine ourselves as simply analysts reporting data; rather we are always witnesses evoking the contested truths and troubled emotions of the local moral world with which we have become a part.

In his chapter in this volume, Ghassan Hage explores the complicated contours of political emotions, drawing out the multiple overlapping strands of personal and collective sentiments that surround political upheaval. In a similar vein, our contribution focuses more directly on the political pole of this affective-analytical-political nexus; that is, we explore how moral experience is constituted in the intersubjective space of the fieldwork encounter. Drawing on Kleinman's consideration of the moral as that which is at stake for individuals and collectivites (2006), we explore the complicated emotions that define these stakes for researchers making fieldwork, at its core, a moral endeavour. Much of the discussion about engagement in anthropology has focused on ethical imperatives, or transcending rules or norms about what is right and good. This has predominantly been framed in terms of exploitation, solidarity, and voice. We see these questions especially within Marxist and feminist turns towards solidarity with the oppressed (Bloch 1983; Collier and Yanagisako 1989; Godelier 1978; Rosaldo and Lamphere 1974), and later in the critical theoretical and textual shifts of reflexive anthropology (Abu-Lughod 1993; Behar and Gordon 1995; Clifford and Marcus 1986; Marcus and Fischer 1986). Rather than exploring these ethical dimensions of engagement, here we explore the complicated shared emotions of fear, guilt, responsibility, and care that form the grounds for what we call moral empathy—the shared stakes that bind us to our informants and our fieldwork sites. We approach this by looking beyond anthropologists as ethical agents and focusing directly on the co-constituted local moral world of the fieldwork encounter. By paying attention to the affective valence of moral experience in fieldwork, including the fraught space of mutual responsibility, we offer our thoughts on the relationship between the common reality of moral action in the field and the ways in which that can be and often is transformed into ethical action.

In our own subfield of medical anthropology, the question of engagement takes on additional urgency because of the field's traditional focus on medical ailments and, more recently, its turn towards empathy and social suffering. As engagement becomes a critical object of inquiry, medical anthropology may offer a unique perspective on the underlying emotions and intersubjective empathetic experiences that frame the terms of ethnographic engagement. The work of the French phenomenologist-ethicist Emmanuel Levinas, which has been drawn on extensively by medical anthropologists studying suffering, has highlighted the preeminence of an ethical relationship in any form of intellectual enquiry, thus providing an epistemological framework in which engagement and analysis may not be separated. Arguing that suffering in and of itself is useless, he suggests that it is the space of empathy in which "the suffering for the useless suffering of the other, the just suffering in me for the unjustifiable suffering of the other, opens suffering to the ethical perspective of the inter-human." The self is thus born in the recognition of the Other in his or her irreducible alterity, but that recognition necessarily comes with responsibility for the Other, which precedes a relationship of exchange, or the social contract. This ethical responsibility to the Other is, for Levinas, the supreme ethical principle and the grounds for "the interhuman order" (1998:100). Participant observation, the practice of being both within and without a local world, is grounded in this interhuman order where recognition of difference is born within a shared local moral world. It is not that we as fieldworkers "go native," but rather that in this ethical emotional recognition or empathy, we affirm, respect, and value diversity because it is the basis for a recognition of ourselves and our informants—a recognition based in a deep responsibility for the Other.

Within anthropological methods training much is made of the first part of this equation—the respect of diversity born in the recognition of the Other. This understanding of fieldwork is decidedly intellectual and valorises participant observation as a unique and valuable way of generating deep data. In this formulation, our intimacy in the field allows for a greater respect of, to quote Levinas, "the irreducible alterity," of the Other. By examining our emotional experiences of empathy, guilt, and responsibility, we seek to pay greater attention to these other aspects of the interhuman: the emergence of the fieldworker's self in a kind of Lacanian mirror stage and the concomitant responsibility for the Other that emerges within this encounter. We suggest that the shared local moral world of fieldwork is born precisely in the responsibility of recognition—a responsibility always tempered by the respect and recognition of the difference and sameness at the base of the interhuman. The moments when we as fieldworkers recognize the interhuman—suffering for the suffering of another, raging at the fierceness of brutality, laughing together in the recognition of an inside joke—mark a moment of internalization of the others' (our informants') worldviews that is as familiar as it is uncanny. We suggest that in paying attention to the emotional grounds of empathy, we can better understand our shared local moral worlds. Moreover, these moments of emotional empathy are certainly not limited to negative experiences. "Going native" is still an insult in our discipline, yet a successful fieldworker is nevertheless expected to "go native" just enough to see the world through his or her informants' eyes, and through that intersubjective, transformative process, he or she is expected to return better able to convey a local moral world to those outside it. Through the process of fieldwork, feelings of joy, sadness, fear, pain, anger, etc., like Levinas' suffering, take on an interhuman quality. Thus engagement, understood as an ethical responsibility to the Other, emerges less from an intellectual or ethical decision and more from these fundamental emotional processes. And yet like life, fieldwork exposes individuals to the complex interweave of values and emotions in the setting of real-world inexpediency and resistance, so that emotion is almost always multiple, complex, and divided. It is this uncertain, multi-sided, and often dangerous human reality that we seek to privilege.

In this chapter, we explore the emotions surrounding engagement. Drawing on our respective ethnographic research on China's Cultural Revolution and Argentina's children of the disappeared, we reflect on this emotional landscape, paying particular attention to processes of transformation wherein a feeling of injustice, even when it is associated with helplessness, can become a motivating sense of responsibility and a paralyzing sense of guilt can become a bridge to engagement. And yet distrust, perfidy, and misunderstanding often turn this bridge into a narrow and crooked path forward.

Buenos Aires, Argentina—Lindsay Smith

Victor came up to the desk where I was working and stuck the day's paper under my nose. Jabbing it at me, he said: "So what do you have to say about this?" I was a month into my internship at the Grandmothers of the Plaza de Mayo, an Argentine family-based human rights group dedicated to finding the five hundred to six hundred babies, now adults, who had been kidnapped almost thirty years ago as part of the systematic state repression known as the "Dirty War." Without even looking at the page, I knew to what he was referring. I had seen the news blurb on the front page of the paper that morning. In a tiny rectangle at the bottom of the page reserved for pieces of international news that the editors find particularly ironic and troubling were the results of a survey done in the United States which found that two out of three Americans found torture to be justifiable in certain circumstances (Pew Research Center 2005).

I was in a shared office, and several others looked up when they heard his question. They crowded around my desk to hear my response, making it hard to breathe in the tense atmosphere. "Lindsay, what do you think of this?" someone repeated. As I tried to formulate a reply, my thoughts went immediately to Angela, the woman now holding the paper. She had been born in a clandestine detention center. Soon after her birth, she was torn out of her mother's arms and given to a military family for them to raise as their own child. Her birth mother remained one of the 30,000 Argentine disappeared. Having discovered her biological identity via DNA tests as a teenager, Angela was forced to come to terms with the perfidy of her adoptive family as well as the large-scale betrayal of the state, which she had previously regarded as a benevolent and protective force. Radicalized by these experiences, she was now working at the Grandmothers to convince families who had a disappeared son or daughter to give their DNA to a national databank so that more missing children could be found.

Desperately thinking about what to say, I was acutely aware of being the "Yankee" and in this moment asked to represent all Americans, a group already despised on principle because of the country's current and historical imperialism. What did I have to say for myself, for my country? My face turned red and my voice became hesitant as I was flooded with shame and overwhelmed by a profound sense of guilt. What was I doing here studying the Argentine situation when things in my country were such a mess? I knew I was motivated to do this project in part because of the current situation in the United States. I felt like life in the contemporary United States was uncomfortably similar to the Argentine repression and wondered if one day history would indict me for my complicity. What was I doing as people were being disappeared and tortured in my birth country? Was I, like the majority of Argentines during the Dirty War, living by a code of *no te metes*—don't get involved? Was I going about my day as if the U.S. government was not disappearing and torturing people suspected of terrorism?

Hesitating and stammering, I explained that I certainly didn't believe in the use of torture under any circumstances. I tried to differentiate myself by describing my antiwar advocacy in the United States and my commitment to fighting precisely the mentality described by the survey. I explained how my work in Argentina was motivated not only by important intellectual questions, or even my commitment to the Grandmothers' project of finding their missing grandchildren, but also by my own concern about these parallel issues in the United States.

My answers were good enough; the group dispersed and returned to work. I wonder if I was able to truly dispel the moment of doubt—that brief moment when my friends began to wonder who exactly they had befriended and what she might believe about them and their history. In the case of the Grandmothers, like many human rights groups in Argentina, loyalty is a high-stakes issue. They had experienced a great deal of betrayal, and it had been measured in lives

lost and friends disappeared forever. Earlier that week, we had gone as a group
to a public memorial service for Azucena Villaflor, the founder of the Mothers
of the Plaza de Mayo. She was disappeared in December 1977 as a direct result of
the infiltration of the Mothers by a young navy lieutenant, Alfred Astiz, pretend-
ing to be a supporter of the movement for human rights (CONADEP 1986:128–
129). As an American I was surprisingly often suspected of being a CIA agent or,
more mildly, a Yankee imperialist with ulterior motives. In a painful reminder
of the distrust that mediated my fieldwork experience, after an accumulated
two years of fieldwork, I once became quite ill, and my friends told me they
were very worried I would die. Feeling flattered, I told them that I appreciated
their concern, but I was fine. Laura, a human rights worker, quickly clarified
that they figured that the CIA would come get them if a girl from Harvard died
around them. Then what would they do? In working with the Grandmothers,
I, like many fieldworkers, faced a deep distrust at the core of our encounter.
This distrust, nonetheless, did not preclude the emotional entanglements of a
shared moral encounter. In fact, the tension described in this encounter made
painfully explicit the constitution of the self and the other as well as the shared
sense of ethical responsibility that forms the core of the interhuman in Levinas'
terms. As a fieldworker, I was also always an American imperialist from an elite
institution, and my colleagues were always also persecuted Argentine activists
working on the front lines of the human rights movements. But I would suggest
that the power made explicit in this encounter at the same time as instantiating
difference also made possible a recognition of mutual, shared responsibility for
each other, as my encounter with Victor later in the afternoon illustrates.

At the end of the day in an Argentine office it's common for each worker to
pass by each desk and kiss everyone good-bye. That afternoon, I stopped Victor
as he came to my desk and asked him how he had felt reading the article. He
said that at first he had dismissed it as the typical North American imperialism
and warmongering, but as he thought more about it, he had felt demoralized
about the similarities between the United States and Argentina. He explained:
these Americans are the same people who look at the Grandmothers and
Mothers circling in the plaza, demanding justice, and they feel sorry for them.
They are horrified at what the Argentine government did, and they want these
old women to find their missing grandchildren. They are the people who nod
in agreement when we publish books and reports titled "Never Again." And yet
this is exactly how "these things" happen again and again.

I told him that I shared his despondency and his drive to do something to change the situation. The discussion that day in the office brought to the fore my own feelings of hopelessness about the situation back in the United States. I was always acutely aware of my own privilege in relationship to my informants and friends. Not only was I a gringa and therefore significantly economically advantaged, but I could also live in times of torture and be one of the people who remained safe. It was an active choice on my part to be aware; my informants did not have that luxury. An encounter that had begun as a test of my loyalty came to mark a new level of intimacy with my informants. I not only saw their frustration but shared in it as well.

Nine months later, in my very last ethnographic interview, I was again called out of my routine and pushed towards engagement through an intense emotional encounter. Irene had invited me to her house for a lengthy interview about her search for her disappeared daughter and grandson. When I called to schedule the interview she explained that she was feeling quite old these days and didn't think she could come to the Grandmothers' office. Would I be willing to come to her? I had happily agreed and was on her doorstep ringing the bell at four p.m., as we had agreed. Her son welcomed me into their small but architecturally stunning home. When I commented on the beauty of the house, she said I should have seen it thirty years ago. It had been just this kitchen and dining room and the two bedrooms in the back. The new additions had been possible through the government reparations she had received because of her daughter's disappearance. Looking up at the skylight with the sun streaming in, she told me that the rooms made her feel in some small way like her daughter was here with her. Irene was more than ninety years old, and thirty years ago her oldest daughter, Ana, had been disappeared by the military dictatorship, leaving Irene with one grandson to raise and another missing. At the time of her disappearance, Ana had recently given birth to a second baby and that child was disappeared along with her. Irene had spent the last thirty years looking for her second grandson. Despite several promising leads and even court-ordered DNA tests of a potential child, she had never found him. She told me it was the great sadness of her life.

Drawn into her story, I was startled when she reached out across the table and grabbed both my hands. With tears in her eyes, Irene begged me to help her find him. She knew of my volunteer work in Buenos Aires with the Grandmothers and asked me to please remember her story, to please keep looking for him. She was getting old, she told me, and would probably die without seeing him. She refused to let me go until I could make some kind of promise to her.

With tears in my eyes, and my heart beating rapidly, I tried to explain to Irene that I was just a volunteer doing data entry. I didn't have any power to find her grandson. I feared I had misled her about my connections and my ability to help her. I told her that I would pass her story on to the lawyers and government workers who were conducting these searches, but that was all that I could do. Pulling me close and looking me in the eyes, she asked me again to promise that I wouldn't forget her or her search.

I had come into Irene's house to collect a life history, like the more than fifty others I had already collected, but Irene broke the routine. In directly appealing to me, she highlighted the unequal exchange in which we engaged. She was sharing her suffering with me so that I could write my dissertation and hopefully one day publish my findings in a book. She hoped that in return I could concretely help her find her grandson. Perhaps I hadn't been clear enough on my limits: I studied scientific technologies and their social meanings, but I could not produce a DNA match for her. I had nothing to offer except that in some far-distant future my book might be translated into Spanish and someone might read it and they might be able to identify her grandson. In the face of her suffering and her tremendous need, I could do nothing. Her anger and determination, despite her powerlessness and lack of success in her search for her grandson, infected my thoughts and emotions. Unlike Victor's despondency in the first story, I couldn't immediately share the intensity of her feelings, even though I felt angry and frustrated at the continued disappearance of so many young adults.

These two very different fieldwork moments, one at the beginning of my fieldwork, the other at the very end, embody for me my continued pull towards engagement. The first interchange cemented my relationship to my informants because the guilt I felt at my country's actions affirmed my solidarity with my friends' suffering. The second case forced me to face the limits of my own engagement and the potential danger in assuming or promising too much. In both cases I was called out of my routine of participant observation through the intensity of the emotional entanglements. I was called into a complex web of reciprocal, emotion-laden exchange, which I came to understand was the privileged position of being welcomed into their local world.

Guilt and fear had been my initial reactions in both of these cases. That which was at stake for me as an anthropologist—data, ethnographic sources, cultivation of social intimacy—seemed insignificant and petty in comparison to the immense issues dominating my informants' lives. Guilt can be an immobilizing emotion, and yet it has remained a common response to power-laden difference that phrases like "liberal guilt" or "white guilt" are common parlance. It is an emotion that emerges when we are faced with our complicity, albeit an unintentional and unwanted complicity, in the suffering of others. Feminist scholars have written about the importance of finding a way of approaching difference that doesn't stop at guilt. Audre Lorde in her pathbreaking article "The Uses of Anger" (1984) indicts guilt as a thoroughly unproductive emotion, often synonymous with helplessness in the face of the status quo. She argues that guilt "is a response to one's own actions or lack of action. If it leads to change then it can be useful, since it is then no longer guilt but the beginning of knowledge" (1984:130). She offers anger as an alternative modality, one that is generative and can produce change. Thus guilt in her formulation leads nowhere.

I would suggest that these initial feelings of helplessness and guilt might be an important part of our recognition of our role as fieldworkers. In the encounter with our informants, we not only learn about them, or even about our own local world, but we also learn something about our roles as fieldworkers and researchers. To return to Levinas, the self is born in the recognition of the Other. For me, these moments in the field were marked by guilt, for I saw and faced the limits of my actions and position. In practice, the fieldwork experience is often delimited by moments where we come face-to-face with our own alterity. And yet, if we take Levinas seriously, this space also opens up the possibility of an ethical recognition of the other, that which we describe as moral empathy. Moral empathy is thus an acknowledgement of our own position and limits along with those of our informants, while still participating in a shared local world that becomes most clear in moments of emotional recognition.

In my own experience, as much as guilt mirrored to me the bounds of my role as fieldworker, it also acted as a bridge to ethical action. It was indeed often replaced by a motivating outrage—burning anger at the institutional disparities perpetrated every day by the majority of Argentines (and Americans) who refuse to believe or simply to care, in acts of what Moody-Adams (1997) calls "affected ignorance"—the choice to perform ignorance in the face of an uncomfortable or contested knowledge. From the cabdriver who longed nostalgically for the military dictatorship to return and deal with the new wave of protesters blocking traffic, to the Argentine businesswoman who in the middle of a dinner party would still loudly claim that all the disappeared are simply hiding out in Italy, a large portion of the Argentine public still chooses not to know what would be easy to know. Although I didn't have the power or the resources to effect major political, legal, or even institutional changes, much less find and identify missing people, I began to realize that I did have some privileges and therefore responsibilities. My guilt turned into anger, and my anger into a concerted effort to break free of the tacit social rules that deny the atrocities of the Dirty War. For example, I told the cabdriver of my work with the Grandmothers and of their very real struggles (even though this meant getting kicked out of the cab late at night in an unfamiliar neighborhood). I disrupted a nice evening among Argentine high society, responding to the businesswoman with statistics about the number of disappeared children identified to date. Even though I was never invited again, I did receive a phone call from one of the other women present at the party, who told me that her husband had been disappeared for five days during the dictatorship. She had never told anyone before. I was able to put her in contact with a supportive community.

Of course, these were the small responses of a fieldworker, not the heroic acts of a political leader or a revolutionary, but they were what I could do at that point in time given my resources and abilities. These engagements, which involved very real fear and a considerable amount of social and physical discomfort, highlighted one tension of fieldwork: they brought me closer to the local moral world of my informants and at the same time reinstantiated its spaces of difference. Of course, I recognize that small efforts do little to address the enormous injustices that Victor, Angela, Irene, and the Grandmothers live with every day. However, small actions and engagements serve to acknowledge the complex, shared emotions of fieldwork and really of every human encounter. Whether guilt, shared happiness, anger, empathy, or the ethical responsibility of Levinas' suffering at the suffering of the other, an attention to emotion is one way to better understand and acknowledge our shared moral experiences. It is in the working through of these everyday entanglements, the day-to-day work of the ethnographer, that spaces emerge for creative action.

Changsha, Hunan—Arthur Kleinman

A late May day in 1978. Heavy rain, swirling into great sky-blocking sheets and thudding in a drumroll against the decrepit walls of our two-story 1930s hotel. Inside, a cool dampness provided evening relief from the balmy heat of the day. We were a delegation of American health officials and researchers sent by the National Academies to study rural health-care conditions in China. We were nearing the end of a two-month trip that took us from remote areas in north and west China to equally remote areas in south China. We were scheduled to take a night flight to Kunming, but we had just been notified that because of the rainstorm our flight would be delayed until the following morning.

Cold beer in hand and nibbling at dry melon seeds, I was relaxing with my roommate and fellow social scientist, David Mechanic. That day we had visited the Hunan Medical School, formerly (before 1950) the renowned Yale-in-China Medical School, but for two decades downgraded to a provincial-level medical school. We had met with the entire faculty in the school's decaying auditorium. We had spoken with deans, department chairs, laboratory researchers, and clinicians, none of whom, to our surprise, spoke English. We had both been eager to interview the three representatives of the Department of Psychiatry. And we had been disappointed by how little they told us. I translated. The spokesman for the psychiatrists was their youngest member: a dynamic broad-shouldered, open-faced man in early middle age—Dr. Shen. He seemed to shield his two older colleagues, who remained silent while he mouthed platitudes about the great achievements of the Cultural Revolution and skilfully deflected our questions about disease rates and mental health practice. In their place he substituted vague generalizations about patients' high spirits; the solidarity of doctors, nurses, and care workers; and the ethos of revolutionising change which infused patients, families, and staff with the power of prevention and healing.

David and I came away shaking our heads in disbelief and with the dispirited sense that we had, once again, learned very little about mental illness and psychiatry in China, a topic we were determined to unearth, because colleagues were either unwilling or unable to provide us with concrete details, just as they had been doing when we arrived in Beijing some weeks before. We commiserated at the failed opportunity, while marvelling at how little long-term influence Yale seemed to have had. Our mood was one of disappointment and frustration.

Then there was a soft knock at our door. Ghost-like, three figures emerged from the dark. They were the same psychiatrists we had met earlier that day. I felt an inward groan. I didn't think I could tolerate further hours of frustrating conversation. I had already written Changsha off in my mind and was preparing for the next day's interviews.

This was the context and background for one of the most memorable and life-changing meetings in my many years of fieldwork in China. That evening, Dr. Shen, who was the Department of Psychiatry's political face, took a back seat. The place of honour went to Professor Ling Mingyou, the former chair of the department and the former dean of the Yale-in-China Medical School. He, Professor Yang Derson, and Dr. Shen all spoke fluent English, as did, they told us, virtually every one of the hundreds of faculty assembled in the school's auditorium. The fear of being labelled with a foreign problem because of language skills and relationships abroad was so pervasive that no one could acknowledge mastery of English or association with the Yale-in-China school. Professor Ling, who wore eyeglasses in which one of the lenses had been shattered into dozens of pieces, told me of the brutality they had experienced during the Cultural Revolution and just how devastating that era of radical Maoism, which had officially ended less than two years earlier, had been for them, their families, and their once-great medical school. Every one of our questions about mental illness and psychiatric care was answered. And our guests helped us to understand a reality that went far beyond anything we had heard earlier or were prepared to hear. I know I felt tremendous feelings of injustice well up inside of me. All that our Chinese guests wanted from us was a promise to help them rebuild their ties to the United States, including receiving books, journals that had been published since 1949, and other forms of information created by the global community of psychiatrists that they sought to rejoin.

So affected was I by the experience of loss, trauma, and the quest for contact that I returned to the United States determined to do something. I set up an exchange program with the Hunan Medical School; I brought Dr. Shen and Dr. Yang to the United States; I raised the funds to send American medical students and researchers to Hunan; I mailed books, journals, and reprints to Changsha; and in June 1980 my family and I went to the Hunan Medical College for six months of research.

During the 1980s I had ample reasons to move my research to Beijing, Shanghai, or Guangzhou—these were the major sites for psychiatry. They were the wealthiest, most powerful, most globally connected cities, and their situations for researchers were far better than those in Changsha. But I refused to do so. I felt a strong sense of loyalty to a damaged school and a peripheral city that I felt needed me. Even in the 1980s, during the early phase of the economic reform that would rework China from a poor country to a global economic powerhouse, strong Maoists led Hunan Province. The city itself had few foreigners from 1949 to 1980. We were the first Americans to conduct research in Hunan since 1949. And it was continually impressed upon Joan Kleinman and me that we were needed, needed desperately. Herein lay the advantages and dangers of engagement.

The fact that there was great need for us and that we could sponsor exchanges and collaborations, participate in scientific development, and help careers and lives meant that we were practically as well as symbolically useful. In 1980 on an excursion boat on the Xiang River to which we were ordered to report by the governor of the province, this leading cadre told me that even if I weren't a good enough researcher to make the collaboration succeed, he would personally see to it that I succeeded, because I represented a connection that had to go forward if the Hunan Medical School and Changsha itself were to modernize. Dr. Ling, who attracted all my empathy and sense of responsibility, told me I needed to do even more. I was responsible for getting his family members to America. Dr. Yang's wife told me that I had to help them set up a special bank account that members of their family could use when they visited America. I came to realise that I had become embedded in a network of exchange that required almost endless reciprocation. At one point in the early 1980s, we got telephone calls on an almost monthly basis from visitors from Hunan who had arrived at Boston's Logan Airport, having been told by our colleagues in Hunan that we would put them up, feed them, help them make travel arrangements, and even lend them money.

And so frustration grew, and from empathy, advocacy, and engagement based in feelings of injustice and solidarity, I began to increasingly dread what I would be asked to do next. I began to contemplate leaving Hunan and breaking the cycle of reciprocity. I became angry as I began to realise that I was being used—that I had so framed my new relationships with Hunanese colleagues that I could be used. My own research became a burden to me. The more I published, the more it was expected I would do to help publicly. What I viewed as a tightening web of relationships outside work was seen by my Chinese colleagues as part and parcel of the research itself. Since the research involved expressions of suffering and reactions to suffering, I was beginning to feel I was purchasing narratives through my acts of engagement. My frustration developed, along with resentment and a desire to break away and end this seemingly endless reciprocity. And that was when I had my "aha!" experience. I was being infected by what my informants and friends were feeling. I had become part of their local world, and they were becoming part of mine. But insight did little to change things. Not until the 1990s, when I transferred my affiliations to Beijing and Shanghai, though not at the same level of intimacy, did I feel the yoke lift off my neck.

Engagement is both ethically required and morally complicated. It is an answer to one kind of problem of values and emotion, and at the same time it engenders a whole new set of questions and difficulties. In this sense it is the most deeply human of experiences—unavoidable to the ethnographer and yet not nearly as clear-cut a response to feelings of injustice as it first appears to be. There is no absolute resolution to most human problems, but that cannot be an excuse for inaction. We must act with responsibility and ideals, even though the hard reality is that moral experience is a messy and demanding business that doesn't naturally end but goes on and on and on as long as we are part of it. Once you enter a local world, there are practical things to be done, but it is also a space of moral meaning and experience, where affect and value are confused and confounded, as they are daily in each of our lives. And this is also the reason why an anti-heroic stance of the ethnographer may be less misleading and less dangerous than the myth of heroic acts (see Kleinman 2006).

Paths of Engagement

In these narratives we have explored a few of the thorny and contorted emotional dimensions of engagement. In particular, we have highlighted the ways in which emotional engagement in the form of empathy or even guilt can draw us into the local worlds we study as ethnographers. Our respective vantage points as a junior scholar and a senior scholar allow us to explore both the initial pull towards engagement and also the more long-term entanglements of sustained advocacy and engagement within a local moral world. Engagement, we suggest, grows out of an ethics of responsibility based in the interhuman space of emotions, understood as inseparable from value. At its most basic level, engagement is an inevitable part of the ethnographic process. At the same time, engaging is anything but straightforward or obvious.

We suggest that first and foremost, any kind of intellectual, emotional, or political engagement begins with a moral act of acknowledgement. Veena Das indicates that it is in speaking as an expression of pain that the sufferer calls out for acknowledgement, even as that speaking fails to express the totality of pain as it is experienced. Following Wittgenstein, she explores how witnessing the pain of others has the potential of transforming individual pain into something shared: "Where is my pain—in touching you to point out the location of that pain—has my pointing finger—there it is—found your body, which my pain (our pain) can inhabit, at least for that moment when I close my eyes and touch your hand?" (Das 1997:70). Language, for Das, is an inadequate medium for the expression of pain, and yet the experience of pain calls out for a response in which one's pain could reside in another's body. The moment of acknowledgement, although it may fall short of witnessing to another's pain, is the first step in an ethics of responsibility, which includes not just empathic witnessing but some direct action to be of use.

Engagement, thus, also involves advocacy. As both of our narratives describe, this often means eschewing the role of impartial observer and choosing instead to preferentially take the side of one's informants. Ruth Behar in her reflection on Renato Rosaldo's "Grief and a Headhunter's Rage" (1994) argues passionately for an anthropology that "breaks your heart" (1996:177), an anthropology based on powerful emotional commitments. She locates the unique contribution of the discipline not in the culture concept or even in the literary form of ethnography, but in the ethnographer's vulnerability. It is in the capacity to experience emotions—one's own or sharing in those of one's informants—and to reflect on those emotions, that the ethnographer is able to produce compelling analyses of particular local worlds. For Behar, the guise of impartiality diminishes this capacity to reflect. It is this most basic form of advocacy—choosing sides—that lays the groundwork for other, more public advocacy.

Of course, engagement also encompasses a wider range of activities that aim to actively improve the social life of the communities we study, of particular individuals in our networks, and of our own communities. In this sense, engagement involves some kind of practical action. The powerful emotions that arise in the processes of acknowledgement and advocacy—often negative and disabling emotions of guilt and powerlessness—can be productively transformed through this move to doing something concrete in the world. This can be large-scale action, like Kleinman's commitment to the physicians in Changsha, or routine challenges like Smith's responses to affected ignorance. In exceptional cases, anthropologists have started NGOs and large-scale programs to address the inequalities they have witnessed (Farmer 1999).

In conclusion, we suggest that the choice to engage is a moral act (Kleinman 1999, 2006). That is, it lies in the realm of what is at stake for anthropologists in the ethnographic project. Undoubtedly, engagement is not simply about the nobility of our discipline; it is also about deeply held core values and feelings about our individual identities and our roles as ethnographers and as real persons. And since the kind of knowledge that ethnography produces about locally lived experience is neither simple nor uncontested, the actions that the ethnographer is likely to undertake must be understood as anti-heroic. Anthropological acknowledgement and advocacy, and even direct action are a kind of tragic practice—a human engagement that can be painful and yet fulfilling, limited yet nevertheless the best way forward, imperative even as it remains, like all action, laden with unintended consequences.

References

Abu-Lughod, L. 1993. *Writing Women's Worlds.* Berkeley: University of California Press.

Behar, R. 1996. *The Vulnerable Observer: Anthropology That Breaks Your Heart.* Boston: Beacon.

Behar, R., and D. A. Gordon. 1995. *Women Writing Culture.* Berkeley: University of California Press.

Bloch, M. 1983. *Marxism and Anthropology: The History of a Relationship.* Oxford: Clarendon Press.

Clifford, J., and G. E. Marcus. 1986. *Writing Culture: The Poetics and Politics of Ethnography.* Berkeley: University of California Press.

Collier, J. F., and S. Yanagisako. 1989. "Theory in Anthropology since Feminist Practice." *Critique of Anthropology* 9 (2): 27–37.

CONADEP. 1986. *Nunca Mas: A Report by Argentina's Commission on Disappeared People.* London: Faber and Faber.

Das, V. 1997. "Language and Body: Transactions in the Construction of Pain." In A. Kleinman, V. Das, and M. Lock, eds., *Social Suffering,* 67–92. Berkeley: University of California Press.

Farmer, P. 1999. *Infections and Inequalities: The Modern Plagues.* Berkeley: University of California Press.

Godelier, M. 1978. *Perspectives in Marxist Anthropology.* Cambridge: Cambridge University Press.

Kim, J., J. Millen, A. Irwin, and J. Gersham. 2000. *Dying for Growth: Global Inequality and the Health of the Poor.* Monroe, ME: Common Courage Press.

Kleinman, A. 1999. "Experience and Its Moral Modes: Culture, Human Conditions, and Disorder." In G. B. Peterson, ed., *The Tanner Lectures on Human Values,* 20–39. Salt Lake City: University of Utah Press.

———. 2006. *What Really Matters: Living a Moral Life amidst Uncertainty and Danger.* Oxford: Oxford University Press.

Levinas, E. 1998. *Entre Nous: Thinking-of-the-Other.* New York: Columbia University Press.

Lorde, A. 1984. "The Uses of Anger: Women Responding to Racism." In *Sister Outsider: Essays and Speeches by Audre Lorde,* 125–133. Freedom, CA: The Crossing Press.

Marcus, G. E., and M. M. J. Fischer. 1986. *Anthropology as Cultural Critique: An Experimental Moment in the Human Sciences.* Chicago: University of Chicago Press.

Moody-Adams, M. M. 1997. *Fieldwork in Familiar Places: Morality, Culture, and Philosophy.* Cambridge, MA: Harvard University Press.

Pew Research Center for the People and the Press. 2005. "Do you think the use of torture against suspected terrorists in order to gain important information can often be justified, sometimes be justified, rarely be justified, or never be justified?" http:// ncronline.org/NCR_Online/archives2/2006a/032406/032406h.htm (accessed January 15, 2007).

Rosaldo, M., and L. Lamphere, eds. 1974. *Woman Culture and Society*. Stanford, CA: Stanford University Press.

Rosaldo, R. 1994. "Grief and a Headhunter's Rage." In E. Bruner, ed., *Text, Play, and Story: The Construction and Reconstruction of Self and Society*, 178–195. Washington, DC: American Ethnological Society.

III

Non-cognitive Field Experiences

8 Emotional Topographies

The Sense of Place in the Far North

Kirsten Hastrup

THIS CHAPTER FOCUSES ON the fieldworker's "sense of place" as imbued with emotional significance and value, internalised along with other social values. The ethnographer's perception of landscapes and paths is grounded in both the intersubjectivity explored in the field and the intertextuality inherent in the anthropological tradition. It will be argued that intersubjectivity itself is mediated by place, and that regionalism in the anthropological tradition is not simply a discursive issue but also a material one, in that the nature of place in itself contributes to the emotional marking of the field. On the basis of field experiences in Iceland and Greenland, I shall discuss some of the moods related to the study of the North.

In a recent article I argued that anthropology is on the verge of a topographic turn, implying a renewed consideration of the material and spatial dimensions of social life (Hastrup 2005b). Our sense of belonging to a particular "formatted" social space is closely related to our sense of topography (James 2003). The formatting of the social space concerns social organisation and differentiation, grouping and individuality, and it comprises evaluation and emotion—all of which combine into a particular space for orientation. My primary focus here is on the emotional dimension of topography, i.e., the sense of place that is spurred by particular landscapes. Stressing the notion of a *sense of place* is in line with the attempt to develop an ethnography of lived topographies as instigated by Steven Feld and Keith Basso (1996), in which the perceptual engagement with the surroundings is critical to the conceptual ordering of space (Feld 1996:91). The relationship is reciprocal, of course.

My background for approaching this topic is the combination of extensive field experience in Iceland, more recent field trips to Greenland, and a general interest in the Arctic. The last began as an interest in the history of Danish anthropology, growing out of the many Arctic expeditions under the leadership of Knud Rasmussen (1879–1933) (Hastrup 2006), whose books, unpublished diaries, and reminiscences I have studied, along with many other works from different periods of Arctic research. The reason I mention this is simply to point out the obvious importance of intertextuality in any anthropological argument; "the Arctic" is certainly narrated (Bravo and Sörlin 2002).

When I first went to Greenland, in 2004, I was struck both by the beauty and magnificence of the landscape and its people and by my own strong feeling of being immediately "at home" there. There were remarkable reminiscences of the Icelandic landscape—but more marked, more extreme. Upon reflection, I concluded that the likeness was not simply one of geographical features; it also had to do with a perceived similarity in the relationship between people and place, and between people themselves. In what follows I shall refer to the Arctic landscape for both Iceland and Greenland when I speak in general terms, although strictly speaking, Iceland is subarctic in geographical terms—as is part of Greenland. My theoretical point of departure in many ways echoes Edward Casey's suggestion that "as places gather bodies in their midst in deeply acculturated ways, so cultures conjoin bodies in concrete circumstances of emplacement" (Casey 1996:46). "Emplacement," in its turn, reminds us of the mutuality of physical and social coordinates.

On the surface of it, "emotions in the field" comprise an assortment of feelings and sensations, but for a study of such emotions to be productive in anthropology, I suggest that it be related not simply to the agents as subjects but also to the concrete and shared field of reasoning and feeling. The "field" itself has strong spatial connotations, and this is one of its merits, even if its physicality has too often been bracketed or seen as simply a backdrop to social life. As a renewed anthropology of landscape has shown, the landscape is part of social life in a profound way (Hirsch and O'Hanlon 1995). This is where a discursive approach to emotions (e.g., Lutz and Abu-Lughod 1990) must be supplemented by a close consideration of topography if we are to understand the "feel for place" by which people live. Incidentally, this is also where we must be careful not to separate ontologically what Michel de Certeau has distinguished analytically, namely place and space (de Certeau 1984)—a distinction that is too often invoked to separate the physical place from the social space and by consequence to reserve the latter for anthropology. Entering the field means incorporating a particular sense of place, which is experientially inseparable from the social space, and becoming captured within it—often unawares.

I concentrate here on some analytical perspectives and concepts by which we may come to terms with the emotional topography of a particular field. Neither time nor space makes it possible to give a truly ethnographic account, even if that is generally where any anthropological argument comes to life. I shall have to do with anecdotes and clippings and refer to my writings on Iceland and on Arctic imageries. I shall start by portraying the Arctic landscape as encapsulating a particular *poetics of space*, and discuss some correlative questions of scaling. In the second section, my focus is on people and the relations between them as mediated by space, and as resulting in particular *chronotopes*. In the third section, I turn to the ethnographer, getting to know the inarticulate dimensions of the space, not least in what I shall call *raw moments*. Through these three closely interwoven sections, we hopefully will arrive at a point where we may embrace the idea of emotional topographies in a more consistent analytical language and sense their impact on ethnographic writing.

The Arctic: The Poetics of Space

First I shall present the Arctic landscape in terms influenced by Gaston Bachelard's work on the poetics of space (1994). My aim is to show how the emplacement of people co-produces particular sensations, which also affect the fieldworker deeply. It is impossible, therefore, to separate the ethnography as written from the place as sensed. This pertains to any ethnographic account.

In modern life, contact with the natural environment has become increasingly indirect and limited to special occasions (Tuan 1990:95); by contrast, in fieldwork anthropologists are often exposed to nature, if for no other reason than that the notion of the *field* in itself generates a heightened attention to the spatial parameters of social life. The defamiliarising strategy that fieldwork entails cuts the ethnographer loose from familiar neighbourhoods and landscapes and gives access to a different sense of place—highlighting a relationship beyond words but within feelings.

Merleau-Ponty suggested that "space and perception generally represent, at the core of the subject, the fact of his birth, the perpetual contribution of his bodily being, a communication with the world more ancient than thought" (Merleau-Ponty 1962:254). The emotional implications of this ancient spatial communication with the world are related to the features of texture, shape, and fecundity that, according to Wendy James, "provide a base line to our human lives, not only our pragmatic activities, but to our conceptual understandings of the organized qualities of differentiated space, and our orientation within it" (James 2003:213).

The texture and shape of Arctic landscapes is a remarkable mixture of emptiness and solidity, of extremely sparse and widely scattered populations and very close social relations. The long seasons of summer and winter are repeatedly torn by bursts of violent gales and snowstorms that make life rather precarious. The slow rhythm of nature in the high latitudes, the long seasons of light and darkness, somewhat paradoxically demand an acute attention to the moment by everybody, lest the one seal of the week, the stray grouse, or the few days of spawning cod are missed. People must constantly be aware of the environment in its totality so as not to miss their moment. Even today, in Greenland a rumour of seal makes most men leave whatever else they are presently working on and jump into their boats, guns in hand, as I have witnessed in Ilulissat (western Greenland). Such rumours and other human sounds contribute to a soundscape that is dominated by sounds of freezing and melting, the breaking of ice, permanently running water and sometimes wild and unpredictable glacier bursts, sea waves and howling winds, volcanic activities and floods—sometimes in the form of regular tsunamis. The intonation of nature in this part of the North Atlantic should not be underestimated.

In such circumstances, the poetics of space is not simply a matter of allegory; it is also a matter of space itself being akin to a poetical image, in the sense suggested by Bachelard (1994). The singular composition of the landscape by ice and fire, glaciers and rivers, barren slopes, migrating prey, and perceived riches of the (frozen) sea is not simply an image that is conferred upon people by their chroniclers, but an image that has taken root in them and is referable to a direct ontology—like the poetic image itself (Bachelard 1994:xvi, xvii). The place makes itself *felt*. In north Greenland, as I traveled for some hours by a simple dinghy deep into the fjord to visit a distant settlement inhabited by a mere fifteen people, I sensed not only movement and distance but also the increasing cold (and threat) emanating from the icebergs, and the thunder-like sounds of calving glaciers. At the same time, I—like the hunter steering the boat—found myself on constant lookout for seal, narwhal, and the dreaded killer whales that this year had decided to visit the fjord. Everything fused into a kind of awareness simultaneously above and within the landscape. Needless to say, hardly any words were exchanged.

Bachelard writes: "The poetic image is an emergence from language, it is always a little above the language of signification. By living the poems we read, we have the salutary experience of emerging" (1994:xxvii). By living the Arctic landscape, I argue, one succumbs to this feeling of perpetual emergence; subjectivity has to be constantly reclaimed in a landscape of such momentousness, within which the manifest insignificance of people readily displaces any comprehensive language of signification. Instead, the people emplaced in the Arctic resort to vivid sagas of aboriginal cunning, of heroic hunts, of narrow escapes from disaster, of disappearance at sea, of falling down glacier rifts, or of the willed death of the old and impaired wandering out into oblivion. Narration makes the subject emerge and underscores a particular *topophilia*.

Yi-Fu Tuan defines topophilia as "the affective bond between people and place or setting" (1990:4). This bond affects perception, here seen as an activity that immerses people in their environment. This immersion is carried out by all the senses; in modern society and in urban settings we have come to privilege sight and vision, and to rely on objects, boundaries, and perspectives for orientation. In the Arctic, however, the visual field potentially extends so far and the air is so clear that it effectively prevents space from being boxed in and organised into different distances and perspectives (Tuan 1990:11). The consequence is that if the landscape is simply "seen," it looks empty, and relative size and distance evade any scale. Thus bear may be mistaken for hare when a white lump is seen moving in the distance. Truth evades the gaze, just as the landscape evades narrative and confounds with poetry, where no human-made structures assemble to form an implicit yardstick of other forms.

In such places, size and distance can be ascertained only through *movement*. This stresses the point made by Tuan that "perception is an activity, a reaching out to the world. Sense organs are minimally operative when they are not actively used. Our tactile sense is very delicate but to tell the differences in the texture or hardness of surfaces it is not sufficient to put a finger on them; the finger has to move over them" (Tuan 1990:12). On a larger scale, we have to move bodily within a particular landscape to sense it properly. In Iceland, that was how I learnt the power and poetics of the landscape; by rounding up stray sheep in the mountains, by gathering berries on the slopes, and by participating in various other activities alongside my Icelandic hosts, I became aware of the hidden histories and portents of places and names (Hastrup 1998). If one only looks, there is nothing to be seen, no recollections to make, but by moving about, one may eventually get a feel for the place.

I felt this even more strongly in north Greenland, where during my first visit I kept looking for action but saw only ice and snow and immeasurable distances. When finally I succeeded in getting a ride on a dogsled joining a party of seal hunters, I understood why nothing was to be seen from the village. Once over the ice foot that marked the border between the ice-covered land and the frozen fjord, we were submerged in a rugged landscape of ice where ice rocks that seemed tiny from shore proved to be of immense size, often hiding the sleds from one another, and where the apparently smooth white surface was in fact extremely uneven, making it necessary to hold tightly to the sled until I learned to read the landscape and predict the movement. Only then did I realise how much life there was on the ice-clad fjord; by feeling small and insignificant myself, I was later able to interpret the tiny black dots on the ice as sleds, going in particular directions for seal. I had understood neither the magnitude of place nor the near-invisibility of people within it until I truly started moving about myself.

The perceived extensional indeterminacy of the open Arctic landscape may momentarily transform into a strong sense of indistinctiveness. During the long winter, it is not uncommon to experience everything as being of one and the same greyish substance, blocking out any distinction between land, sea, and sky. Again, to move about, one has to supplement one's vision with other senses (Tuan 1990:11). We are not the first ones to acknowledge this; already Boas (1964 [1888]) had noted how the Eskimos depended on the smell of the winds, for instance, to orient themselves in space. In general, if the idea of place as sensed is pursued, we shall have to acknowledge that sensing a place rests on a broad spectrum of clues: visual, auditory, olfactory, etc. (Feld 1996:98). The main point is that the Arctic landscape presents itself as a totalistic image that is akin to the condensed image of a poem. A poem works on the mind as a whole, by evoking a comprehensive sensation of emotional fulfilment through a *complete form* rather than by a narrative unfolding of plot.

The poetics of space is implicitly subject-referring, of course, since poetics in this sense is a matter of perception, not one of physics per se. I would like to argue the other way round as well, seeing that in the Arctic subjectivity itself is implicitly place-referring and thus not entirely coterminous with individuality. It has been claimed, for instance, that a proper understanding of the ancient Icelandic sagas is contingent upon dwelling within the Icelandic landscape and language (Kristjánsson 1988:7). No less important is the fact that in Iceland, genealogy—of both people and places—plays an important part in the mental mapping of social relations (Hastrup 2008a). Somehow, one's emergence into society is part of who one is.

Even more marked, perhaps, is the situation in north Greenland, where the small community of hunters until recently moved about between different camps, following the game, and where today they will still lay out the track by which they came to live in the village for the inquisitive ethnographer wanting to know "who" they are. Itineraries make people; they emerge along the way of their dwellings.

Significantly, it has also been a persistent trope in Arctic ethnographies that people are of a particularly poetical bent. In Iceland it is very much a trope entertained by the Icelanders themselves; it is still common for ordinary people to compose a poetical tribute to others, for instance in obituaries, or secretly offered to sweethearts, or to stray anthropologists inducing illicit desires. The Eskimo encountered by Boas in the 1880s were no less profoundly steeped in the Arctic landscape; they too displayed a strong poetical bent (Boas 1964 [1888]:240). Boas noted how tradition had become "abridged" over time, the content being supposedly known. This poetical compression allowed people to sense their tradition in its totality. The compression of knowledge is a feature also of history being literally shared in communities so strongly marked by fewness. This, again, is co-productive of the perceived silence in these places, or the sparse recourse to an unmarked language of signification—unless new-comers arrive.

Rasmussen noted that the Eskimos were "poets unawares" (Rasmussen 1929:33); I would still claim that in north Greenland such poets give voice to the poetics of space that I am after here. In narrative the voices are represented by characters, while in poetry the voices are represented by "changing registers of diction, contrastive rhythms, and varieties of tone" (Vendler 1995:6). Emplacement within the Arctic landscape and its contrastive rhythms and changing registers of sound correlates with a muting of characters—as autonomous subjects of speaking and acting. Somehow, the landscape acts upon you and not the other way round, as I experienced. Once, during a coffee break on the seal hunt, I tumbled down from the top of the ice foot, landing ungraciously and painfully on my back. My companions roared with laughter, which at first I found rather distressing, not only because I felt silly but also because I was as yet unaccustomed to the *impersonal* reason for laughter—just as I was in-experienced in walking on ice in bearskin kamiks. It is a landscape of such magnitude that it cannot be told; it can only be experienced as a whole image, compressing vastness into intensity. This is where referential language must give way to either silence or compressed feeling.

This leads us to questions of scale, which we usually think of in quantitative terms. In anthropology, the holistic ambition entailed an idea that *whole* societies or cultures had to be known, and they therefore had to be quite small (or at least portrayed as such). It is not as simple as that. Scale is more than a matter of size or extension; it also has to do with complexity, dynamics, and quality. The demand for comprehensiveness that still qualifies the anthropological object—and without which fieldwork would be meaningless—has less to do with quantity than with quality. Already in 1978, Fredrik Barth suggested that a qualification of scale—in terms of numbers, extension of territory, and intensity of interaction—should be part of any empirical description (Barth 1978). Yet we have still to come to terms with analytical concepts for intensities, not to speak of feelings, beyond quantification.

Clifford Geertz has offered an operative analytical distinction that captures some of the complexity of this, with regard to the distinction between moods and motivations. He qualifies them thus:

> The major difference between moods and motivations is that where the latter are, so to speak, vectorial qualities, the former are merely scalar. Motives have a directional cast, they describe a certain overall course, gravitate toward certain, usually temporary, consummations. But moods vary only as to intensity: they go nowhere. They spring from certain circumstances but they are responsive to no ends. Like fogs, they just settle and lift; like scents, suffuse and evaporate. When present they are totalistic: if one is sad everything and everybody seems dreary; if one is gay, everything and everybody seems splendid. . . . But perhaps the most important difference, so far as we are concerned, between moods and motivations is that motivations are "made meaningful" with reference to the ends toward which they are conceived to conduce, whereas moods are "made meaningful" with reference to the conditions from which they are conceived to spring. We interpret motives in terms of their consummations, but we interpret moods in terms of their sources. (Geertz 1973:97)

My point would be that the relative intensity of moods strongly affects the perceived success of consummation. In other words, moods and motivations are co-incident; the directionality and temporality of will, life-course, and history are fuelled by wellsprings of intensity and feelings. In the Arctic, motivated actions are fuelled by the built-up moods and tensions of enforced hibernation, as it were, when unpredictability reigns outside and condensed tradition is recycled inside.

Within this poetical framework of the landscape as a whole, people naturally move about and invest their own submerged narrative into the space within which they find themselves. Thus space itself capacitates people in particular ways; it is a dimension of agency (Corsín Jiménez 2003:138).

The People: Chronotopes in Life

To capture the poetical landscape from the point of view of the dwellers, whose own trajectories are rather more like narratives, I shall borrow Bakhtin's notion of the chronotope (1996). In the *literary* chronotope, "spatial and temporal indicators are fused into one carefully thought out, concrete whole. Time, as it were, takes on flesh, becomes artistically visible; likewise, space becomes charged and responsive to the movements of time, plot, and history" (Bakhtin 1994:84). This resonates well with what we might call *lived* chronotopes, and just as different literary genres may be defined by their distinct chronotopes, so may different ways of emplacement. And just as in literature the chronotope is always coloured by emotions and values (Bakhtin 1996:243), so also is it in landscapes.

Lived chronotopes relate to different ways of perceiving the *territory*, among other things. I am here referring to the notion of territory as discussed by Deleuze and Guattari, claiming that a territory "is first of all the critical distance between two beings of the same species: Mark your distance" (Deleuze and Guattari 2004:352). We know how birds mark their territory by sounds, and we know how people all over the place draw boundaries—around their personal, familial, or national spaces—by various other means. So, clearly, territory defines a field of social relations.

In the far North, the territory in this sense is relatively unmarked. There is a long tradition of commons and of free access to the natural environment in the Nordic countries, including Iceland. In the polar North the Inuit are by tradition even less territorial—at least between themselves; they migrated, moved apart, regrouped, and exchanged news and wives as a matter of course. This in itself is a huge difference from living within more confined spaces, where territory is closely related to property rights and other well-defined codes for social relationships. Territorialisation is a precondition for the emergence of specialised functions and "occupations" (Deleuze and Guattari 2004:354), which in the Arctic are absent—or were until recently. Space, once again, capacitates people in different ways, and conversely, "space is an emerging property of social relationships" (Corsín Jiménez 2003:140).

The perceived lack of territoriality in the Arctic is related to both the expansiveness of the land and the precariousness of living. People would leave surplus game under heaps of stones for others to take if they were in need, and they would share whatever they had with each other. Generosity towards passing strangers is still a strong feature in both Iceland and Greenland, as I have often experienced. There is a remarkable openness to travellers, reflective of the shared knowledge of the hazards of exposure to the landscape, and the sudden need for shelter. The directionality of narrative and travel is constantly punctuated by nature, forcing people to regroup and redefine the social space; conversely—we should never forget that we are talking about the mutual impacting of place and social possibilities—place effects peculiar encounters and social events, allowing for narrative gestures slightly "above" the language of signification.

A distinction between open and enclosed spaces seems generally relevant, and we know that each affects people differently (Tuan 1990:27–28). The comparative experience of different fields in anthropology clearly resonates with a deep-seated sensation of the importance of the distinction between open and enclosed spaces, and of the existential significance of the opening and closing of horizons, affecting both experience and interpretation (Crapanzano 2004). What is peculiar to life in the Arctic is the remarkable presence of both extremes—in terms of openness and closure—in experience. Expansiveness and free movement over infinite expanses, travelling from one node in a vast network of acquaintances and relatives to another, is repeatedly cut short by enforced stillness within the confined space of the dwelling or the snow-blinded field of vision. Freezing and melting are part of social as well as natural processes. The tiny settlements along coasts that until recently were inaccessible for long periods of time and still are so by relative standards—in both Iceland and more markedly in Greenland—contribute to an inversion of the feeling of extension; places become marked by intension. This distinction is owed to Deleuze and Guattari, who explain:

> Although in extension the territory separates the interior forces of the earth from the exterior forces of chaos, the same does not occur in "intension," in the dimension of depth, where the two types of force clasp and are wed in a battle whose only criterion and stakes is the earth. There is always a palace, a tree or a grove, in the territory where all the forces come together in a hand-to-hand combat of energies. The earth is this close embrace. This intense center is simul-

taneously inside the territory, and outside several territories that converge on it at the end of an immense pilgrimage. . . . Inside or out, the territory is linked to this intense center, which is like the unknown homeland, terrestrial source of all forces friendly and hostile, where everything is decided. (Deleuze and Guattari 2004:354)

I would argue that the territorial expanse and indistinctiveness actually and somewhat paradoxically afford a peculiar prominence of intension in the Arctic, where the centre of the dwelling itself signifies the converging of inside and outside, of stillness and action. This is echoed in social relationships, equally formatted by both their extension and their intension. The tradition of migration and the perpetual movements of herders and hunters have a counterpoint in a remarkably strong sense of *home* as the centre of the world, and the source of spiritual nourishment, of new beginnings and long histories. The centre is defined as such by a compression of experience. I here sense an echo of what Michael Jackson writes:

The compression of experience at times of birth and death has an exact analogue in the way in which we regard the places we hold dear to us and make central to our lives. We speak of intense experience in terms of mass. Images of bedrock and stone stand for what is real, while water, air, and sand suggest what is ephemeral. *Homeplaces are the spatial correlatives of the moments that have changed our lives.* These places of orientation, from which we perpetually start out and to which we perennially return in our imaginations, are steeped in the memory of births and deaths (emphasis in original). (Jackson 1995:135–136)

In such places, which in the Arctic become places of both communion and of communal confinement, anger cannot be tolerated, as Jean Briggs (1970) realised in her study of the emotional texture of social life in a confined Canadian Inuit community. Hostility must be tempered or resolved, for instance through the drum dances and singing contests in traditional Greenland, where maddened or disturbed people might also leave for the wilderness—to disappear or to calm down. When intension becomes overwhelming, people resort to spatial strategies—either by way of words that fabricate a new space or by way of re-placement.

As a moment of social engagement, movement and travelling in the Arctic are greatly appreciated, also by ethnographers, whose patience is under considerable strain when weather-bound in confined communities. Travelling and the means of transport are not immaterial to the resulting description. I have described this for Iceland (Hastrup 1998), and I perfectly understood Knud Rasmussen when he said about his Eskimo expeditions: "From the bottom of my heart I bless the fate that had me born at a time where polar research by means of dog sledges had not yet become outdated" (1932:ii). The chosen mode of transport was a means not only to get from one place to another but also to become inscribed into the Arctic topography (Hastrup 2006). The sled still lingers as a powerful image in the self-perception of the (northern) Greenlanders and mediates their sense of place and distance, as can be easily ascertained by the present-day ethnographer.

Engaging people where they are—in a community of hunters this means travelling along with them by sled for most of the year and by boat for a few months during summer. When travel takes over and dogs are as important as people in sustaining social life, the entire lifeworld as well as human agency takes on a particular texture that by its nature subsumes sociality under a larger vision of the world. Travel is a *social* practice, even when one travels alone; by inscribing himself into the Arctic topography along with the local people, the ethnographer may report on their social *life*—such as it is, deeply embedded in a landscape inhabited by both humans and their prey. In this world, skills and knowledge are two sides of the same coin; to quote Tim Ingold: "The more skilled the hunter, the more knowledgeable he becomes, for with a finely tuned perceptual system, the world will appear to him in greater richness and profundity. New knowledge comes from creative acts of discovery rather than imagining, from attending more closely to the environment rather than reassembling one's picture of it along new conceptual lines" (Ingold 2000:55–56). Movement, enskillment, and perception go together.

Within the all-embracing poetics of space, people create lesser narratives through their movement. Returning to the idea of chronotopes, we might say that the lived narratives are governed by the chronotope of the *road* (Bakhtin 1996:243).

> People who are normally kept separate by social and spatial distance can accidentally meet; any contrast may crop up, the most various fates may collide and interweave with one another. On the road the spatial and temporal series defining human fates and lives combine with one another in distinctive ways, even as they become more complex and more concrete by the collapse of *social distances*. The chronotope of the road is both a point of new departures and a

place for events to find their denouement. Time, as it were, fuses together with space and flows in it; this is the source of the rich metaphorical expansion on the image of the road as a course. (Bakhtin 1996:243–244)

Perhaps somewhat paradoxically, the vast and certainly unpaved Arctic landscape has often been likened to one big road—the point being that movement occurs wherever possible (and almost impossible). It is part of local ground knowledge that time and season account for openings and closings of particular parts of the extensive road. Openings were to be seized; if one was prevented from moving oneself, one could always hope for others to come by, on the road to nowhere in particular. Such encounters would temporarily release the stunted language of reference in the cross-narration of experiences and events.

It is logical that in Bakhtin's scheme, the chronotope of the road is closely related to the chronotope of the *encounter*; the latter is marked by a higher degree of intensity in emotions and values, and by a predominance of time over space (Bakhtin 1996:243). The extreme case would be so-called "first encounters"; it is significant that being "the first" was for a long time a persistent trope in ethnographic writing. I have written about that elsewhere, and shall simply say here that most depictions of "first encounters" are replete with other first encounters (Hastrup 2007, 2008a). This also goes for the famous arrival stories in anthropology that serve the literary purpose of inserting the ethnographer in the field—and immersing him or her in a particular chronotope: imagine yourself as part of another story (Hastrup 2005a).

If, as I suggested earlier, the poetics of the Arctic space capacitated people in particular ways, we are now in a position to suggest also that this space affects intersubjectivity deeply, because intersubjectivity is embedded in place. To phrase it dfferently, I would suggest that intersubjectivity is not simply a matter of relationships between persons but involves relations between people and places and ideas about places; the ethnographer in the field becomes similarly emplaced and emotionally embraced by the chronotopes at play.

The Ethnographer: Raw Moments of Knowing

Because geography poses a real challenge for survival in the Arctic, it is also a major challenge of perception. Snowstorms, icebergs, mists, and gales, not to mention strange visual effects and temporary absences of differentiation between earth, sky, and sea, demand an exceptional perceptual acuity. It has often been noted how the Inuit are able to travel hundreds of miles across expansive landscapes by taking cues from the environment that are less visual than acoustic, olfactory, and tactile. The Inuit is "guided by the direction and smell of winds, and by the feel of ice and snow under his feet" (Tuan 1990:77).

The tuning of perception is not exclusive to the Arctic people, of course, but the particular training of the senses is specific to the topography (Feld 1996). The question becomes how we may access such tuning in the field. Part of the answer lies in the amount of time spent and the quality of the training, as once so vividly described by Turnbull (1990). Another part of the answer lies in the openness and susceptibility of the ethnographer to what I shall call *raw moments*, again following an inspiration from Deleuze and Guattari, who say about them that "the essential thing is the disjunction noticeable between the code and the territory" (Deleuze and Guattari 2004:355). In raw moments, an unknown territory arises on the margins of the coded space, and the entire topography seems to shift around through a process of transcoding. The raw moments are thresholds of knowledge, and in lived narratives they reflect Bakhtin's chronotope of the threshold (1996:248), also by their being highly charged with emotion.

The raw moments are different from diagnostic events, as we usually talk about them in anthropology, because they are intensely emotional and related to the feelings of the fieldworker rather than the analytical habitus. The raw moments strip us bare of conceptual prejudice and deliver us to pure sensation. I shall relate my meeting with a *huldumaður*, a man of the "hidden people," who have always lived in rocks, caves, and knolls in the Icelandic landscape (see also Hastrup 1987).

During the autumn collection of sheep in the steep mountain ridges behind the farm where I worked, I was once left on a rock ledge to hold on to a sheep that we had just recovered from another ledge where it had been trapped. Alone, rope in hand and sheep beside me, I sat marvelling at the view down towards the coastal flatlands where the farmstead was located, and sideways to the huge glacier that towered over everything. At the time I had learnt to read the landscape historically for remains of older turf farms, for original settlements, and so on. I felt completely at ease with myself and with my combined position as shepherdess and surveyor.

Suddenly a dense fog came rolling down from the upper mountains, and with it an icy cold; the fog enclosed me completely on my ledge. In the subarctic, one knows never to trust the sun, and I was prepared to meet the cold,

but in the long run, woollen clothes could not prevent a degree of fear creep-
ing in. It was not primarily a fear of getting lost, even though I knew I could
never descend the steep slopes on my own. It was a sense of trepidation of
a different order, closely related to the place where I found myself. In that
place, the fog made a particularly *Icelandic* landscape emerge, which I could
no longer objectify. As it happened, a nebulous human figure appeared in the
mist, on the outskirts of my narrow field of vision. I instantly sensed that it
was a man of the "hidden people" (*huldufólkið*) who visited me; ever since the
Middle Ages *huldumenn* have been known to seduce Icelandic womenfolk,
and especially shepherdesses in the misty mountains. Whatever it was, it was
certainly a very strong sense of *presence*, emerging out of the landscape within
which I was captured. Afterwards this experience allowed me to engage in
completely different conversations with my hosts on both the hidden people
and the landscape; as solitary as the experience was, it immersed me even
more strongly in the social space.

I want to suggest that in the far North, as I deal with it here, the raw moments, the overpowering emotional experiences of transcoding, are singularly
attached to the landscape and to the extreme sense of solitude that descends
upon locals and foreigners alike when they are lost in space and find themselves to be somewhat removed from time as well. It is frightening to lose one's
footing in time and space, but there is no way to back out from such experiences in a place where thought, emotion, and action unite in a singular experience of the boundaries between the self and the environment dissolving
completely. The topographical approach allows for a realisation of the role
played by places and passages in our perception of the field—and the perception of ourselves within the field.

The anecdote illustrates the point made by Merleau-Ponty that "perception
does not give me truth like geometry but presences" (1964:14). It also shows
that the professional self is configured and reconfigured through sensory experiences that can never be fully translated into cognitive schemes. When, only
this summer, I walked along the stony beach, where after a major storm in-
numerable ice-rocks of considerable size had stranded, and kept hearing the
sound of breaking glaciers and icebergs, and took it all in, I also suddenly felt
myself frightened by (imagined) polar bears lurking among and indistinguish-
able from the ice-rocks. I had just read a report of the reemergence of the bear
in the area, but my fright did not spring from this reading alone; it came from
a perceived presence on the beach.

Anecdotes are useful for conveying the configuration of the professional self, and for intimating that not all experience is reducible to knowledge, as Michael Jackson has reminded us (Jackson 1995). There is a vast amount of experience—on the part of people and of anthropologists—that may linger without necessarily contributing explicitly to the larger order as presented, but still providing sources of insight and understanding. On the basis of such experiences, we access a larger truth of time-space-self being tied into one knot—a holistic configuration, if ever there was one.

Wherever we go in the name of anthropology, the shifting time-space-self configurations destabilise the subject-object relationship that was part and parcel of modernist anthropology and its heroic venture. The raw moments are indicators of transcoding as much as they are the reason for it. One cannot see a *huldumaður* without already being present in space where he appears; neither may one feel fright of a polar bear if its possible presence is not acknowledged—and this might be fatal. The rawness of the moment is a symptom of a momentary loss of any fixed horizon of expectation and orientation. In some fields or at some times, fieldwork is experienced as a series of jumps between raw moments; in others, there is a greater sense of a gradual gaining of knowledge. The *tempo* of fieldwork cannot be forced beyond a certain point, and raw moments cannot be cooked up.

Within the present argument, raw moments are not any moment of angst in the field, of course; they are moments where emplacement *within* the field impinges upon subjectivity and allows for an unmediated perception of something that cannot be called up but that manifests itself as a presence—even if unaccounted for by the rationality of Western science, including anthropology. I read Jon Mitchell's "moment with Christ" (1997) as such a raw moment, where the physicality of both the sculpture and the act of cleaning it that he had volunteered for changed his perception of belief in Malta forever. The raw moments, as I suggest we use the notion, are not simply decisive moments of understanding that we may retrospectively identify when back at our desk; they are sensed very strongly while they happen as having sensational, if unfathomable, ethnographic significance.

There is no way in which we can measure "how much" we must know of the social world or culture under study for such moments to be ethnographically significant. What we can say is that if they register as turning points in the social relations, including relations of co-feeling, they have demonstrated themselves as "raw" in the sense used here, as transgressive and unmediated experiences of local stakes. I use the word "local" deliberately here, because the raw moments are symptoms also of those practices through which the "present" is fabricated as a regional world (see also Corsín Jiménez 2003:141). The social world happens by our spatial engagement with it.

The Refrain: Topographic Salience

In this chapter I have repeatedly referred to literary concepts. This is to suggest that the ethnographic—like the poetical—image may be seen as a sudden salience on the linguistic surface, which makes us "recognise" what we did not know. And just as poetry makes a voice out of those voices that surround it (Geertz 1983:117), ethnography makes an image of a people out of those images that surround it. This displaces the author from the position of absolute authority. The ethnographer cannot hide his or her presence as author, but the pen is governed as much by the embodied experience of thresholds and raw moments as by his or her will—by moods and emotions as much as by motivations and theoretical goals.

Through the particular "participant experience," the ethnographer incorporates an emotional topography, where the scalar qualities of moods are as important as the vectoral qualities of direction. The topographic salience encountered in the field is a unity of sensation and thought, of activity and reflexivity. As Tim Ingold says:

> The differences between the activities of hunting and gathering, on the one hand, and singing, storytelling and the narration of myth on the other cannot be accommodated within a dichotomy between the material and the mental, between ecological interactions *in* nature and cultural constructions *of* nature. On the contrary, both sets of activities are, in the first place, ways of dwelling. The latter . . . amount not to a metaphorical representation of the world, but to a form of poetic involvement. (Ingold 2000:57)

The explicitly analogical method used by ethnographers in their quest for knowledge gives access to local topographic salience as simultaneously material and emotional. In turn, this mediates relations between people living by particular chronotopes. In this chapter I have wanted to show how the sense of place in the far North is formatted by a certain Arctic poetics that capacitates people in particular ways. In turn, place affects intersubjectivity—always so much more than simply a relationship between persons, because place enters into the equation. Place also infuses the feeling of raw moments where prefabricated categories give way to pure sensation. "Getting it right" in anthropology requires that the emplacement of people and of the ethnographic encounter be acknowledged (Hastrup 2004c). Agency is a matter of exploring the possibilities of place, and hence of social relationships. To "act" is to make a move within a territory, which sets the scene for the imagined outcome. The action itself realises the illusion of wholeness in the social (Hastrup 2004a, 2004b).

To conclude, I shall once again invoke the work of Deleuze and Guattari, namely their notion of *the refrain*. They define a refrain as "any aggregate of matters of expression that draws a territory and develops into territorial motifs and landscapes" (Deleuze and Guattari 2004:356). The notion derives from assemblages that are dominated by sound, such as the singing of birds, or—one might like to add—by the ringing of church bells or the voices flowing out of minarets at particular times—but refrains can be optical, gestural, architectural, and much more, including combinations of them all. The point is that the refrain "holds together" the heterogeneous elements of the territory; it is the refrain itself that affords it with a sense of consistency. In the Arctic the refrain is a complex whole of motifs related to a peculiar combination of extension and intension; of vastness of vision, extreme climatic changes, and the sounds of wind and breaking ice on the one hand and of confined spaces, muted emotions, level human voices, and storytelling on the other. The refrain assembles the poetics of space and the chronotopes of life in nodal points of sensory experience.

As I reread this chapter in Greenland, where in late April the snow was still piled up and snowstorms sometimes confined me to the comforts of the computer, the refrain took on a new literal meaning with the chorus of (chained) sled dogs singing their sad songs at certain moments of the day. Often one pack would set off its neighbour, and thus the song would spring from one house to the next—except when feeding had them all howling at the same time. This sonorous reminder of the relationship between people and their means of transport and hunting is a significant part of the Arctic refrain amidst the larger silence bestowed upon people by their emplacement. The chant sessions of the Greenlanders, like the sonorous repetition of the Icelandic sagas, can be seen as means of reclaiming a fraction of the poetics of space by the otherwise silenced, a collective intonation of community, however small and insignificant, within the expansive wilderness.

I would suggest that the topographic and sensory approach which I have here proposed lends strength to a new sense of "the field" as a distinct whole that does not depend on preconceived notions of society or culture, or, indeed, of scale. By opening up to an idea of emotional topographies, we may be able to write about the unspeakable without losing our foothold in the concrete. Anthropological writing is an art of conveying composite worlds beyond the ontology of solids. Finally, we may realise also that anthropology itself is held together by a particular refrain that we all recognise—the refrain of fieldwork and ancestral invocations—creating the sonorous background for insights that may be unprecedented but are nevertheless recognisable as anthropological knowledge.

References

Bachelard, G. 1994 [1958]. *The Poetics of Space: The Classic Look at How We Experience Intimate Places.* Boston: Beacon.

Bakhtin, M. M. 1996. *The Dialogic Imagination.* Austin: University of Texas Press.

Boas, F. 1964 [1888]. *The Central Eskimo.* Lincoln: University of Nebraska Press.

Bravo, M., and S. Sörlin. 2002. "Narrative and Practice: An Introduction." In M. Bravo and S. Sörlin, eds., *Narrating the Arctic: A Cultural History of Nordic Scientific Practices.* Canton, MA: Science History Publications USA.

Briggs, J. 1970. *Never in Anger: Portrait of an Eskimo Family.* Cambridge, MA: Harvard University Press.

Casey, E. 1996. "How to Get from Space to Place in a Fairly Short Stretch of Time: Phenomenological Prolegomena." In S. Feld and K. H. Basso, eds., *Senses of Place,* 13–52. Santa Fe: School of American Research.

Corsín Jiménez, A. 2003. "On Space as a Capacity." *Journal of the Royal Anthropological Institute* 9:137–153.

Crapanzano, V. 2004. *Imaginative Horizons: An Essay in Literary-Philosophical Anthropology.* Chicago: University of Chicago Press.

de Certeau, M. 1984. *The Practice of Everyday Life.* Berkeley: University of California Press.

Deleuze, G., and F. Guattari. 2004. *A Thousand Plateaus: Capitalism and Schizophrenia.* Trans. B. Massumi. London and New York: Continuum.

Feld, S. 1996. "Waterfalls of Song: An Acoustemology of Place Resounding in Bosavi, Papua New Guinea." In S. Feld and K. H. Basso, eds., *Senses of Place,* 91–135. Santa Fe: School of American Research.

Feld, S., and K. H. Basso, eds. 1996. *Senses of Place.* Santa Fe: School of American Research.

Hastrup, K. 1987. "The Challenge of the Unreal—or How Anthropology Comes to Terms with Life." *Culture and History* 1:50–62.

———. 1998. *A Place Apart: An Anthropological Study of the Icelandic World.* Oxford: Clarendon.

———. 2004a. *Action: Anthropology in the Company of Shakespeare*. Copenhagen: Museum Tusculanum Press (University of Copenhagen).

———. 2004b. "All the World's a Stage: The Imaginative Texture of Social Spaces." *Space and Culture* 7:223–236.

———. 2004c. "Getting It Right: Knowledge and Evidence in Anthropology." *Anthropological Theory* 4:455–472.

———. 2005a. "Performing the World: Agency, Anticipation, and Creativity." *Cambridge Anthropology* 25 (2): 5–19.

———. 2005b. "Social Anthropology: Towards a Pragmatic Enlightenment." *Social Anthropology* 13:133–149.

———. 2006. "Knud Rasmussen (1879–1933): The Anthropologist as Explorer, Hunter, and Narrator." *Folk Journal of the Danish Ethnographic Society* 46/47:159–180.

———. 2007. "Ultima Thule: Anthropology and the Call of the Unknown." *Journal of the Royal Anthropological Institute* 13:789–804.

———. 2008a. "Icelandic Topography and the Sense of Identity." In M. Jones and K. R. Olwig, eds., *Nordic Landscapes: Region and Belonging on the Northern Edge of Europe*, 53–76. Minneapolis: University of Minnesota Press.

———. 2008b. "Images of Thule: Maps and Metaphors in the Representation of the Far North." In S. Jakobsson, ed., *Images of the North*. Iceland: Reykjavík Press.

Hirsch, E., and M. O'Hanlon, eds. 1995. *The Anthropology of Landscape: Perspectives of Place and Space*. Oxford: Oxford University Press.

Ingold, T. 2000. *The Perception of the Environment: Essays in Livelihood, Dwelling, and Skill*. London: Routledge.

Jackson, M. 1995. *At Home in the World*. Durham, NC: Duke University Press.

James, W. 2003. *The Ceremonial Animal: A New Portrait of Anthropology*. Oxford: Oxford University Press.

Kristjánsson, J. 1988. *Eddas and Sagas: Iceland's Medieval Literature*. Trans. P. Foote. Reykjavík: Hið íslenska bókmenntafélag.

Lutz, C. A., and L. Abu-Lughod, eds. 1990. *Language and the Politics of Emotion*. Cambridge: Cambridge University Press.

Mauss, M. (in collaboration with H. Beuchat). 1979 [1906]. *Seasonal Variations of the Eskimo: A Study in Social Morphology*. Trans. James J. Fox. London: Routledge and Kegan Paul.

Mitchell, J. P. 1997. "A Moment with Christ: The Importance of Feelings in the Analysis of Belief." *Journal of the Royal Anthropological Institute* 3 (1): 79–94.

Rasmussen, K. 1929. *Intellectual Culture of the Iglulik Eskimos*. Report of the Fifth Thule Expedition 1921–24. København: Gyldendalske Boghandel.

———. 1932. *Den Store Slæderejse*. Copenhagen: Gyldendalske Boghandel.

Tuan, Y. F. 1990. *Topophilia: A Study of Environmental Perceptions, Attitudes, and Values*. New York: Columbia University Press.

Turnbull, C. 1990. "Liminality: A Synthesis of Subjective and Objective Experience." In R. Schechner and W. Appel, eds., *By Means of Performance: Intercultural Studies of Theatre and Ritual*, 50–81. Cambridge: Cambridge University Press.

Vendler, H. 1995. *Soul Says: On Recent Poetry*. Cambridge, MA: Belknap Press of Harvard University Press.

9 What Counts as Data?

Tanya Luhrmann

IN SOCIOCULTURAL ANTHROPOLOGY, when we study culture, we often study form and not content. We study the representation of kinship, the imagery of the ordered social relationship, but not actual biological relatedness. We shy away from a discussion of the nature of madness to look at the way madness is shaped by local culture—the way it has been named, defined, treated, responded to. That is what our theory invites us to do. In David Schneider's famous first line, "This book is concerned with American kinship as a cultural system: that is, as a system of symbols" (1980 [1968]:80). In that theory, we mean by "culture" the categories a society generates around and out of its social order—concepts of witchcraft, symbols of divinity, images of the bad and the good. The definition of culture as concepts and categories which express and maintain the social order first emerged out of the early seminar room discussions in the era of British structural functionalism. It soon became instantiated in American anthropology and indeed became a professional credo of the American style of anthropology, as Talcott Parsons divided up the responsibilities of the social sciences. When Clifford Geertz, borrowing from Clyde Kluckhohn, asserted that symbols were models of and models for reality, he was enacting Parsons' division of intellectual mission from the great mélange of Harvard's Department of Social Relations: mind to the psychologists, social structure to the sociologists, culture to the anthropologists. For the British, sociocultural anthropology retained the responsibility for both social structure and culture, but still in British anthropological theory, culture remained a thing of concepts and categories, signifiers rather than the signified.

Yet what anthropologist does not have a story of his or her own stunned astonishment as the cultural symbols of those who are studied—abstract, other, distant, the fanciful beliefs about which we strive not to show our unbelief—become for a moment as real as flesh? Kirsten Hastrup calls these "raw moments." As an anthropologist of Icelandic people, she was studying, among other quaint concepts, their folkloric notion of hill men who emerged out of the dense clouds shrouding the peaks. One afternoon she was on one of these peaks alone, having corralled an errant sheep, when the mist descended. And then she saw a gaunt and purposeful hill man through the clouds. Paul Stoller (1987), come to study sorcery among the Songhay of Niger, visited a famed sorceress and discovered during the night that she had bewitched him into paralysis. He could not move.

Those raw moments, and the frustration that an anthropology focused upon categories cannot capture lived experience, have become the impulse behind the new turn to a theory of "embodiment." "In Nepal," Robert Desjarlais reflects, "I found that 'knowing through the body' often centers on knowledge of the body, for how I came to hold my limbs in Helambu led to a tacit assessment of how villagers themselves experience somatic and social forms. . . . Experiencing my body in this manner influenced my understanding of Yolmo experiences" (Desjarlais 1992:27). Thomas Csordas, perhaps the leading contemporary spokesperson for this position, frames the argument as a rejection of the classic binary. Drawing from Merleau-Ponty, he argues that "on the level of perception it is thus not legitimate to distinguish between mind and body" (1994:9). For him the puzzle becomes the creation of the object of the self out of social practice. Such theorists take experience as their object of study. They resist the idea that discourse alone could account for the complex phenomena they describe. They urge fellow scholars to understand that cultural categories become inscribed upon the body, and that it is the inscription which is the proper study of the anthropologist. Such scholars hesitate at the distinction between the cultural and the experiential. That is the power of the theoretical commitment to "embodiment"—it resists the binary distinction between culture and the body and the insistence that culture alone is the proper focus of the anthropologist.

Yet false distinctions can be useful heuristics. This volume invites us to adopt a "radical empiricism." It asks that we treat as "data"—that word which signifies so much to a science-minded community—not only what we see as ethnographers but what we experience as well. Knowing the limits of the distinction between cultural categories and bodily experience, I want, for the purposes of analysis, to use the distinction to force us to pay attention to our own experience as ethnographers. When we treat our own raw moments as data, they demand that we take seriously the limitations of a category-centric approach. They force us to take seriously the different ways in which we pay attention to cultural categories. And that, in turn, can teach us something about the process through which embodiment takes place. This chapter contributes to the recent development of the anthropological theory of embodiment by focusing on what and how we learn.

.   .   .

I was sitting in a commuter train to London the first time I felt supernatural power rip through me. I was twenty-three, and I was one year into my graduate training in anthropology. I had decided to do my fieldwork among educated white Britons who practiced what they called magic. I thought of this as a clever twist on more traditional anthropological fieldwork about the strange ways of natives who clearly were not "us." I was on my way to meet some of them, and I had ridden my bike to the station with trepidation and excitement. Now in my seat, as the sheep-dotted countryside rolled by I was reading a book written by a man they called an "adept," meaning someone regarded by the people I was about to meet as deeply knowledgeable and powerful (The book was *Experience of the Inner Worlds*, by Gareth Knight). The book's language was dense and abstract, and my mind kept slipping as I struggled to grasp what he was talking about, which I wanted so badly to understand. The text spoke of the Holy Spirit and Tibetan masters and an ancient system of Judaic mysticism called kabbalah. The author wrote that all these were so many names for forces that flowed from a higher spiritual reality into this one through the vehicle of the trained mind. And as I strained to imagine what it would be like to be that vehicle, I began to feel power in my veins—to really feel it, not to imagine it. I grew hot. I became completely alert, more awake than I usually am, and I felt so alive. It seemed that power coursed through me like water through a chute. I wanted to sing. And then wisps of smoke came out of my backpack, into which I had tossed my bicycle lights. One of them was melting.

This impressed me. I had gone to graduate school because I was fascinated by the problem of mind: how humans think, what constrains our thought, and in particular, the problem of irrational thought, which is the problem of how apparently reasonable, pragmatic people can accept beliefs which skeptical observers—more "rational" observers—simply can't believe. In the literature, magic is always used as the best example. A man puts a special amulet in his field to keep people from stealing the crop, the skeptical observer can't believe that the amulet works, and yet the man puts the amulet in his field year after year. What is he thinking?

Then I took that train ride to London. I didn't quite know what to make of the experience. In fact, I think I didn't even mention it to anyone for months. In the meantime, I began to learn to practice magic.

In the world I had entered, people are trained in what are considered to be basic skills, which are thought to enable them to recognize, to generate, and to manipulate magical forces. The exact purpose of the training varied from group to group (people who called themselves witches talked more about generating power, while those who thought of themselves as practicing "high magic" talked about manipulating existing power), but the actual training structure was common. Moreover, all groups recognized the need for training, and all groups identified some people as more skilled than others, and a smaller group of people as experts. Some groups even had formal take-home courses. Before I could be initiated into the most elaborately hierarchical and secretive of magical groups, I was required to take a nine-month home-study course complete with supervisor and monthly essays. It was one of two home-study courses I took. These courses were not dissimilar from other published courses offered to new students in magic. Lessons typically demanded that the student learn the knowledge associated with that kind of magic (how magical power was understood, which symbols represented it), and they typically asked students to personalize that knowledge, to see it as relevant to and embedded in their lives. But they also demanded the acquisition of two attentional skills: meditation and visualization. Each course required that the student learn to quiet the mind and to focus on some internal experience (an image, a word, or the apparently empty mind itself). Each course also required that the student learn to relax and to see with the mind's eye some unfolding narrative sequence. Here is an example from on one of my early lessons, which I did, in some form, for fifteen minutes a day for nine months:

> Work through these exercises, practicing one of them for a few minutes each day, either before or after your meditation session.
>
> 1. Stand up and examine the room in which you are working. Turn a full circle, scanning the room. Now sit down, close the eyes and build the room in imagination. Note where the memory or visualizing power fails. At the

end of the exercise briefly re-examine the room and check your accuracy. Note the results in your diary.

2. Carefully visualize yourself leaving the room in which you are working, going for a short walk you know well, and returning to your room. Note clarity, breaks in concentration, etc, as before.

3. Go for an imaginary walk; an imaginary companion, human or animal, can accompany you. Always start and finish the walk in the room you use for the exercises. Note the results, etc, as before.

4. Build up in imagination a journey from your physical plane home to your ideal room. Start the journey in real surrounds then gradually make the transition to the imaginary journey by any means you wish. Make the journey to and from the room until it is entirely familiar.

The idea behind this (what I came to think of as the theology of magic) was that if you could learn to see mental images clearly, with borders, duration, and stability, those images could become the vehicle for supernatural power to enter the mundane world.

What startled me, as a young ethnographer, was that this training worked. At least, it seemed to change the way I experienced mental images. After about a year of this kind of training, my mental imagery *did* seem to become clearer. I thought that my images had sharper borders, greater solidity, and more endurance. I began to feel that my concentration states were deeper and more sharply different from the everyday. And I began to have more of what a psychologist would call "anomalous experience," the kind of thing that had happened to me on the train. I had a vision, or more technically, a hallucination. It was, admittedly, an early-morning vision. (It is more common to have visual and auditory hallucinations when you are on the verge of sleep.) I had been reading a novel written by this kind of magical practitioner, really trying to imagine what the characters were experiencing, and one morning I awoke to see some of the characters standing by my window. I shot up in bed when I saw them, and they vanished. But for a moment, I really saw them. And I felt different in rituals, when we shut our eyes, sank into meditative states, and visualized what the group leader told us to. At those times, when I was trying so hard to see with my mind's eye and to be completely relaxed but mentally alert, it seemed as if there was something altered about the way I experienced the world—in my sense of self, sense of time, sense of focus, but also, and less metaphorically, in what I sensed: in the way I saw, heard, and felt, even when I knew that what

I sensed was internal and imagined. This was not true for all ritual gatherings, but in those rituals in which I felt fully absorbed, the difference from the everyday was striking. Of course I was socially immersed in this world, and I was learning new ways to interpret my awareness and my experience. But it didn't feel to me that I was "just" acquiring knowledge. I felt that I was acquiring new psychological skills, and that the skills could be taught and mastered. And as I acquired those skills, the world became drenched in meaning. Nothing happened by accident anymore. A phone call, the kind of fruit the greengrocer sold, a book I glanced at in a window—everything seemed connected to my thoughts, my visualizations, and my dreams.

I was still cautious about telling anyone outside my little magical world about these experiences. I mentioned them on a page or two in the book I eventually wrote about magic (*Persuasions of the Witch's Craft*, 1989), but I buried the account on page 348. That was cowardly, if perhaps also wise. Those experiences completely changed the way I thought about magic.

I had gone into the field looking for discourse, broadly conceived. Whether you understand that word from a Foucauldian perspective or from the perspective of cognitive science, I was looking for the words people used and the narratives they spun and the consequences of their interpretations for their choices and actions. Like most anthropologists before me, I assumed that to study magic was to study the way people organized knowledge—the way they identified what counted as evidence for these forces, the way they compared (or failed to compare) the "outcome" of rituals over time, and the metaphors and narratives they used that might lead them to think differently about magical forces than they might think about an experimental procedure in a laboratory. I thought I would be telling a cognitive story—an account of the kinds of categories people acquired, how those categories were structured, and the way they were learned. In the crudest rendering, I assumed before I did the fieldwork that people who believed in magic had different cognitive models—different ideas—and that those ideas were what led them to think differently about cause and effect.

Instead, what the unusual experiences taught me was that people who believed in magic had different *bodily feelings* (again, broadly construed) as well as different ideas. They certainly acquired a set of cognitive models, but those models became meaningful, salient, for them because they confirmed those ideas in their own personal experience of their world. They felt the power, they heard the gods, and they saw the spirits. Something was going on that was more complicated than simply the acquisition of discourse.

My unusual experiences would not, of course, have taught me this if no one else seemed to have such experiences. If that had been true, I would have learned, I think, about my own psychic health and not about the local culture. But in fact other people did report unusual experiences, and they did so with pride. Moreover, they attributed them to the training, or at least to the process of becoming skilled in magic. They all thought that training was important; they all thought it was hard and took work; and they all thought that it changed the way that they experienced their world. Moreover, the training they advocated had shared features found around the world in what are often called "spiritual disciplines." There is a great deal of historical and ethnographic evidence that the attentional skills of meditation and visualization have been taught throughout history and across culture, that they are learnable skills, and that mastery of those skills is associated with intense spiritual experience.[1] These practices encourage what I would now call absorption, a simple behavioral pattern in which a subject displays intense attention to internal sensory stimuli with diminished peripheral awareness. The techniques probably encourage absorption by related means. Meditation probably inhibits sensory responsiveness to external sensory stimulation by dampening reaction, while visualization probably discourages such responsiveness to the external by intensifying internal stimuli and in effect drowning out external sensory stimulation. We use the word "trance" to describe deep absorption. An interest in trance states is even more widely distributed than the specific attentional practices of meditation and visualization. Trance states play a role in nearly every known culture, although their role seems to wax and wane. And whether or not the specific attentional techniques of meditation and visualization are culturally encouraged, typically the trance is entered through the use of some kind of sensory manipulation—chanting, altering the light, fantasy, pain, rapid whirling—techniques which decrease peripheral awareness and enhance absorption in internal sensory stimuli.[2]

At the time I modeled this process as "interpretive drift." If you looked at what individuals were implicitly and explicitly taught about magic in the different everyday settings in which they engaged it, you discovered that two different kinds of learning took place. On the one hand, there was discourse, the ideas which people acquired from books and from each other: cognitive models and representations. I could see that the social interactions between people practicing magic provided a newcomer to magic with a host of phrases, associations, and symbolic representations with which to think about magic. There was didactic teaching in courses run by practitioners and the knowledge presented by the many books people bought about magical ritual and the various symbolic systems associated with it: astrology, mythology, the tarot, kabbalah, alchemy, and the like. Casual conversations were also crucial in providing individuals with a way of thinking about magical ideas, and newcomers learned from the ways in which more experienced magicians talked about them how the ideas hung together as a system, loosely construed, and how they could be used to identify and explain events. This kind of formal and informal learning centered on the domain of ideas: categories which are learned in social discourse, which can be understood as schemas, and which hang together and are acquired through narratives, concepts, systems of information.

On the other hand, there was what one could loosely call practice and its psychological sequelae. New magicians learned to meditate and to visualize. They would learn to close their eyes for fifteen minutes a day, sink into an absorbed state, and see in their minds eye a trip to a sacred garden in the clouds. There they would clean their altar, fill their chalice, and converse with spirits. They learned to journey on what they called the astral plane, experiencing themselves as flying over London and swooping down as hunters, pre-Potter wizards with no need for brooms. Their daydreams grew more intense; their images grew more vivid; they experienced themselves as losing time in this world as they traveled into others. They recorded their dreams in bedside dream books, and their dreams became drenched in symbolism. This was not the same learning experience as simply acquiring cognitive models in casual conversation. To be sure, they used those cognitive models to interpret the experiences. They studied alchemy, and alchemical symbols appeared in their dreams. But the learning was of a different nature.

Back then I also described what I thought of as a third form of learning, around the way individuals learned to manage conflicting self-representations. In magical practice, this was important because people who practice magic are on the one hand committed to their practice and invested in being magicians; yet on the other hand, as middle-class, well-educated individuals, they realize that many of their peers believe that they are foolish or even crazy to practice magic. Individuals who practiced magic learned to use particular metaphors to capture and explain this apparent dissonance to themselves: they spoke about magical power being "on another plane" or "part of another reality." They then had a variety of philosophical reflections on these dual "worlds" which were more or less important to them, depending on their sense of disjunction between the two "worlds." This now seems to me to be an issue of epistemo-logical commitment, a way of negotiating how true, how real, you hold these claims to be. For the moment I will put that learning domain to the side. Instead I want to emphasize the difference between learning the categories and learning the practice, and I want to point out that my own bodily feelings forced me to recognize that categories are not enough. Newcomers to magic did not simply accept the cognitive models of magical practice with which peers and experts presented them. They confirmed those ideas in their every-day experience of their world, and when their practice led them to experience magical power in their bodies, the discourse seemed much more real.

It is a risky business to use your own bodily experience—your own raw moments—to draw inferences about the lives of people in other social worlds. The word "empathy" is supposed to refer to the listener's capacity to feel at the moment, to some extent, what the speaker is feeling. It is the attempt by a listener to understand, from the inside, what the speaker's experience is like. That is, of course, an impossible task. But it is partially possible through the use of our own emotional response. I think the best account of the ethnogra-pher's main goal is that the ethnographer attempts to grasp the task that the field subject must master in order to be minimally competent in his or her domain—that task of being a Bororo man or woman, the task of being a com-petent psychiatrist, the task of living an agricultural life to the rhythms of a subcontinental monsoon. Like psychoanalytic patients, field subjects rarely say all that that must be said to understand them, although in the case of the field subject the issue may be less unconscious conflict than the absurdity of asking a fish to describe water. Part of understanding that task is to understand the emotional cost and consequence of the enactment of the task, what it feels like to manage your life decisions according to the outcome of the poison oracle. And there our personal experience as ethnographers can be an important guide to the emotional experience of others. One reason why E. E. Evans-Pritchard's Azande were so engrossing was that he said that he himself could live by the rhythms of the local divination. He was able to manage it and not be driven mad, and so we readers were willing to accept, if given further evidence, that even the Azande were logical, in their own way. Had I not paid attention to my own experience in the field, I would have missed the phenomenology of magical training, which is both its most interesting aspect and the aspect not captured by the scholarly approaches to irrationality which focus on cognitive heuristics and biases.[3]

And yet it is terribly risky. The psychodynamically minded describe this danger as "countertransference": an emotional judgment that rises out of the listener's own life circumstances, not out of anything the speaker has said.[4] You find yourself furious at someone because he or she unwittingly echoed a demeaning voice from the past. You use your own emotional experience to interpret the way other people are responding: and you are wrong. Psychoanalysts require that their candidates themselves go through analyses, and while few believe, as perhaps they once did, that such analyses make it possible to listen free of your own emotional entanglements—to listen, as they put it, without memory or desire—it probably helps. Margaret Mead famously thought that all ethnographers should experience personal therapy for the same reason. It's not a bad idea. Training in psychotherapy probably makes one a better ethnographer.

In my own case, however, the danger of inferring from my own experience was more blunt. When I began interviewing Christians who were encouraged to train in the spiritual disciplines as seriously as the magicians, I discovered that only some had the unusual experiences that many of the magicians I knew had reported.

In 1997 I began to do fieldwork in the growing points of American religion, in spiritualities where the participation had expanded significantly since 1970. I spent months in a black Catholic church, months in a new age Anglo Cuban Santeria house, months in a shul for newly orthodox Jews, months in an evangelical church. All these are examples of the intense American interest in developing an intimate relationship with the divine through unusual moments of spiritual experience. There are many theories of the causes and consequences of this shift in American religion toward a more concrete experience of God: Vincent Crapanzano (2004), Wade Clark Roof (1993), Robert Wuthnow (1999), Robert Bellah (1970), Thomas Frank (2004), and others. Unlike most of these theories, my focus here is not political but practical. I am interested in understanding how it is done, how someone comes to hear the audible voice of God and to feel wrapped in God's embrace. This is the problem of how God becomes real for people. It is an old problem and a deep one, whether or not you believe in God.

I have done my most intensive interviewing in Chicago, in a new paradigm Christian church called the Vineyard Christian fellowship, now with more than six hundred churches nationwide. "New paradigm" Christian churches pair conservative theology with liberal social conventions (their congregants dance, see movies, date, and even drink in moderation) (Miller 1997). Such churches meet in gyms, not churches; they use a rock band, not a choir; most people, including the pastors, dress casually; and they target the young, often deliberately planting seedling churches in college communities. They are Bible-based, by which is meant that the written Bible is seen as the only decisive authority, and the words of the Bible are taken to be literally true. They are also entrepreneurial, well organized, and technologically sophisticated. They spring from the same reformist principle that has animated Protestantism from the beginning: to throw out the middleman of institutional religion and to connect the believer directly to God. "What drew us together?" the national leader of the Vineyard asked in a recent gathering. "A dislike for church and a hunger for the holy spirit." And yet Sunday mornings at a Vineyard are relatively tame. People do not speak in tongues or fall, smitten by the Holy Spirit, during the service. But new paradigm churches do want people to experience an intimate relationship with God. They set out to make God real by modeling a relationship to God as the point of life—and incidentally, of going to church—and modeling prayer as the practice on which that relationship is built. These churches democratize God, and they democratize intense spiritual experience. They expect all their congregants, not just the elite, to experience God as a best friend as well as a holy majesty, and they expect that intimacy to develop during prayer. They also expect that prayer is hard and requires training and practice; and they expect God to answer back in dialogue, through images, impressions, and unusual sensory experience. As one of the most popular books asserts: "Prayer is two-way fellowship and communication with God. You speak to God and He speaks to you. It is not a one-way communication."[5]

It would be hard to overestimate the importance placed on prayer and prayer experience in a church like this and, indeed, in Christian America today. Many of the best-selling Christian books are books on prayer technique, and they sell in the millions. One such example is Richard Foster's *Celebration of Discipline*. The book is a straightforward and accessible summary of the classic spiritual disciplines, and it leads with chapters on each of what he calls "the inward disciplines": meditation, prayer, fasting, and solitude. He describes prayer as a learning process, and meditation—his first discipline—as most effectively achieved through the imagination. "Perhaps some rare individuals experience God through abstract contemplation alone, but most of us need to be more deeply rooted in the senses" (2003:25). He says that meditation cannot be learned from a book, but only from its practice, and advises the reader to find a comfortable position that won't be distracting, to relax, and to focus on the written word of God. "Seek to live the experience, remembering the encouragement of Ignatius of Loyola to apply all our senses to the task. Smell the sea. Hear the lap of water along the shore. See the crowd. Feel the sun on your head and the hunger in your stomach. Taste the salt in the air. Touch the hem of his garment" (2003:29–30). This is the basic structure of the Ignatian Spiritual Exercises, and it is also the structure of the training I was given in magic so many years ago.

Such books often begin by presenting concrete sensory experience of God in the Hebrew Bible as the everyday relationship for which the ordinary believer should strive. In the well-known evangelical text *Hearing God: Developing a Conversational Relationship with God*, the author, Dallas Willard, begins by saying that God's face-to-face conversations with Moses are examples of the "normal human life God intended for us" (1999:18). The text then tries to lead the reader to have this experience. In *God Whispers*, another manual, the author says: "From the first moments in the garden of Eden, mankind was introduced to the voice. Adam and Eve communed with their creator. When they called out to God, they didn't get silence" (Feinberg 2005:3). *Experiencing God*—four million copies sold—tells the story of Abraham and Moses and asserts: "In the Scriptures knowledge of God comes through experience. We come to know God as we experience Him in and around our live." (Blackaby and King 2004:7). Throughout, unusual sensory experiences are presented as spiritual guidance, and as God's communication to his followers. Here is an example from another beloved text, *Is That Really You, God?* "Suddenly I was looking at a map of the world, only the map was alive and moving! I sat up and shook my head and rubbed my eyes. It was a mental movie.... Then just as suddenly as it had come, the scene was gone" (Cunningham 1984: 32–33).

There is persuasive evidence, then, that the congregant learns the cultural idea that God should be experienced by the senses. A psychological skeptic could argue that what congregants learn is to talk as if experiencing God with the senses—but nothing more. Clearly some of what they learn is interpretation. They are being taught in part to interpret everyday experience as bearing the signs of God's presence. This interpretation is explicitly part of the learning process described in *Dialogue with God*, another well-known book.[6] The author begins by saying that he used to live in a rationalist box. He yearned to hear God speak to him the way God spoke to others in the Hebrew Bible—and he believed that God still spoke to others the way he did in ancient Canaan.

Alas, he was unable to hear God speak to him until he realized that God's voice often sounded like his own stream of consciousness, and that the Christian just needs to know how to pay attention to his own awareness in order to hear God speaking directly and clearly. "God's voice normally sounds like a flow of spontaneous thoughts, rather than an audible voice. I have since discovered certain characteristics of God's interjected thoughts which help me to recognize them" (1986:29). That is the point of the book: to help you to identify what, in your experience of your own mind, are God's thoughts. "You need to learn to distinguish God's interjected thoughts from the cognitive thoughts that are coming from your own mind" (1986:31). God's voice, the book explains, has an unusual content. You will recognize it as different from your ordinary thoughts. You feel different when you hear God. "There is often a sense of excitement, conviction, faith, vibrant life, awe or peace that accompanies receiving God's word" (1986:30).

At the same time, there is persuasive evidence that congregants learn that prayer practice is very important. It is also clear that congregants are being taught the classic attentional techniques that have been used to generate religious experience across the ages. *Dialogue with God* begins by saying that a man who knew how to hear God's voice "knew how to go to a quiet place and quiet his own thoughts and emotions so that he could sense the spontaneous flow of God within" (1986:6). The author provides explicit exercises to help his readers do likewise. He sells a "centering cassette" for that purpose on his Web site. In fact, he recommends a "prayer closet," a place where you can go, unplug the phone, and be fully quiet in prayer. He recommends journaling to write down and discard distracting thoughts; he recommends simple song to focus the mind in worship; he recommends breathing techniques to breathe out your sin and breathe in the healing Holy Spirit; he recommends the complete focus of the mind and heart on Jesus. He acknowledges that many of these techniques seem very Eastern, but distinguishes them from Zen and other forms of meditation on the grounds that Eastern meditation contacts "the evil one," while he uses the techniques to contact God.

And indeed, as I found when studying magic, the accounts that people gave suggest that congregants learn more than discourse and more than a style of interpretation. Much of the ethnographic account one would give of spiritual experience in the Vineyard church that I studied is similar to the ethnographic account I gave of the magic. People reported unusual experiences. These experiences seemed to be heightened by what I would describe as prayer "training." Training was perceived as essential and as hard, and it was perceived by congregants to have consequences. At the beginning of the spiritual journey, new believers often did report an unusual powerful experience, like hearing God speak audibly or feeling the Holy Spirit flood through them. Such experiences were rare in the worshipper's life, but they were very important. As new believers began to pray, if they prayed assiduously and in a focused way, they were likely to say that they received images, impressions, and sensations during prayer, and that these were God's often coded communications. They were also likely to report that the images got sharper over time, that they became more absorbed in their prayers, and that they became better prayers.

Andy, for example, became a Christian during college. His conversion experience was dramatic, a classic experience of the Holy Spirit.[7]

> She [the leader] said some of you might be feeling the spirit on you now, and I noticed about myself that my breathing was getting like really deep and like I was starting to shake a little bit. I just feel like my body has so much energy, and it's like I'm gonna just leap out of my seat and just go running like 50 miles or something. [She's . . .] like some of you may be sweating, and I'm like yeah, I'm sweating. She's like some of you might have oily palms, and I'm like yeah, I got oily palms, and she's like some of you might be shaking and heavy breathing, and some of you might just be like jittery. And I'm like check, check, check, check, I've got all that.
>
> I could hear people praying around me and saying certain things, and, and, I mean it was kind of like you could say that it felt like I was in a bubble and everything outside of this bubble just would not exist. Like it was just time for me and God in this one little tiny capsule and the rest of the world can go by it like a billion miles per hour and I wouldn't care.

He no longer has such powerful experiences, although he wishes that he did. "Like, I was like the first day I got this whole cake, and then from now you get to have little servings of it from time to time again, but sometimes it's bigger and sometimes it's smaller." At the beginning, he didn't know what people meant when they said that God spoke to them. "I'd always hear Christians talk about how they heard God speak to them. At the beginning of my Christian walk for like the first nine months I was totally, like I wish I could hear him talk." Then he began to pray seriously, reading through five biblical chapters each day and trying to see them and be in them and have them be alive. And he began to feel that God was interacting with him, nudging him to do this or that. He began to pray for people, and he would experience what he called "impressions," ideas about what he should pray for and how, which he believed had come from God. And he began to feel that God was a person for him. "It is like having an imaginary friend, in a sense, because I talk to him all the time like he's always next to me, but [it's not imaginary because] you know that he's there." He has heard God speak to him, audibly, although on only a few occasions.

Amy grew up in a more sedate Christianity. She never expected to have direct contact with God, although she was always a believer. Then she began to go to the Vineyard. "I always saw prayer as talking to God, but I didn't realize that he was also gonna talk to me and I needed to just sit there and just listen." She began to pray seriously, about forty-five minutes every day, focusing on the Bible and on people she felt she needed to pray for. Now, when she is praying for someone, she will sometimes see something in her mind's eye, an image or a verse, that will change what she prays for them. When she is praying out loud for someone with her hands on them—at the Vineyard this is called prayer ministry—she will feel God speaking to her at the same time that she is speaking to the person she is praying for, as if she and God are talking at the same time she prays aloud. "I would feel like God would show me something that, you know, he wants me to speak out to them to encourage them, you know, at the same time that I'm praying, you know, I'm talking to him about what's going on." Sometimes when she is praying alone, something will come to her mind that she feels are the right words to pray for the other person and she'll tell them about it the next time she sees them, that this was what she was led to pray.

Amy feels that the images she gets in prayer have become clearer, and she feels more confident recognizing when her thoughts are in fact what God is saying to her, and not the detritus of an ordinary human mind. "The more you do something the better you get at it, you know. If you play a piano piece and you just play it over and over and over again, and then you finally get it, so you can play it perfect every time—it's a lot like that. When you get that first word [of God], you're like 'whoa, that was awesome,' and then you ask, and you keep asking for another one, and eventually that comes."[8] And for her the relationship with God has become vivid and personal. He feels like someone she can talk to throughout the day, chatting about the little things that matter to her. "Sometimes I imagine he's walking there right alongside me. I actually can sometimes imagine that there's a physical person there, going along with me, and we're having a great conversation." She has felt his arms around her, and she has heard him speak out loud—not often, but occasionally and audibly. Once, sitting by the lake, she heard him say, in a voice she heard outside her head, "sit and listen." But those dramatic moments are unusual and unimportant compared to the vividness of the everyday relationship. Amy loves her relationship with God. Sometimes she'll go on what she calls "date night" with God. She'll walk out to the lake, maybe with something to eat, and just sit there, feeling his arm around her shoulder, sometimes talking out loud to him.

But not everyone in the church experiences God that way, despite the explicit encouragement to do so in the books that people read, in the sermons on Sunday morning, and in the casual conversations people have with one another. Jake grew up in a Vineyard church. When he was in high school the church had a revival. Many people were saved, and many people who were already saved found that they had vivid experiences of God's presence. That never happened to Jake. "I remember really desperately wanting to draw closer to God," he recalled, "having one of these inspired Holy Spirit moments that maybe sometimes get more attention than they deserve . . . mountain top experiences, tangible signs and wonders. I wanted those and I sought those out but I never really found myself encountering them." It was hard for him, and he was demoralized when nothing happened. "There was a time when I was seeking God during that period of high school where that was very frustrating. Why doesn't God speak to me in ways that I hear when dad speaks to me or mom speaks to me?" Now he has made his peace with his sense that he is just not someone who experiences God that way. He experiences God as close, but he does not have the chatty relationship with God that Andy and Amy seem to have. He doesn't find himself talking to God routinely throughout the day. "I mean they'll be sporadic prayers, quick prayers mostly, not, you know, deep long prayers." He doesn't have many images when he prays, and they don't seem important to him. "I don't picture anything when I pray. I know some people picture things when they pray or praise an image of God or something. I don't."

Nor is Jake so unusual. "Please pray that I will hear God speak in a booming voice," Zeke pleaded one evening in Bible study. Like most people in the church, he wanted concrete encounters with God, and he felt bad because he did not have them. When I sat down with him in an interview, he was glum. "I don't have these superpowerful experiences that make me fall to my knees."

What this taught me anthropologically was that there was more to the theoretical account of learning that I gave in the construct of interpretive drift. It now became clear, based on the difference between Amy and Andy on the one hand

and Jake and Zeke on the other, that there was some kind of difference in *procliv- ity*, a difference in the capacity for and/or interest in having such unusual sen- sory experiences. And indeed there was ethnographic material to support a claim about proclivity. Both in the magical world and in the evangelical world there is recognition that some people are better at the spiritual disciplines than others. In both worlds, there is recognition that there is something like "natural" talent, and that those who have such talent are more likely to become expert when trained. In both worlds, there are names for such experts. In the magical world they are called "adepts"; in the evangelical world, "prayer warriors." And in those different worlds there is often widespread agreement about who counts as an expert. This should be enough to persuade one that there is more to being a Christian than just learning discourse. If all they learn is discourse, after all, all good, compliant Christians should report the same spiritual experiences. But they don't.

Just as my own raw moments were crucial in leading me to understand that there was more to understanding than discourse, I knew that if I wanted to un- derstand the problem of proclivity—in effect, the puzzle of the way people were different from me, not alike—I would have to use a method that let me see past my own predispositions and interests—my own transference, if you will—in order to grasp something of the way people differed. I turned to methods bor- rowed from academic psychology, where the researchers' personal experience is written out. Academic psychologists are as allergic to the personal experience of the observer as clinical psychologists are sympathetic to it. Their method— what they call "science"—depends upon removing the emotional experience of the observer from the observations. It is their way of removing the risk of seeing on the basis of your bias.

By the time I began to do fieldwork in the Vineyard church, I had decided to supplement my ethnographic participant observation and my open-ended interviews with more-focused interviews which asked people specifically about their spiritual experience, and about what a psychologist would call anoma- lous experience. Because I was also interested in the psychological routes to these experiences, I had people fill out all kinds of different questionnaires.[9] Most of them failed—by which I mean that people didn't like them and didn't say yes to many items, and I soon stopped using them. One of them, however, seemed to pick out the difference between people like Andy and Amy and people like Jake.

This was the Tellegen Absorption Scale, developed and introduced in 1974 by Auke Tellegen and Gilbert Atkinson, who had set out to find a pen-and-paper measure of hypnotic susceptibility. The scale correlates only modestly with the current gold standard measure of hypnotic susceptibility, and modestly with dissociation. It seems instead to capture something broader than trance itself. The questions tap subjects' willingness to be caught up in their experience— particularly in their imaginative experience, and in nature and music. Tellegen and Atkinson argue that the attentional style captured by the questions created "a heightened sense of the reality of the attentional object, imperviousness to distracting events, and an altered sense of reality in general, including an empathically altered sense of self" (1974:268). What the instrument seems to capture is someone's willingness to allow him- or herself to be absorbed in internal or external sensory experience for its own sake, to enjoy the involvement in itself rather than experiencing it primarily as a means to some other goal. And that, of course, is precisely the domain that magical training and prayer training encourage. That kind of spiritual training specifically asks the practitioner to focus with absorbed attention on internal sensory experience. Tellegen even argues, in an aside, that the attention to one's internal thoughts "hangs together" with vivid imagery and altered states, suggesting that the construct of absorption captures that combination of imagery, internal focus, and altered state that seemed central to magical practice as I described it ethnographically.

Later, Tellegen argued that there were clusters of experiential response within the scale. He identified eight such clusters: 1. *Imaginative involvement* in items like these: "If I wish I can imagine (or daydream) some things so vividly that they hold my attention as a good movie or story does" and "When I listen to music I can get so caught up in it that I don't notice anything else." 2. *Emotional responsiveness* in items like these: "I can be deeply moved by a sunset" and "I like to watch cloud shapes change in the sky." 3. *Responsiveness to highly inductive (e.g., hypnosis-inducing) stimuli* in items like these: "When listening to organ music or other powerful music I sometimes feel as if I am being lifted into the air" and "The sound of a voice can be so fascinating to me that I can just go on listening to it." 4. *Vivid re-experiencing of the past* in items like these: "Sometimes I feel and experience things as I did as a child" and "I can sometimes recollect certain past experiences in my life with such clarity and vividness that it is like living them again or almost so." 5. *Expansion of awareness* in items like these: "I sometimes 'step outside' my usual self and experience an entirely different state of being" and "At times I somehow feel the presence of someone who is not physically there." 6. *Powerful imaging* in items like these: "If I wish I can imagine that my body is so heavy that I could not move it if I wanted to" and "Sometimes I can change noise into music by the way I listen to it." 7. *Imaginal thinking* in items like these: "My thoughts often don't occur as words but as visual images" and "Sometimes thoughts and images come to me without the slightest effort on my part." 8. *Cross-modal experiencing* in items like these: "Different colors have distinctive and special meanings for me" and "I find that different odors have different colors" (Tellegen 1981:220–221).

There is surprisingly little empirical work with the scale, particularly on normal populations. What work has been done has tended to focus on "openness to self-altering experiences," "imaginative involvement," or fantasy (McCrae and Costa 1983; Glisky et al. 1991; Wild, Kuiken, and Schopflocher 1995). One well-known paper demonstrates that those who have a "fantasy prone" personality style are more likely to score high on absorption (Wilson and Barber 1983). Other papers demonstrate that high absorption, as measured by the Tellegen scale, correlates with enjoying reading novels and listening to music (Nell 1988; Snodgrass and Lynn 1989) and with the ability not only to have altered states but while in such states to experience greater alterations in imagery and awareness (Pekala, Wenger, and Levine 1985). More recent work, done primarily with people reporting psychiatric pathology, has demonstrated that people who report that they have been abducted by aliens have on average higher Tellegen scores, and those who report repressed memories of childhood sexual abuse also have higher Tellegen scores, although those who report childhood sexual abuse which has not been repressed do not. And while absorption as measured by this scale seems modestly connected to both hypnotic and dissociative experience, the relationship is real. The Dissociative Experiences Scale, probably the most widely used measure of dissociation, bases a third of its items on absorption. (Another third measures amnesia, and the final third, depersonalization). Spiegel and Spiegel (2004) suggest that hypnosis can be thought of as one-third absorption, one-third suggestion, and one-third dissociation. Many studies have found a moderate correlation between response to the Tellegen and hypnotizability (Nadon et al. 1991). And while there are still debates on the relationship between dissociation and hypnotizability, there is no doubt that absorption is clearly moderately to strongly correlated with both (Whalen and Nash 1996).

Now, with a potential measure of proclivity in hand, I went back through my interviews in a more systematic manner. I re-interviewed people, and interviewed more of them. I gave them the Tellegen, I asked them a set of specific and open-ended questions, and I did some post hoc coding of the responses to see whether the experiences they reported varied systematically with their Tellegen scores.[10]

First, I asked them how long they prayed. There was no relationship between the time they devoted to prayer and their Tellegen score. I put together a series of questions about the sensory experience of God: whether the subjects reported experiencing God with their senses; whether they described getting images often when they prayed; whether they said that they got sensations or thoughts when they prayed; whether they said something that indicated the vividness of those experiences, as, for example, when one woman said, "It's almost like PowerPoint sometimes." I included in this category "pseudo-hallucinations," or what the subject experienced as momentarily veridical and external but knew immediately were not. For example, Amy commented that she had begun to see things occasionally as she walked down the street, but she knew they weren't really there. I included hallucinated smells and hallucinated touch; the hallucinations people had between sleep and awareness, like hearing someone call their name and waking them up out of sleep; and fully awake hallucinations, as in the experience of a woman who distinctly heard God tell her to get off a bus because she was about to miss a stop. And I included in this category any spontaneous comment the subject made about loving the Holy Spirit side of God. I gave subjects a point for any of these questions which they answered in the affirmative. Here there was quite a clear relationship—a statistically significant one, at that—between subjects' Tellegen scores and their reported sensory experience of God.

What does this tell us? To those who are skeptical of such instruments, perhaps not much. After all, it is not clear what kind of psychological process the absorption scale picks up, or even whether it picks up a complexly trained skill or a preexisting trait—although I can say that some congregants score highly on the Tellegen even when they have had little prayer practice, and that people's responses to the scale seem relatively stable over time. That is, as most researchers using the scale have reported, the scale seems to measure a *trait*, like being tall or insecure, which is a more stable feature of a person than a *state*, like being hungry, which changes significantly from hour to hour. And so it seems quite interesting that those who seem to have this trait-like interest or capacity in absorption should have sensory experiences of God. It was also, on a personal note, soothing. I have confessed that I had a hallucination; and I can now say, with quantitative confidence, that more than a third of my twenty-eight subjects have had a hallucination. And if you score above 18 on the Tellegen, you are six times more likely to have a hallucination than some-one who scored lower.

But I also looked at the way people talked about their personal relation-ship with God, the degree to which they did experience God vividly in the way that the books and the pastor suggested that they should. I asked everyone I spoke with whether they would pray to God about something other people might regard as trivial, like a haircut. Some people looked vaguely insulted at the thought of addressing majesty about such a topic; some people laughingly told me about sitting in the salon and praying solemnly that the cut would be a good experience. (You can't get different answers to this question if you ask about parking. Everyone prays to God about parking.) I asked people whether they spoke to God only during moments of formal prayer, or whether they chatted to God freely, walking to class or putting petrol in the car, at different moments throughout the day. I asked people whether they thought of God as their best friend, and how he was different from an imaginary friend. Some people said that the difference between God and an imaginary friend was that God was real; other people quietly said that they didn't think of God that way at all. I asked people whether they got angry with God, not because of a distant tragedy—genocide in Darfur, for example—but because of something personal and intimate. Some people said things like, "Angry? I've yelled out loud at him, in fact only last week," and other people looked taken aback and clearly felt un-comfortable with the idea. I asked people whether there was a teasing, playful side to their relationship with God, whether they ever tried to make God laugh, or whether he ever teased them. I gave a subject a point for each item (trivial prayer, chatting, best or imaginary friend, personal anger, play) that they af-firmed. I also made a judgment, based on their description of their prayer ex-perience, on whether they experienced prayer as a dialogue, and gave them a point if I thought they did.

Here again, the vividness is significantly related to the Tellegen. And if you regress vividness against the time that someone prays, it turns out that both play a role, although the numbers are so small that the effect nearly disappears. If you hold the Tellegen score steady, the more the subject prays, the more vivid God becomes for him or her.

This is a much more interesting finding. The church teaches that con-gregants should be in a personal relationship with God—that God should be almost like a buddy, a chum, as well as a mighty and majestic lord. Books and sermons and conferences model a God who is a confidant, who cares about your trivial personal issues, someone big enough to handle your little games and rages. And still it is only some people who have this experience, who find themselves in intimate personal closeness with God.

This takes me back to the beginning of the chapter, but from a different angle, and helps me to make the argument with which I began. Discourse and categories are not enough. Becoming a believer in this kind of church—the kind of church that arguably now dominates the American landscape—is not just about adopting a set of ideas that someone else has handed you. It is about being able and willing to confirm these ideas in your own experience.

And so a more sophisticated model of learning religion would include not only belief and practice, the two linchpins of the model I called "interpretive drift," but proclivity as well. Even if we do not know exactly what the underlying psychological mechanism is, we know that not all people who are members of this cultural community experience the ideas of the culture in the same way. They must have something else: a willingness, a capacity, perhaps an interest in allowing those cultural ideas to change their lives. Culture does not change the world for everyone in the same way.

There is a sobering message here for our understanding of the ethnographic method. The lesson that proclivity affects the way an individual responds to cultural models and social practices is as true for the ethnographer as it is for those he or she studies ethnographically. The judgments we make about other societies are affected by our own bodily and psychological orientations, the way we bend and flow. Our own personal interests and psychic uncertainties of course affect the topics we choose, and the issues to which we are drawn; we knew that. But it may also be true that the person who writes about religious experience may write differently if she has been knocked sideways in an invocation. If you have heard the mermaids singing, you are more likely to ask people about mermaids in different ways than if you have not. As anthropologists, we have grappled with these issues before, most famously when Alasdair MacIntyre and Peter Winch collided over the question of whether a person who did not believe in God could understand the experience of one that did. But in that debate, as so often in our field, the emphasis was upon cognition and knowledge: the concepts you believed in, the knowledge you held to be true. We are slower to think about anthropologists as having different proclivities, different psychological and bodily capacities, but they are at least as important. We know that those who believe in God and those who do not may write differently about religious practice—but we have been slower to recognize that those who have vivid imaginations, perhaps those who have had a hallucination, may attend to different features of religious experience, whatever beliefs they hold.

Which is fine. But just as we acknowledge that we should admit to our own beliefs when writing about belief, or at least recognize the possible impact of those beliefs, we should acknowledge that our own proclivities could be impediment or advantage when writing about certain topics. Some years ago a book on mental imagery was published. The editor, a well-respected philosopher,[11] began the volume with a subtle and sophisticated argument against mental imagery, on the oddity that the phrase even existed in our descriptive vocabulary, as if we believed that we had pictures in our minds. Then there followed a series of articles, among them Stephen Kosslyn's essay describing the famous experiments through which psychologists have demonstrated that most people do, in fact, behave as if they have pictures in their minds, and process their evidential experience through the use and manipulation of these pictures. The editor had a summary piece at the end in which he commented that perhaps he, the editor, just didn't have mental images. Perhaps philosophers, he suggested, were just the kinds of people who were less likely to experience themselves as having pictures in their minds. If psychological and bodily proclivities make a difference to the way people use and understand cultural models, it is to the advantage of the anthropologists to understand their own proclivities and the way those proclivities may shape the way they learn about culture in the field. Otherwise they run the risk of sounding foolish, like someone who doesn't remember his dreams and treats cultural models of dream interpretation as metaphors, or someone who doesn't realize that hallucinations are uncommon and treats all reports of unusual experience as descriptions of the world as it is.

If this can be seen as an attempt to cut culture down to size, as Clifford Geertz described the point of his own work to be so many decades ago, it becomes also a testament to how powerful these cultural ideas can be in the lives of those who take them on. This kind of religious belief is a commitment to a sensory override of the most basic mechanisms of our body: our ability to see, to hear, to feel, to smell. The fact that the true override—the hallucination— happens so rarely is testimony to how hard it is, and how deeply culture reaches into the minds of those who experience the true override and its partial correlates, the capacity to feel God's touch, to listen to his voice, to be with his spirit as one is with an ordinary human. And that, as Rita Astuti points out,[12] becomes a moving insight into how hard people work to create out of dull materials a world which conforms to the moral vision they seek.

In the end, the ethnography that the ethnographer delivers must persuade the audience independently of the ethnographer's experience in the field. The more you know about yourself, the way you learn, and the way those tendencies are distributed among human beings, the more wisely you will gauge the way your own experience will inform you about the experience of others and about what and how they learn. But it is always worthwhile to pay attention to your experience. If I hadn't paid attention when what felt like power shot through me on the train, I would have missed half of what was going on with magical practice.

Even so, I never figured out what was going on with the batteries.

References

Astuti, R. Forthcoming. *Revealing and Obscuring Rivers' Pedigree: Biological Inheritance and Kinship in Madagascar.*

Austin, J. H. 1999. *Zen and the Brain.* Cambridge, MA: MIT Press.

Bellah, R., R. Madsen, W. M. Sullivan, A. Swidler, and M. S. Tipton. 1985. *Habits of the Heart.* Berkeley: University of California Press.

Beyer, S. 1978. *The Cult of Tara.* Berkeley: University of California Press.

Blackaby, H., and C. King. 2004. *Experiencing God.* Nashville: Broadman and Holman.

Block, N., ed. 1981. Imagery. Cambridge, MA: MIT Press.

Bourguignon, E. 1979. "Hallucination and Trance: An Anthropologist's Perspective." In W. Keup, ed., *Origins and Mechanisms of Hallucinations,* 183–190. New York: Plenum.

Carruthers, M. 1998. *The Craft of Thought: Meditation, Rhetoric, and the Making of Images.* Cambridge: Cambridge University Press.

Claridge, G., ed. 1997. *Schizotypy.* Oxford: Oxford University Press.

Crapanzano, V. 1990. *Tuhami: Portrait of a Moroccan.* Chicago: University of Chicago Press.

———. 2004. *Serving the Word.* New York: New Press.

Crocker, C. 1985. *Vital Souls.* Tucson: University of Arizona Press.

Csikszentmihalyi, M. 1990. *Flow: The Psychology of Optimal Experience.* New York: Harper Perennial.

Csordas, T. 1994. *The Sacred Self.* Berkeley: University of California Press.

Cunningham, L. 1984. *Is That Really You, God?* Seattle: YWAM.

Desjarlais, R. 1992. *Body and Emotion.* Philadelphia: University of Pennsylvania Press.

Evans-Pritchard, E. E. 1937. *Witchcraft, Oracles, and Magic among the Azande.* Oxford: Oxford University Press.

Feinberg, M. 2005. *God Whispers.* Orlando: Relevant Books.

Foster, R. 1978. *Celebration of Discipline.* San Francisco: HarperSanFrancisco.

Frank, T. 2004. *What's the Matter with Kansas?* New York: Metropolitan Books.

Frischholz, E., L. Lipman, B. Braun, and R. Sachs. 1992. "Psychopathology, Hypnotizability, and Dissociation." *American Journal of Psychiatry* 149:1521–1525.

Fromm, E., and S. Katz. 1990. *Self-hypnosis.* New York: Guilford.

Glisky, M., D. Tataryn, K. McConkey, B. Tobias, and J. Kihlstrom. 1991. "Absorption, Openness to Experience, and Hypnotizability." *Journal of Personality and Social Psychology* 60:263–272.

Goleman, D. 1977. *The Varieties of the Meditative Experience.* New York: Dutton.

Happold, F. C., ed. 1963. *Mysticism.* Harmondsworth: Penguin.

Kleinman, A. 1980. *Patients and Healers in the Context of Culture.* Berkeley: University of California Press.

Knight, G. 1975. *Experience of the Inner Worlds.* Toddington, Gloucestershire: Helios Books.

Luhrmann, T. M. 1989. *Persuasions of the Witch's Craft.* Cambridge, MA: Harvard University Press.

———. 2004. "Yearning for God: Trance as a Culturally Specific Practice and Its Implications for Understanding Dissociative Disorders." *Journal of Trauma and Dissociation* 5:101–129.

Luhrmann, T. M., H. Nusbaum, and R. Thisted. 2010. "The Absorption Hypothesis: Learning to Hear God in American Evangelical Christianity." *American Anthropologist* (March).

McCrae, R., and P. Costa. 1983. "Joint Factors in Self-Reports and Ratings: Neuroticism, Extraversion, and Openness to Experience." *Personality and Individual Differences* 4:245–255.

Miller, D. 1997. *Reinventing American Protestantism.* Berkeley: University of California Press.

Nadon, R., I. Hoyt, P. Register, and J. Kihlstrom. 1991. "Absorption and Hypnotizability." *Journal of Personality and Social Psychology* 60:144–153.

Nell, V. 1988. "The Psychology of Reading for Pleasure." *Reading Research Quarterly* 23:6–50.

Pekala, R., C. Wenger, and R. Levine. 1985. "Individual Differences in Phenomenological Experience: States of Consciousness as a Function of Absorption." *Journal of Personality and Social Psychology* 48:125–132.

Roche, S., and K. McConkey. 1990. "Absorption: Nature, Assessment, Correlates." *Journal of Personality and Social Psychology* 59:91–101.

Roof, W. 1993. *A Generation of Seekers.* San Francisco: HarperSanFranicisco.

Schneider, D. 1980 [1968]. *American Kinship: A Cultural Account.* Chicago: University of Chicago Press.

Snodgrass, M., and S. Lynn. 1989. "Music Absorption and Hypnotizability." *International Journal of Clinical and Experimental Hypnosis* 37:41–54.

Spiegel, D., and H. Spiegel. 2004. *Trance and Treatment.* Washington, DC: American Psychiatric Association Press.

Stoller, P. 1987. *In Sorcery's Shadow.* Chicago: University of Chicago Press.

Tellegen, A., and G. Atkinson. 1974. "Openness to Absorption and Self Altering Experiences ('Absorption'): A Trait Related to Hypnotic Susceptibility." *Journal of Abnormal Psychology* 83:268–277.

Virkler, M., and P. Virkler. 1986. *Dialogue with God.* Gainesville, FL: BridgeLogos.

Whalen, J., and M. Nash. 1996. "Hypnosis and Dissociation: Theoretical, Empirical, and Clinical Perspectives." In L. Michelson and W. Ray, eds., *Handbook of Dissociation,* 191–206. New York: Plenum.

Wild, T. C., D. Kuiken, and D. Schopflocher. 1995. "The Role of Absorption in Experiential Involvement." *Journal of Personality and Social Psychology* 69:569–579.

Willard, D. 1999. *Hearing God.* Downer's Grove, IL: Intervarsity Press.

Wuthnow, R. 1999. *After Heaven.* Berkeley: University of California Press.

Notes

1. Systematic visualization practice is found in Asian monastic tradition and in medieval Christianity, and it remains the cornerstone of arguably the most successful spiritual conversion practice in Catholicism, the Ignatian Spiritual Exercises. The practice of visualization is also widely distributed in shamanic or shamanic-style religions, although the training may appear less systematic to an observer, in part because it is apprentice-based and taught in a preliterate context. Most ethnographies of shamanism are clear that the shaman must be apprenticed and trained. Those ethnographies that describe the training in detail suggest that such training consists in expert coaching to enable the apprentice to enter an altered state and to see certain kinds of images clearly and reliably. The practice of meditation is equally widely distributed, and famously present in many Eastern spiritual systems, where it is presumed to be a skill that can be learned and that, when learned, will deliver to the practitioner a series of intense spiritual experiences. Meditation has garnered the lion's share of the scientific study of spiritual practice, and because of this we know that consistent practice may produce physiological changes. Discussions include: Austin 1999; Beyer 1978; Bourguignon 1979; Carruthers 1998; Crocker 1985; Csikszentmihaly 1990; Fromm and Katz 1990; Goleman 1977; Happold 1963; Noll 1985.

2. See the discussion in Luhrmann 2004.

3. I have in mind the work of Tversky and Kahneman, which, while brilliant, underestimates the experiential dimension of the frame, that people may not only have different interpretive frames but even differential evidence with which to make their judgments.

4. The classic ethnographic study of transference and countertransference in anthropology is Crapanzano, *Tuhami: Portrait of a Moroccan* (1990).

5. Blackaby and King, *Experiencing God* (2004:174).

6. I came across this as a teaching text for a Vineyard weekend course titled "The Art of Hearing God." The course was technically offered by a group that was separate from the Vineyard, but it was taught in a Vineyard church by a Vineyard pastor.

7. It took place in the Alpha course Holy Spirit retreat. The Alpha course is a very widely used course to introduce non-Christians to Christianity.

8. Amy's quotations have been edited for clarity, as she uses many repeated words and phatic phrases. The sense has not been altered.

9. For example, the Dissociative Experiences Scale, the Launay-Slade Psychosis Proneness Scale, the Curious Experiences Scale, Claridge's Schizotypy Scale, and so forth.

10. These results are also reported in Luhrmann, Nusbaum, and Thisted 2010.

11. Block, *Imagery*.

12. Astuti, forthcoming.

10 Ascetic Practice and Participant Observation, or, the Gift of Doubt in Field Experience*

Joanna Cook

LONG-TERM PARTICIPANT OBSERVATION enables the learning practice at the heart of anthropological enquiry. Unsurprisingly, such a task brings its own doubts and anxieties. If such anxieties are recognised when they occur they may be used as an enabling aspect of the field experience rather than something that inhibits research. In this chapter I put forward the argument that consciously viewing doubt or anxiety as a part of fieldwork can enable further learning while also ameliorating some of the anxiety of the novice anthropologist. Rather than reducing emotion to an unfortunate impediment, such an approach allows the anthropologist to understand her field experiences in ways that provide insight into the conditions of the field. The application of local interpretive models to the anthropologist's own interiority may provide the anthropologist with a crucial source for learning culture that is not limited to previously interna-lised directives or pre-defined modes of understanding. My aim is to show that considering methodology as open-ended and incomplete may enable the re-searcher to explore local understandings of self and emotion.

I draw an analogy between the learning involved in becoming a *mae chee* (Thai Buddhist nun) and that transpiring in anthropological research. Both as-cetic practice and fieldwork are structured learning processes, and up to a point, the Buddhist attitude toward doubt—to acknowledge and observe it rather

* The research upon which this chapter is based was conducted over fifteen months in a monastery in North Thailand with the support of an ESRC Award for Postgraduate Training. Further support was generously provided by a British Academy Small Research Grant. I am grateful to Susan Bayly, Matei Candea, Laura Jeffrey, James Laidlaw, and Nick Long for their comments on earlier drafts of this chapter.

than allowing it to become controlling—is one that the field researcher can learn from. My own fieldwork in a monastery in North Thailand was characterized by a heavily participant form of participant observation. My ongoing subjective experience of monastic life gave me important insights into the meaning and use of emotions in the field. Without resulting in self-indulgence or navel gazing (apart from as a meditative tool), my awareness of my own doubts about the processes of fieldwork and commitment to the monastery clarified my understanding of monasticism in ways that I could not have foreseen.

My Field Site and Research

In many ways the monastery where I lived and carried out fieldwork is a typical Thai monastery, where monks and *mae chee* live lives of renunciation and contemplation. The idea of detachment is central to the monastic community's imagining of itself. At the same time, much daily activity in the monastery surrounds collective commitment to the monastery's well-being and observance of monastic hierarchy. Moreover, this monastery is set apart from other similar institutions in Thailand by the teaching of *vipassanā* meditation (see below). The widespread adoption of meditation by the laity since the 1950s is identified by some scholars as the greatest single change to have come over Theravada Buddhist countries since the Second World War (Gombrich and Obeyesekere 1988:237). Today this is a widely popular and influential movement, with meditation being taught in monasteries throughout Thailand, Sri Lanka, Burma, and, most recently, Nepal. The monastery in Thailand where I conducted fieldwork has functioned as a *vipassanā* meditation centre since it was founded in the 1970s. It has a stable monastic community, the largest *mae chee* population in the region, and during one year approximately four thousand laypeople attend the monastery to do a retreat. For individual monastics, periods of retreat are tempered by long periods of time during which they work and teach. The scale of teaching, and the work involved, make it difficult for members of the community to experience extended periods of isolation, and monastics have relatively little opportunity to do retreat themselves, though all work in the monastery is ideally a site for mindful awareness and provides an opportunity to develop the state of mind engendered by meditation. The work of teaching also fosters a great sense of community amongst people who feel that they are doing good by combining this-worldly activity with withdrawal from the world.

In my research (Cook, in press) I try to convey how becoming a monastic changes one's relationship with mental, physical, and emotional processes as well as the way in which one interprets subjective experiences. Further, I examine how these changes are similar to those engendered by ascetic practice for laity, but also the way in which they are crucially different. Thus I try to describe the kinds of feelings, practices, explanations, and rituals with which monastics engage. The experiences of meditation can be described and identified; they are vivid and emotive and must be made sense of by the experiencer as she makes sense of herself and the changes that she effects, and intends to effect, through meditation practice. Talking about meditation in the monastery is frowned upon. It is considered that learning is by doing, not by talking, and there is a limited amount that can be transmitted verbally. Meditation may be understood as a prescribed embodied practice. It may be considered with respect to associated psychological states, such as "mindfulness," that are the result of physical and mental discipline. And it may also be considered in the context of the ways in which these states and practices are articulated and understood by individuals. Experiential knowledge of meditation was of paramount importance if I was to have any understanding of how meditation becomes meaningful and why people commit themselves to what is often a gruelling practice. In order to translate theoretical issues of individuality, renunciation, and practice into researchable empirical questions, I spent fifteen months in the monastery and for one year of this time I took ordination as a Buddhist nun (*mae chee*).

Becoming a *Mae Chee*

I had some experience of my field site before I began research. While travelling around Southeast Asia at the age of twenty-one I did a one-month meditation course at the monastery and was ordained as a *mae chee* for four months, taking a vow of silence for much of this time.[1] As a child I had been taught various meditation techniques by my parents, and our family holidays were often organised around meditation retreats in a variety of traditions. Thus, when I first entered the monastery I already had some experience of meditation and the tenets of Buddhism. I took ordination at this time because I saw it as a way of developing my meditation practice, and I disrobed in order to complete my undergraduate degree. My later research on meditation presented a way of returning to the monastery and taking ordination for a longer period of time.

Before embarking upon my first serious long-term research, I imagined that ordination and my life as a *mae chee* would be straightforward. Having had a brief flirtation with ordination a few years previously, I naïvely thought that I knew what it entailed. However, nothing prepared me for the effect and challenges of the relative longevity of my second ordination period. My ordination as a *mae chee* was both central to my research and a monumental personal commitment. It was understood by people in the field and by me as a demonstration of respect for monasticism and the monastic project.[2] My religious position was unambiguous: I was a Buddhist and I was committed to the ordination and meditation. It was known in the monastery that my ordination would be limited to one year and that I would be doing anthropological research.

My commitment to the monastery and my social status within the monastic community were officially marked by my ordination and the subsequent meditation retreat that all new ordinands undertake. As a very senior *mae chee*, called Jau Mae, dressed me in the robe during the ceremony, she whispered, "You are my daughter now; I have given birth to you in the *dhamma* family." After the ceremony I offered alms to all senior monastics (and everyone was my senior) in the form of an envelope containing a small sum of money. Throughout fieldwork I was fully involved in the monastery, performing my daily monastic duties and participating in rituals as a monastic. I would wake at four a.m., meditate or chant for two hours before breakfast, and work in the office during the morning giving information and meditation instruction to foreigners. I observed fast for eighteen hours a day (from noon until six a.m.) and conditioned myself to sleep for six hours a night. I translated the abbot's meditation teaching for foreigners during the daily meeting between teacher and meditation students. I received alms from the laity and donated alms to the monastery and monks.[3] I tried to maintain six hours daily meditation practice when not on retreat. I also assisted in the meditation retreats of groups of Thai laity. These were frequently as large as a hundred people, usually comprising schoolchildren, university students, or work colleagues. My duty was to speak on the microphone about the benefits of meditation. At such times my status as a young scholar from Cambridge was always emphasised and it was suggested that my level of education at a renowned institution and my ordination directly resulted from my meditation practice. I was thus endowed with symbolic capital which reflected well on the monastery, the community, and the monastery's project to teach meditation to large numbers of people. Throughout fieldwork I regularly undertook a two-week meditation retreat during which I slept for four hours a night and meditated for a minimum of sixteen hours a day. Each retreat ended with a period of days without sleep, meditating continuously. The shortest of these was three days and two nights; the longest was five days and four nights. Living a monastic life, I also had ample time on my own that was not occupied by religious duties. Monastics have time each late afternoon and evening to themselves in which they can do as they choose. Most evenings I and other *mae chee* would meet for tea and conversation before returning to our rooms. Thus, built into the daily routine there are legitimate periods of free time that monastics can enjoy for their own ends. I used this time for relaxation, washing, and, importantly, writing field notes and reports. Throughout my ordination I self-identified and was identified by others as a *mae chee*. I had shaved my head and renounced the world and was trying to be good: I strove to be mindful in my thinking, speech, and comportment and to cut attachment to a sense of self.

While my duties and reasons for ordination were similar to those of some *mae chee* and monks, they differed from those of others. Monastics constitute a heterogeneous category, and in any given community, motivations for monastic commitment and experience of monastic life will be varied. There is huge variance in age, reasons for ordination, educational attainment, and social background. Before ordination, monastics had occupations ranging from civil servants, farmers, hoteliers, office workers, policemen, shopkeepers, and society ladies to labourers. While one *mae chee* had no education and had been a construction labourer prior to ordination, another was a wealthy Laotian princess.

Reasons for ordination were equally varied. Many monks and *mae chee* felt motivated to ordain after doing a meditation retreat. One monk who had been ordained for twenty years did so after being inspired by the *dhamma* teaching of a monk who encouraged him to meditate.[4] Before ordination he had worked on his family's rice farm; he ordained because he believed that this was the way to find peace. Another *mae chee*, who had been ordained for twenty-eight years, had ordained at eighteen as a result of her faith in the religion. She recounted crucial points in her adolescence, such as a *dhamma* teaching she attended with her grandmother, the death of a friend at fourteen, the example of the hardships of her mother's life, as cementing her faith in meditation and renunciation. One *mae chee* had promised that she would ordain for a month if her father recovered from a life-threatening illness. Once in the robes, she decided to stay. A monk from a poor family took ordination in order to receive an education and was confident that he would disrobe once he completed his master's degree. Another monk took ordination because he had promised his mother that he would. More than one elderly *mae chee* took ordination after husbands had passed away, stating that it was appropriate for them to dedicate their energies towards meditation now that they were no longer focused on family life.

Mae Chee Bun, who had been ordained for three years and was forty-four years old, told me in an interview that she came to practise meditation because she felt that she was leading a bad life:

> The first time I ever tried meditation I did it because I felt bored. Nothing was good in my life and I felt so bad for myself that I did no good for my family, my friends, or me and it hurt my heart. When I came to practice I cried for a long time. Then I decided to be a *mae chee* because I could do good. I could stop doing bad.

The duties of monastics are assigned on the basis of their skills. Duties are varied, and the collective commitment to individual responsibilities ensures the ongoing maintenance of the community. As well as organising and officiating at ceremonies, meditating and teaching large numbers of people to meditate, monks' duties include construction, renovation, and maintenance of monastery property, which is ongoing and labour-intensive work. *Mae chee* work in the kitchens, the shop, run the main office, and are responsible for much of the cleaning in the monastery. As well as the duties to meditate, study *dhamma*, and chant, individuals from both groups have duties to sit on the various administrative committees that oversee the running of the monastery, and also to teach in the large meditation "camps." Allocation of duties depends on an individual's abilities and inclination. For example, a *mae chee* who was a property developer before ordination enjoys running the main office, and a *mae chee* who was a chef in lay life heads one of the teams who work in the kitchen.

Fieldwork Doubts

For the first six months of fieldwork I was concerned about doing enough "formal" research and about the quantity and quality of the "data" that I was collecting. At such times I fell back on standardised techniques, each of which led to the formation of different kinds of data. Clearly, just to *be* a *mae chee* is not methodologically sufficient for anthropological research. Thus, as well as writing field notes in notebooks of varying sizes, I busied myself conducting surveys, doing formal and informal interviews, collecting life histories, documenting rituals, researching the meaning of symbols, and so on. When I spoke with my contemporaries, it seemed that such concerns were a common aspect of the fieldwork process. This led me to consider two important points which I shall later develop: firstly, that a certain amount of anxiety is endemic to the practice of anthropology, and secondly, that once such responses to the pressures of fieldwork are recognised by the conscientious researcher, they become potentially methodologically fruitful. While employing formal research methods is of benefit to the anthropologist, such methods are, by and large, in addition the anthropologist's methodological bread and butter: participant observation. Furthermore, I suggest that while anxiety and doubt within the researcher are not of primary concern in the implementation and analysis of formal methods, ongoing participant observation necessitates the researcher's awareness of her own psychological responses to her participation in cultural practices. Despite the reflexive turn in anthropology since the 1970s (see Davies, chapter 3, this volume, for an overview of this scholarship), there remains a perception of anthropological fieldwork as dependent largely upon the adaptability and effort of the individual anthropologist. This has led to an understanding within anthropology suggesting that our greatest methodological asset is not only informal and individually variable but also, to some extent, imponderable. As Evans-Pritchard argued back in the 1970s, the exact nature of any particular fieldwork cannot be known in advance, and "much will depend on the man, on the society he is to study, and the conditions in which he is to make it" (Evans-Pritchard 1973:1). Though pre-field training has advanced considerably since Evans-Pritchard's day, young researchers often perceive fieldwork as a methodological black box, the contents of which cannot be known until they are experienced by the researcher herself. To flag some of the common concerns generated by the learning process of anthropological research may be a fruitful exercise, not just as an analysis of the fieldwork experience for its own sake but also as a practical help for junior colleagues preparing to embark on fieldwork for the first time.

With the benefit of hindsight it is possible to see that while the anxiety about fieldwork felt by my contemporaries and me prompted us to employ a proliferation of methods, that anxiety was itself an aspect of the process of participation.[5] I suggest that problematising doubt and anxiety as an aspect of, rather than a hindrance to, anthropological research may go some way toward anticipating some of the common concerns of fieldwork.[6] In the field the anthropologist is learning, among other things, to understand the world around her through a new interpretative framework. If we view long-term fieldwork as a knowledge practice, it is reflection on precisely such states in the researcher that enables her to gain further in-depth understanding of the field. In the field, methodological anxieties—Is this research? Am I doing enough? Does this count? Will this look like anthropology one day?—are compounded by the anxieties of entering and navigating previously unknown contexts. As well as the personal commitment of ensconcing herself in social contexts in which she is uncertain, the anthropologist must also contend with the accompanying knowledge that she is to return from this journey ready to spin her data into the yarn of anthropology. There is, then, a perceived pressure on the anthropologist to find something in the encounters of the field that may be recognised as having worth beyond that of the immediate experience. The worry that one will not know what to do with the collected data follows hot on the heels of anxieties about not recognising significant experiences, as and when they occur, or whether indeed that they will occur at all.

During fieldwork I felt fortunate to have frequent e-mail contact with my colleagues, and I was reassured that not only was I not alone in feeling uncertain about fieldwork but it was not unprofessional to voice such doubts: we were all having them. However, for much of the fieldwork period neither I nor my peers understood our doubts to be *part* of the fieldwork process, believing them to be rather the result of inadequate fieldwork practice. Common worries included questions about doing too much or not enough, what counts as participant observation, how to define the boundaries of the research, self-questioning about the role of the anthropologist (the methods employed, the "data" being collected), and finally concerns about what will result from so much investment on the part of the researcher herself. Anthropological research requires that the researcher commit herself to practices and processes often entirely new to her domain of experience. And while it is comforting to hear news of family, friends, and colleagues, what James Davies has identified as a "strategy of withdrawal," such news does not necessarily assist the progress of fieldwork, though it may temporarily relieve some of its pressures. The researcher must contend with the anxieties of fieldwork and yet continue to do fieldwork. Thus, while many researchers in the field today now have recourse to communication media in a way that our predecessors did not, I suggest that the intellectual isolation recognised by Malinowski and the generation that followed him remains an identifiable aspect of the fieldwork process because there is little that can be done by others to actually assist the anthropologist in doing fieldwork. While it was reassuring for me to receive e-mails from my colleagues complaining of similar anxieties in their respective field sites, such reassurances were of no practical assistance in the day-to-day negotiation of the situations in which I found myself.

Meditation as Methodology

It is in part the prolonged encounter of fieldwork that enables anthropological understanding of the subtlety of interpersonal awareness. As a *mae chee*, I had a duty to explicitly offer an example of monastic piety for the laity and to act as daughter to senior monks and *mae chee*. Learning what was appropriate in my behaviour with particular people was also central to learning about what it means to be a monastic in Thailand. It was through this process of "gradual familiarization" (Hastrup and Hervik 1994:7) that I learnt how to act and behave sensitively and become aware of the feelings of those around me.

The emphasis placed upon the experiential dimension of meditation makes it a particularly thorny challenge for anthropology: in many ways research about meditation is an attempt to "eff" the ineffable. In translating the teachings of the meditation teacher, I was struck by the number of questions that were met with responses such as "acknowledge" or "meditate and you will know." Houtman found that because of similar strictures in a Burmese meditation centre it was difficult to cultivate social contacts. He makes the further point that, in comparison with a monastery not focused on meditation, in the meditation centre the pursuit of a very limited type of knowledge was encouraged:

> In the monastery my every question was taken seriously by the monks, but in the meditation centre questions about the organisation of the centre, and the way people experienced meditation, were all considered tangential to the knowledge they thought I *should* be seeking—If you meditate yourself you will find all answers to your questions. (Houtman 1990:131)

The knowledge engendered by meditation is highly valued and considered the only appropriate area of enquiry for meditation students: "While in the monastery knowledge can be received in a social context and transmitted between people, in the meditation centre knowledge is not conceived in its 'received' form but only as an experiential knowledge derived from lengthy private dedicated 'work'" (Houtman 1990:156). By choosing to ordain and practise meditation I experienced the effects of religious practice on my own feelings and sense of self. Long-term participant observation enables the anthropologist to think about a multiplicity of bodily practices in order to examine cultural processes of physical learning. This emphasises "a mode of fieldwork that focuses on the mediations of corporeal experience and that locates what has been called 'the mind' . . . in the body" (Fernandez and Herzfeld 1998:110).

I suggest that, while being careful not to generalise from the individual to the collective, the anthropologist who wholeheartedly participates in cultural practice can draw on such experiences when reflecting on the stated impact of such practices for other people. As Tanya Luhrmann writes:

> Often human experience is stimulated in similar ways by similar activity. Being deprived of food in an initiation ceremony, undergoing group-led imaginative "journeys," dancing until exhausted in a group ritual—all these have a signifi-cant subjective impact upon the participants, and some features of the subjec-tive response to each will be common to many. (Luhrmann 1989:14–15)

Through one's own involvement one can begin to understand what others may have been experiencing. Without resorting to assumptions about mental actions one may cautiously develop some awareness of the psychological land-scape in which assertions are made.

In the meditation monastery the primary monastic duties of the commu-nity were to practise meditation and facilitate the meditation practice of others. Following the work of Luhrmann (chapter 9, this volume) it is possible to inter-pret meditation as a social learning process. In so doing, I shall consider some of the socially taught rules by which the cognitive categories of Buddhism are identified in the experiences of the practising monastic. The practitioner learns to engage with and interpret internal and external sensory phenomena in spe-cific ways. Thus the development of meditative discipline and monastic identity involves a process of learning to reinterpret subjective experiences and learning to alter subjectivity. The monastic learns to experience thoughts and emotions not as the uninteresting slough of the daily grind but rather as evidence of the fundamental truths of Buddhism: that all phenomena are conditioned by non-self, impermanence, and suffering. These three tenets become the context in which all logical analyses and apperceptions of phenomena are carried out. Thus the renunciate learns to experience her own mental and physical activities as evidence of the importance of the project of renunciation. Mae Chee Sati, a young woman who had been ordained for nine years, explained the significance that meditation held for her when she said:

> I can say to you that meditation is the most important thing in my life and it's what I was born for. I want to practise and I want to improve my mind. Practice gives you more understanding of yourself and of life. You can do good more easily; you can see right or wrong more easily also. And then you're good for

other people too. It changes the way that you see yourself; I can see my greed very easily. I look at my greed and I say to myself, "Can you cut it?" "Yes." I can see my power, if it's strong enough or not; first, understanding and after that, doing. When I cannot cut it, little by little this improves through practice. With other people I have more kindness and more forgiveness; more loving-kindness and less selfishness. Practice is not easy. You go little by little for learning. But it's not too difficult. There's more and more to learn, so that you don't follow your defilements. It's hard, but it's good. When you take medicine it tastes bitter but it's good for you.

Thus meditation, which we might think of as being a solitary activity, in fact has important social dimensions that are collectively understood and taught. The renunciate who comes to experience his or her subjectivity as congruent with religious tenets has done so through active learning and engaging with specific, socially taught techniques by which subjectivity is intended to be shaped.

By sharing the process of socialisation, each monastic is subject to the same requirements and practices that are intended to alter the ways in which the world is perceived; such processes throw up their own challenges and doubts as subjectivity is altered over time. For example, Mae Chee Bun understood the measurement of her success in developing mindfulness to be her interactions with other monastics:

> Before I would get angry so often. But when I practise [meditation] it goes away little by little. Outside [the monastery] if someone talks no good to you then you cannot accept it, but if someone talks no good to you on the inside then you can say thank you to them. It's the opposite. When you talk no good then you are my mirror. I can look at myself and see my reaction. If you don't say bad things to me I cannot know how I will respond. I cannot see my face; I cannot know my voice. When you say I've done something wrong I can accept it.

Acknowledging Doubt in Meditation

The effect of practising *vipassanā* meditation is to develop awareness of the conditions of the body and the mind in the present moment, thereby gaining insight. This insight is not conceptual but comes to the practitioner through direct experience in her meditation; doubt is eradicated and with it ignorance (*avijja*), understood as the cause of suffering. Doubt in meditation may take many forms: doubt about the truth of Buddhist teaching, doubt as to one's own ability to practise meditation or compatibility with the technique, doubt about the value of committing oneself to hours of meditation, and so on. Irrespective of the reason behind doubting, all doubt is to be dealt with in the same way. The meditator uses a process of mental noting in order to develop awareness of and cut attachment to the condition of doubt. It is not the case, therefore, that doubt is necessarily a hindrance to meditative progress. As long as doubt is recognised and used as the focus of meditative awareness, it is of benefit to the meditator. It is when doubt is not acknowledged in this way, but rather conditions meditative experiences, that it is inhibiting.

The meditation technique begins with focusing on the rise and fall of the stomach as the practitioner breathes in and out. As the stomach rises the practitioner mentally notes "rising," and as it falls she mentally notes "falling." Any distraction from "rising-falling" is briefly taken as the object of the meditation and labelled three times, for example "thinking thinking thinking," and then the attention is returned to "rising-falling." With practice the meditator is able to maintain mindful awareness of the breath for increasing periods of time. Distractions from this focus are not necessarily bad or unhelpful as long as they are recognised and acknowledged quickly. For example, it is possible to spend a long time lost in daydreams rather than focusing on the breath. For the purposes of meditation it is unimportant whether thinking is about the past or the future, about serious matters or total fantasy—it is acknowledged as a thinking process in the present and this acknowledgement enables the meditator to remove herself from the thoughts themselves and return her attention to the breath. Similarly, emotional conditions such as anger or doubt are not considered in terms of the reasons behind them or their validity. Rather, they are understood as emotional conditions in the present moment that are to be acknowledged. For the purposes of meditation it is unimportant whether the meditator is justified in her anger or doubt: indeed, it is thought that exploring the reasons for such states does nothing to help the meditator cut attachment to them.

A central tenet of *vipassanā* is to experience, not just to know, that there is no "self" which exists.[7] The Buddhist principle of non-self (*anatta*) is intended to be realised as a psychological reality through the practice of *vipassanā*: it is intended that through this self-willed ascetic practice volition may be eradicated. The body is broken down into its constituent parts, the feelings are isolated and examined apart from their causes, bodily desire is subdued, and the mind is quietened. During retreat this mental discipline slowly extends to a conscious awareness in minute detail of what one is doing both bodily and mentally in each moment. The practitioner uses the process of mental noting to observe and detach from the normal processes of the body and mind, such as grief, sleep, pain, doubt, restlessness, or desire. In order to do this it is necessary to see all mental and physical phenomena as neutral, responding to them with neither desire nor aversion but rather developing a position of equanimity and balance. By observing the conditions of the body and the mind (both of which are ethnographically relevant concepts) in this way, the practitioner detaches herself from her involvement with these conditions sufficiently to be able to *look at* them rather than *look through* them. The practitioner is no longer exclusively identified with these conditions, and this creates a psychological "space" or perspective, from which change is effected.

While the conditions of the body and mind are not eliminated, the practitioner suffers less because she has less attachment (and conversely, less aversion) to them. For example, if she is in pain, then that pain is to be acknowledged, along with any associated thoughts, fears, or emotions surrounding it, without actually acting on the pain by moving or taking medicine. "Good" feelings or emotions are thought to be as problematic as "bad" ones, for though the practitioner may believe herself to be happy or suffering, this feeling is produced by a delusional sense of self and permanence. For example, a teacher at Boonkanjanaram Meditation Center is recorded (1988:128) as guiding a student in retreat by saying: "*Foong* [restless mind] and *Samadhi* [concentration], while opposites, have the same effect as objects. They are of good benefit to observe and have *vipassanā paññā* [insight wisdom] occur. You don't like *foong* because it makes you uncomfortable and because you like to feel peaceful."

I suggest that an ethnographic consideration of involvement in Buddhist meditation as a structured learning process casts light on the challenges of doubt and anxiety in fieldwork. In both, anxiety and doubt need not be crippling if approached with an enquiring perspective. This is to say, the surfacing of these emotions need not necessarily be a bad thing. Rather, what is of real significance is how we respond to them—that is, once they are experienced, it is of central importance that they are employed in a way that enables the practitioner to continue to learn. Thus understood, anxiety and doubt may be used fruitfully in both meditation and fieldwork but for different ends. The danger of ignoring doubt in both instances is that it will inhibit further learning. "Why am I sitting with all this suffering?" is a valid question in meditation and in fieldwork, and how one answers that question in the two instances will be very different: done well, both will recognise the anxiety behind the question and employ it for different ends.

Mindful Performance and Monastic Duty

Through intensive meditation, monks and *mae chee* attempt to go beyond the intellectual cognition of reality and gain an experiential understanding of ultimate truth. Truth in this context may be understood in the sense of absence of deformation. It is not a falsifiable proposition about the world; it is rather that without a delusional sense of self one's perception of the world "hangs true." Meditation combines ruthless introspection, self-attention, and, at the same time, the dissolution of the self. This entails a fairly complex understanding of "reality," which combines the virtues of ultimate reality and individual attainment and purification with the social engagement and responsibility of conventional reality. On the one hand one must be a "lamp unto oneself," while on the other one transcends conventional reality by actually being a part of it.

During fieldwork and analysis a paradox became apparent between internal processes of renunciation for individual monks and *mae chee* and the importance of public demonstrations of "non-self." Multiple displays of sensory and physical control become a central focus in renunciates' lives, but this necessarily creates a dynamic paradox between understandings of self and the moral context of public action. In his discussion of the body in Theravada Buddhist monasticism, Steven Collins argues that for monks and nuns correct physical decorum is a requirement of public life (Collins 1997:198). Their social position within a community requires what he knowingly terms "a spotless performance." He suggests that the reputation of individual monastics is gained and maintained through composed comportment and through social interactions in which they are treated as superiors. The spectacle of the monastic body thus provides the laity with access to Buddhist wisdom and morality:

> The composed, pure, and autonomous body of the monk or nun presented in social life instantiates for lay supporters the immediate existence of that sacred, immaterial, and underlying Truth which their own bodily concerns make impossibly distant from them, and with which they can thus be connected by their material support of its human embodiments. (Collins 1997:203)[8]

This image of the style of deportment appropriate for monks is well established in Thailand. Michael Carrithers comments on the same image of monks in Sinhalese Buddhist society as typified by slow, low-range movements:

> Perhaps our nearest equivalent is the deportment of a well-brought-up lady: the voice is gentle, the knees kept together, the arms held close to the body. The glance in public is controlled. (Carrithers 1983:57)

Carrithers suggests that training in deportment has the social function of inspiring confidence in lay supporters and creating smooth relations within the *sangha*. I have argued elsewhere (Cook, in press) that appropriate deportment for monastics is not only communicative but also constitutive and that the performance of religious identity is one way in which the moral self is formed *and* communicated. Monastic performance may actualise Buddhist ethical principles while simultaneously being a question of social and gendered hierarchy, judgment, and duty.

The level of this emphasis on physical control and demure comportment was reflected in my education as a *mae chee*. While learning to be a *mae chee*, I followed the example of more-experienced *mae chee*, usually by copying everything that they did. Occasionally my behaviour would be addressed directly by another *mae chee*; for example, I was told, "You shouldn't sit with your legs crossed, it makes you look like you think you're something." Every action was to be done slowly and mindfully. One way I was encouraged to appraise my own behaviour was to consider whether my actions were silent: if my robe swished around my ankles when I walked, then I was walking too fast; if the dishes chinked in the sink as I did the washing up, it was because I was not being sufficiently mindful. *Mae chee* who sat silently with their knees and ankles together and backs straight and who spoke quietly with little bodily gesticulation were pointed out to me as suitable people to emulate. *Mae chee* who sat with their legs apart, who spoke loudly, or who were emotionally expressive explained to me themselves that this was the result of their lack of education, but that they could nonetheless use their behaviour as a means for improving their mental control of themselves and that they had already seen a marked improvement in their behaviour and emotionality since ordaining. Monastics around me were in some cases teachers and in others embodiments of full participation in the monastery to which I, as a young *mae chee* and relatively inexperienced meditator, could aspire.[9]

As we have seen, *vipassanā* meditation involves a process of detaching from a sense of self. Such detachment is evidenced through the level of sartorial

neatness exhibited by the individual. The appearance of the body of the monastic reveals an inner state of moral attainment: others bear witness to moral
qualities and virtues in monastic physical performance. Sitting up straight,
speaking quietly, eating slowly, and so on, therefore become a question of morality for the monastic.[10] Ideally, appropriate emotional and physical control
comes as an automatic result of ascetic practice. Yet when behavioural characteristics are refined and held up as indicative of a virtuous state of mind, one's
behaviour becomes a question of not only individual morality but also social
responsibility. As such, the correct behaviour of monastics does not always
result from an attitude of detachment. As one monk told me, "Sometimes in
ourselves we know that we are not doing good but we want to keep it to ourselves so that it is only our own demerit and no one else has to share it."

Monastics are "on show" to the laity for much of the time. If the monastic
appearance communicates how the monastic is to be treated *by* the laity, then
it also communicates how the monastic is to behave *for* the laity. The appearance of the monastic both physically and performatively acts as a buffer zone
between the social world and the bounded self. It is the space in which lay
impressions of renunciates are realised, and where renunciates communicate
themselves to others in the light of the religious ideal. The body may speak to
others about one's personhood, but after ordination one's body becomes part
of the public domain—one has a moral duty to behave in an appropriate way.
As a monastic, one is related to by the laity as one who has renounced a sense
of self, but there is necessarily a discrepancy between this and one's own awareness of the ongoing process of renunciation, between oneself as a spectacle of
asceticism and the reality of one's own imperfection. Through articulating my
own anxieties about my duty to maintain appropriate performative control, I
was able to understand the ways in which such experiences were understood
by others. Often, counsel came through illustrative examples from the lives of
others and the ways in which their understanding of the experience of emotion
had changed as a result of further meditation and mindfulness. For example, in
response to my concern Mae Chee Sati told me:

> When you become a *mae chee* people respect you. Automatically you have to
> look at yourself to see if you are worthy of respect. So you have to act properly.
> If you didn't act properly then people would follow. Sometimes I forget to do
> some things properly. It is forgetting to be mindful, or acknowledge what we are
> doing. Like when we are working together and someone is joking, at that time

you laugh loudly and *mae chee* shouldn't have loud voices. It's not good for another to hear it, but already it's forgotten. Mindfulness is knowing exactly what you are doing. Just only sitting, but you will know how about your hand, how about your leg, how about your mind, how about your feelings; you will know.

Periods of doubt are a recognised part of a monastic life. This was made explicit in sermons given by senior monks for which the whole community gathered once a week. During these sermons monastics were encouraged to act as "*dhamma* friends" (Pali: *kalyana mittata*; variously translated as "good friend," "virtuous friend," "noble friend" "admirable friend") for those experiencing doubts and anxieties. "*Dhamma* friendship" refers to spiritual friendship and support in a Buddhist community: a special relationship either between teacher and student or within a communal peer group that encourages the development of skillfulness and ethical virtues. As in Mae Chee Sati's response to my doubts above, the responsibilities of a *dhamma* friend are to offer counsel and example when others are experiencing doubts about their abilities to maintain discipline in their lives.

The doubts that people experienced were in part in reaction to the responsibility to offer an example of moral perfection to the laity. Monastics who worried that they were not sufficiently disciplined in their behaviour and meditation practice would often avoid those members of the community who were revered for the level of their ascetic discipline. It was commonly assumed that younger monks and *mae chee* would have "struggles" with their ordination because the lure of a worldly life was stronger at a young age. Doubts, as with renunciation, unfolded over time. Recounting periods of doubt after the fact was often a way of illustrating the ways in which mindfulness had developed. Monks and *mae chee* would recount doubtful periods from the past, particularly during the first few years of ordination, as a way of demonstrating how they had overcome doubt through the gradual development of mindfulness.

Of course, being mindful is not merely a monastic injunction upon public emotionality; it is valued in and of itself. It is indicative of a deepening level of wisdom as a result of ascetic practice and bespeaks a level of spiritual attainment. While it may be performed as a duty rather than as a genuine reflection of equanimity, the value of mindfulness is ideologically sustained. The empirical evidence for the state of virtue is to be read from a monastic's conduct—by themselves as much as by others. By doing one's duty selflessly and performing the role of the ideal renunciate, one hopes to "fill the robe from the inside" as the precepts "settle in the heart." The full weight of others' moral expectation lies on one's personal morality as it is expressed through the body; the external world impinges on the internal through the robe. As Sue Benson (2000:252) writes of Euro-American tattooing practices, so do I understand renunciation partially as "a consequence of engagement, imagined as detachment" because in the context of the monastery self-willed practice is enhanced by the moral expectation and elicitation of others.

Process and Emotion in Renunciation and Fieldwork

Throughout fieldwork the ongoing challenge of maintaining an attitude of mindful awareness and equanimity aided me in an understanding of the lived significance of monastic duty and ascetic practice. As a *mae chee* striving to act with mindful awareness in all things, including research, I underwent what felt to me like large personal and emotional changes. The things that one learns during fieldwork may be of academic merit but they may also be emotionally and personally compelling. For example, Evans-Pritchard reflects upon the personal impact of his relationship with the Nuer after his conversion to Catholicism, when he writes: "I would say that I learnt more about the nature of God and our human predicament from the Nuer than I ever learnt at home" (Evans-Pritchard 1973:5). However, the personal impact of field experience is often not visible in anthropological writing. Though sharing the monastic duty to be physically and emotionally controlled was an important aspect of my methodology, when writing my account I was concerned that there was a danger of capitalising on my emotional experience at the expense of ethnography. During the course of my fifteen months of fieldwork, I was deeply touched not only by the friendships and bonds I formed in the community but also by blissful, challenging, and transformative experiences in meditation. I experienced phenomenological conditions far more intense than anything I had previously discovered: at times I felt as though energy coursed through my body and my heart was rent open. The air smelled sweet, time was suspended, and there was no discontinuity between myself and others. At other times I felt bored and claustrophobic as a result of the monastic duty to be physically and emotionally controlled, and I did not feel inclined to use mindful awareness to address such inappropriate (but unexpressed) emotions. I felt deeply frustrated by the restrictions and inhibitions that I had to observe in order to be a good *mae chee*.[11] However, my behaviour in the field was defined by my status as *mae chee*, and so I was unable to modify my behaviour in response to my own subjective commitment to the monastery or the changing weather of my emotions. The moral standards for my behaviour were prescribed and absolute. When a new *mae chee* ordained eight months into my ordination, my behaviour was held up by others as exemplary and I was struck by the extent to which I was embodying the decorum that monastics had been so at pains to teach me.

During fieldwork I participated in numerous meditation retreats both as a personal practice and so that I might develop more understanding about meditation. Initially this process was greatly aided by personal conviction and faith in the technique and the teacher. Intensive embodied practice of this sort provided a way of understanding abstract concepts of "truth" in the field while remaining "true" to the roles of *mae chee* and meditator adopted in the field—alternative "me's" in relation to the cultural world I had come to inhabit. Through executing my duties to behave impeccably, practise meditation, and observe monastic hierarchy, I increasingly felt independent from the good or bad opinion of others. However, I could not maintain this level of practice, and after twelve months I did not want to continue doing intensive retreats. My fieldwork was distinctive in that I committed myself to ordination as a Buddhist nun and to intensive meditation practice, but my experience of being a *mae chee* was coloured by my reasons for ordaining and my experiences of meditation in the past. I understood the different meditation techniques that I had learnt from an early age as options that I could draw upon depending on how I felt. This mix-and-match approach to spiritual practice was very different from the belief in the monastery that *vipassanā* meditation was the only path to enlightenment. It presented a clear contrast between my own understandings of meditation and those of the people around me. Surprisingly, given the hybridity of the Thai religious landscape (Jackson 1997; Keyes 1978; Kirsch 1977; McCargo 2004; Pattana 2005; Taylor 2001), I never encountered monks or *mae chee* in the monastery encouraging any other meditative techniques. While other techniques, traditions, and religions were discussed, they were understood to be inferior to the practice of *vipassanā* and the view was that practising them would be a waste of time. For example, in a discussion about spirits and channeling with a group of *mae chee*, I was told that "the meditation and the teaching [of the abbot] is pure wisdom, the pure teaching of the Buddha, but some people need something to believe in." Even common Thai Buddhist meditations such as *samatha*[12] techniques were discouraged in discussions with meditation students. In contrast, while I had practised *vipassanā* intensively for five years, I had not conceived of this to be at the exclusion of other possible techniques on anything other than a temporary basis.

Ultimately, I experienced doubts about my own vocation as a Buddhist nun and my commitment to *vipassanā* as my sole meditative practice. Thus, my doubts were less a question of belief—whether or not meditation "works," whether the principles of Buddhism are true—than a question of my own commitment to Buddhist monasticism as a vocation. The way in which doubts are dealt with in the monastic community more broadly is to a certain extent self-selecting. Many people who ordained for short periods only ever intended to be in the robes for a limited time, while those who experienced doubts about their vocation as a monastic and were unable to overcome them disrobed. For example, one woman disrobed after six years as a *mae chee* because she doubted that ordination was right for her. Over a number of months she discussed these doubts with the abbot, who encouraged her to undertake several meditation retreats to consider them. Finally she felt that she could not use the doubts as a meditative tool and continue as a *mae chee*. She now lives close to the monastery as a laywoman with a young family. She continues to practise *vipassanā* exclusively and visits the temple on a daily basis.

Although my fieldwork involved a heavily participant form of participant observation, it had limits: it was informed by my doubts as to whether or not I could remain as a *mae chee*; that these appeared *as* doubt is indicative of the degree to which I committed myself to participating *as* a *mae chee*. My doubts about my vocation were limited in terms of the amount I learnt from them as a monastic. Ultimately, I did not acknowledge these doubts with mindful awareness in order to cut attachment to a sense of self. I was, in fact, drawing different conclusions. While I gained insight into monastic practice by entering into it to the extent that I did and applying a new interpretive framework to the social context and my own responses to that context, some of what I was learning was consistent with monastic practice, while some of what I was learning was the result of my role as an anthropologist conducting participant observation. Nonetheless, the learning process of fieldwork meant committing myself to learning through participant observation, including meditation, and thus as the fieldwork progressed I was both able to address doubts and to erode the perceived justification for them.

For me, the greatest trial of the fieldwork period was lack of exercise. Prohibition on exercise is intended to enable monastics to cut attachment to the body. Prior to entering the monastery I was surfing and dancing regularly, and I found that after a number of months of ordination without exercise my body became sluggish, my skin became sallow, and I had very low energy. Further-more, though it is prohibited to eat after noon,[13] monastics in this monastery are allowed to have yogurt, chocolate, and ice cream because they all have liquid forms. Every evening I and a group of *mae chee* would have sweet tea with condensed milk and a piece of chocolate. By the end of my ordination my blood sugar was fluctuating wildly and I frequently felt hypoglycaemic. When I expressed concern about my health to a *mae chee* the same age as I was, she responded that if we were crippled later in life it would not matter because we would have no attachment to our physical form. I was not so convinced. I tried to improve my physical condition by doing the exercise that *is* appropriate for monastics. I swept the paths of the monastery rigorously and hand-washed my robes and towels more than I needed to. Towels were particularly useful because once wet they took effort to lift. When I disrobed I went on holiday in the south of Thailand. I relished the sheer physicality of Frisbee, swimming in the sea, the sun on my skin, and eating green vegetables regularly.

The way in which I perceived my own and other people's bodies changed dramatically during fieldwork. I was given a photographic atlas of the body as a meditative tool to assist me in cutting attachment to the body. At first I found the images of dissected corpses upsetting, but soon I became fascinated by the construction of the human body and the ways in which the pictures on the pages corresponded to my own imagining of my body. In a short time this coloured my perceptions of other people as well: I would be aware that their skulls were made up of plates that meshed together, or that with a turn of the head count-less tendons and muscles were activated in the neck. I was encouraged, and was keen to view the corpses at funerals I attended. In ways I had never experienced before I became aware of not only other people's mortality but also my own. In the context of the meditation this was a fascinating experience: I felt as though I was experiencing and accepting the Buddhist principles of non-self, imperma-nence, and suffering (*anatta, anicca, dukkha*) in my own self-perception.[14]

In the monastery doubt and the dispossession of certainty appear to play a qualified role in relation to the "power" of the religious experience. In the practice of *vipassanā* emphasis is placed on dealing with the attitude produced by feelings such as doubt or grief, rather than in examining the causal chain of what has generated such feelings; to consider cause is to be part of this worldly truth and identified with maintaining a sense of self. Doubt is not what drives the initiate; as a condition of the mind it is one tool amongst many used in the cultivation of detachment.

If we assume that the anthropologist is affected or changed by the process of participant observation, this does not necessarily suggest a before and after, so often seen in the narrative structures of entry stories such as the flight from the cockfight immortalized by Geertz (1973). As Beatty has argued (1999), such epiphanic immersion stories do nothing to hint at the confusion and incompleteness of formative processes of participation. My emotional commitment to ordination positioned me in relation to monastics and laity, but my ultimate withdrawal from the monastic project, my inability to understand my doubt as a site for meditative awareness, in some ways placed me in opposition to my informants. In different ways, then, during fieldwork, I both shared in and resisted ritual experience. However, this ambivalence was fruitful and interesting in and of itself, and my involvement in the monastery, robes and all, led to ways of understanding both myself and monasticism beyond spoken communication.

Renouncing the world and cutting attachment to it through meditative practices are understood by monastics to be ongoing processes, rather than a one-off act. It is possible that a whole lifetime may be spent trying to achieve a state of comparative spiritual excellence without ever actually achieving it. Being a monastic in this sense is taken as a process of becoming, and the continuing "work" that monastics do on themselves through meditation is believed to take lifetime after lifetime to complete. As wisdom is deepened through meditation, a monastic comes closer to the goal of enlightenment, thereby putting her beyond paltry individual or group identity. This is a practical way of understanding the world in which introspection and isolation constitute dominant social norms used in the construction and realisation of the Buddhist self and community. Equally, in the process of fieldwork the subjective and emotional terrain of the fieldworker is unlikely to be monotonously smooth and free from obstacles. Thus, in my experience, while embodying the roles of monastic and fieldworker, each was at times a joyous experience, at others riddled with doubt. Viewing doubt as part of the process of fieldwork *and* the process of renunciation was both personally and methodologically fruitful.

Conclusion: Thai Monasticism
and Anthropological Methodology

Though meditation is a solitary pursuit, the self that the monastic progressively produces through meditation is firmly located within a community of practice. Through my ethnography I have attempted to examine what the continual practice of asceticism means for the monastic as an *ongoing* project of self-formation. Ascetic life is not merely about conforming either to the precepts or to monastic practice; to think of it as such would be an inadequate conception of the relation between values and practice. As James Laidlaw (1995:7) argues of Jain asceticism, a gap between hope/intention and reality does not necessarily suggest a deviation from the religious system or a dysfunction of social organisation. It is in that dynamic tension between precept and practice that asceticism is really lived. In a community typified by sartorial neatness and physical control, striving for an ideal of non-self, the ultimate act of giving is of oneself, and it is *through* renunciation of the body that renunciation *becomes* embodied. Sartorial neatness is understood to result from moral purity and is a monastic duty. The duty to behave in accord with such an ideal creates the cognitive space required to actualise spiritual development, and it is through such a performance that people become members of a community of practice.

In my own experience as a *mae chee*, while I was emotionally and subjectively involved in religious performance and practice, the way in which I understood my ordination was as an ongoing process, one that was at some times liberating, at others deeply frustrating. For many anthropologists the longevity of ethnographic fieldwork makes it hard to maintain divisions between their research and their personal relationships. In my case, I made little attempt to draw such distinctions in the first place. Although I went into the field primed to deal with ethical, theoretical, and methodological obstacles, I was forced to confront emotional and subjective challenges as a result of my commitment to the field— challenges that were themselves ultimately fruitful, personally and ethnographically, but challenges nonetheless. Perhaps my doubts, about what counted as fieldwork and my ultimate reluctance to continue doing intensive retreat, were themselves a result of not being attentive enough to textbook techniques of separating "personal life" and "fieldwork" and thereby managing emotional well-being. But the recognised challenges of ordination are shared by most (if not all) monastics as they learn to develop ascetic discipline. The anxieties of fieldwork were not only shared and discussed by my contemporaries who were experiencing comparable learning processes in their respective field sites, but, as I have argued in this chapter, such anxieties are to some extent unavoidable. Rather than inhibiting research or renunciation, doubt and performance proved to be fruitful and relevant aspects of these different learning processes.

Codified methods for data analysis provide us with useful and at times reassuring ways of collecting different types of data. But to the extent that field experience is circumscribed by such methods, and anthropological knowledge is limited to such data, essential modes of learning and social facts may remain inaccessible to the researcher. In this chapter I have argued for embracing uncertainty and doubt in participant observation. If we deny that anxieties exist, and thereby present fieldwork as clear-cut and well structured, we deny ourselves the possibility of considering the context of such anxieties and their very relevant place in the process of field research. Thus, while official guidelines and methodological training may provide the anthropologist with methods for approaching the field, we must take care that these do not inhibit either the anthropologist's ability to give herself over to local modes of understanding or the learning process of participant observation. Rather than presenting the researcher as detached from the process of fieldwork through intellectual strategies of systematising and objectification, I suggest that the ongoing subjective negotiation of the fieldworker in the field and the incomplete nature of many field experiences are themselves positive and fruitful aspects of the fieldwork process—experiences which, if subjected to sustained anthropological reflection, may reveal dimensions of the studied community that would have otherwise remained concealed. Most anthropological fieldwork entails prolonged commitment to the field. Therefore, reflecting upon doubts or anxieties about this learning process and recognising them as and when they occur, rather than reacting to them symptomatically, are not only part of the solution but also part of the process.

References

Beatty, A. 1999. "On Ethnographic Experience: Formative and Informative." In C. W. Watson, ed., *Being There: Fieldwork in Anthropology*, 74–98. London and Sterling, VA: Pluto Press.

Benson, S. 2000. "Inscriptions of the Self: Reflections on Tattooing and Piercing in Contemporary Euro-America." In J. Kaplan, ed., *Written on the Body: The Tattoo in European and American History*, 234–254. London: Reaktion Books.

Boonkanjanaram Meditation Center. 1988. *Vipassana Bhavana: Theory, Practice, and Results*. Pattaya, Chonburi, Thailand: Boonkanjanaram Meditation Center.

Buddhaghosa. 1976. *The Path of Purification: Visuddhimagga*. Trans. Bhikkhu Ñāṇamoli. Berkeley, CA: Shambhala Publications.

Candea, M. 2007. "Arbitrary Locations: In Defense of the Bounded Field-Site." *Journal of the Royal Anthropological Institute* 13 (1): 167–184.

Carrithers, M. 1983. *The Forest Monks of Sri Lanka: An Anthropological and Historical Study*. Oxford: Oxford University Press.

Collins, S. 1997. "The Body in Theravada Buddhist Monasticism." In S. Coakley, ed., *Religion and the Body*, 185–204. Cambridge: Cambridge University Press.

Cook, J. In press. *Meditation in Modern Buddhism: Renunciation and Change in Thai Monastic Life.* Cambridge: Cambridge University Press.

———. 2009. "Hagiographic Narrative and Monastic Practice: Buddhist Morality and Mastery amongst Thai Buddhist Nuns." *Journal of the Royal Anthropological Institute* 15 (2): 349–364.

———. 2008. "Alms, Money, and Reciprocity: Buddhist Nuns as Mediators of Generalized Exchange in Thailand." *Anthropology in Action. Special Edition: Gift Exchange in Modern Society* 15 (3): 8–21.

Devereux, G. 1967. *From Anxiety to Method in the Behavioural Sciences.* The Hague: Mouton.

Evans-Pritchard, E. E. 1973. "Some Reminiscences and Reflections on Fieldwork." *Journal of the Anthropological Society of Oxford* 4:1–12.

Fernandez, J., and M. Herzfeld. 1998. "In Search of Meaningful Methods." In H. Russell Bernard, ed., *Handbook of Methods in Cultural Anthropology*, 89–129. Lanham, MD: AltaMira Press.

Geertz, C. 1973. *The Interpretation of Cultures.* New York: Basic Books.

Gombrich, R., and G. Obeyesekere. 1988. *Buddhism Transformed: Religious Change in Sri Lanka.* Princeton, NJ: Princeton University Press.

Hastrup, K., and P. Hervik, eds. 1994. *Social Experience and Anthropological Knowledge.* London: Routledge.

Houtman, G. 1990. "Traditions of Buddhist Practice in Burma." Ph.D. diss., School of Oriental and African Studies, London University.

Jackson, P. A. 1997. "Withering Centre, Flourishing Margins: Buddhism's Changing Political Roles." In K. Hewison, ed., *Political Change in Thailand: Democracy and Participation*, 75–93. London: Routledge.

Keyes, C. 1978. "Ethnography and Anthropological Interpretation in the Study of Thailand." In E. B. Ayal, ed., *The Study of Thailand: Analyses of Knowledge, Approaches, and Prospects in Anthropology, Art History, Economics, History, and Political Science*, 1–66. Athens: Ohio University Center for International Studies.

Kirsch, T. 1977. "Complexity in the Thai Religious System: An Interpretation." *Journal of Asian Studies* 36 (2): 241–266.

Kleinman, S., and M. A. Copp. 1993. *Emotions in Fieldwork.* London: Sage.

Klima, A. 2002. *The Funeral Casino: Meditation, Massacre, and Exchange with the Dead in Thailand.* Princeton, NJ: Princeton University Press.

Laidlaw, J. 1995. *Riches and Renunciation: Religion, Economy, and Society among the Jains.* Oxford: Clarendon Press.

Lave, J., and E. Wenger. 1991. *Situated Learning: Legitimate Peripheral Participation.* Cambridge: Cambridge University Press.

Luhrmann, T. 1989. *Persuasions of the Witch's Craft: Ritual Magic and Witchcraft in Present-Day England.* London: Blackwell.

McCargo, D. 2004. "Populism and Reformism in Contemporary Thailand." *South East Asia Research* 9 (1): 89–107.

Pattana, K. 2005. "Beyond Syncretism: Hybridization of Popular Religion in Contemporary Thailand." *Journal of Southeast Asian Studies* 36 (3): 461–487.

Tambiah, S. J. 1970. *Buddhism and the Spirit Cults in North-East Thailand.* Cambridge Studies in Social Anthropology 2. Cambridge: Cambridge University Press.

Taylor, J. L. 2001. "Embodiment, Nation, and Religio-politics in Thailand." *South East Asian Research* 9 (2): 129–147.

Notes

1. Temporary ordination is common in Thailand and remains an important part of the life cycle of most Buddhist men. As a cultural ideal every Thai Buddhist man should ordain as a monk as a rite of passage between adolescence and marriage, usually for one *phansa*, or Buddhist Lent of three months, during the rainy season (Tambiah 1970). Men at this age or older are granted paid leave from government employment in order to ordain temporarily. A disrobing ceremony is necessary at the end of the period of ordination in order to reduce the number of precepts held by the ordinand to those of a layperson. Both monk and *mae chee* ordination is considered as temporary in the first instance, even if the ordinand remains in the robes for a lifetime. This is fitting with the Buddhist principle that all things are impermanent.

2. I do not want to suggest that an ethnographic study of religion by the uninitiated would be impossible or insufficient, only that this approach was fitting for me.

3. For a discussion on the qualified involvement of *mae chee* in giving and receiving alms, see Cook (2008).

4. A *dhamma* talk is a talk based on the teachings of the Buddha, much like a sermon. Laypeople often attend monasteries in order to hear monks giving *dhamma* talks.

5. See Candea (2007) for a skillful account of the ways in which such concerns prompted him to reconsider multi-sited research methods.

6. The benefits of examining the anxieties of research have been given a very different treatment by Devereux (1967). According to him, the researcher should reflect upon that which she observes in the same way as a psychoanalyst would do in her relation to her analysand. He argues that the transference and countertransference that are necessarily generated by the research relationship evoke anxiety and pain. In his opinion, the construction of defenses (such as the application of "objective" methods) in order to avoid such unpleasant feelings is responsible for much analytical distortion in the behavioural sciences because such methods widen the partition between the researcher and her subjects. Research methods, as familiar cognitive activities, may be employed in foreign and unfamiliar contexts in order to mitigate anxiety generated by fieldwork. But in so doing they may also render invisible many important variables

of the study. While I see much to commend in such an approach, my emphasis here is not on a psychoanalytical interpretation of research but rather on the multiple social learning processes with which the novice anthropologist engages. See also Kleinman and Copp (1993) for a consideration of the ways in which an incorporation of emotional responses to field experiences may enhance qualitative research.

7. For a discussion of the distinction between experience and knowledge, see Cook (in press).

8. The *Visuddhimagga* gives considerable attention to the good conduct of a monk:

> A *Bhikkhu*, is respectful, deferential, possessed of conscience and modesty, wears his inner robe properly, wears his upper robe properly, his manner inspires confidence whether in moving forwards or backwards, looking ahead or aside, bending or stretching, his eyes are downcast, he has [good] deportment, he guards the doors of his sense faculties, knows the right measure in eating, is devoted to wakefulness, possesses mindfulness and full-awareness, wants little, is contented, is strenuous, is a careful observer of good behaviour, and treats the teachers with great respect. (Buddhaghosa: 1976. VM.I.48)

The *Visuddhimagga*, meaning "Path of Purification," was written in Sri Lanka in the early fifth century A.D. by the scholar monk Buddhaghosa. It has long been and remains the most authoritative text in Theravada Buddhism apart from the *Tipitaka* itself.

9. See Lave and Wenger (1991) for a fascinating discussion of learning as a dimension of social practice.

10. See Cook (in press) for an extended discussion of the relationship between morality, mindful performance, and merit making.

11. At one point, I took my robe off in private and drop-kicked it across the room. While it sounds like a simple thing, it made me feel much better knowing that in my small rebellion I had kicked the habit.

12. The effect of *samatha* meditation is to calm the mind and develop one's pointed awareness and concentration. It is often associated with the development of supernormal powers.

13. The monastic precept to refrain from eating at wrong times prohibits consuming solid foods after twelve noon.

14. In the monastery this meditation technique (*asubha kammatthāna*) is used as an aspect of *vipassanā*. See Klima (2002) for an interesting discussion of *asubha kammatthāna*.

Index

References to notes are indicated by n and the number of the note, e.g., 30n8.

Absence, sense of, 87–88
Absorption, 218, 219, 228–233
Abu-Lughod, L., 172, 192
Accident: importance in fieldwork, 60
Acknowledgment: moral act, 184–185, 185–186
Action, ethical, 172, 179, 184–185, 185–186
Adjustment transference, 80
Adler, Patricia, 12
Adler, Peter, 12
Adorno, Theodor, 9–10, 30n12, 52
Advocacy, 185–186
Affect and value, confusion between, 184
Affected ignorance, 179, 185
Alienation, preservation of, 63–64
Alpha course, 238n7
Altered states, 229, 230, 237n1
Altering, 80
Alterity, 173, 179
America, Kuranko suspicion of, 50–51
Amnesia, 19
Anderson, Barbara, 7
Anderson, Robin, 97n4
Anger, 75, 115, 120; anti-Israeli, 137, 142–143, 145, 146–149; Arctic homeplaces, 201; burdensome network of exchange, 183; extent of sharing, 178; rhetorical function, 70
L'Année sociologique, 15
Anomalous experience, 228
Anthropology, justification of, 47

Anthropormorphisation of nations, 138
Antidepressants, 123
Anti-Zionism, 135
Anxiety, 22, 40, 41–43, 49, 50–51; fieldworkers, 102, 244–246, 262, 264n6; sense of fragmentation, 141; separation, 40, 48–50, 52; stress and, 112
Apartheid, 68–69
Apollo missions: reactions of Kuranko, 50–51
Appraisal: in field encounters, 63
Arctic landscapes: impact on social life, 191–211
Argentina: generals: interviews with, 100
Argonauts of the Western Pacific (Malinowski), 5
Aristotle, 70
Asper, K., 120
Astuti, Rita, 234
Atkinson, Gilbert, 228–229
Atkinson, P., 12
Australian National University, 36
Authorization: the Third, 73–74
Autonomy: regained through divination, 49
Awareness, mindful: Buddhist monasticism, 240, 241, 249–260, 265n8
Azande, 220

Bacchiddu, Giovanna, 88–89
Bachelard, Gaston, 193, 194–195
Bachnick, J. M., 62
Bakhtin, M. M., 199, 202–203, 204
Barber, T. X., 230

Barrett, R., 106, 121, 123, 125n2
Barth, Fredrik, 198
Basso, Keith, 191
Beatty, Andrew, 260
Behar, Ruth, 13, 172
Belief systems: coping mechanisms, 48
Belief, unintended, 90–92
Beliefs: commitment to, 220; testing of
    anthropologists', 66–70
Bellah, Robert, 89, 221
Belonging, sense of: social space, 191
Benjamin, Walter, 52
Benson, Sue, 256
Berdyaev, Nikolai, 9
Bernard, H. R., 12
Berreman, Gerald, 6
Betrayal, 175–176
Beyond the Pleasure Principle (Freud), 50
Bias: intellectualist: debate on divination, 48;
    methods and, 7; personal experience, 228
Biehl, João Guilherme, 30n13, 105
Blackaby, H., 223
Bloch, M., 172
Boas, Franz, 4, 6, 196, 197
Bodily proclivities: fieldworkers, 21
Body: boundaries: traffic across, 50; Buddhist
    monasticism, 252–257, 258–259, 261;
    individual: impact of body politic,
    156, 165, 168–169; knowledge of, 213;
    knowledge of: and magic, 217, 220; mind/
    body distinctions, 92, 121, 213
Body politic: impact on individual body, 156,
    165, 168–169
Bohannon, Laura, 6
Boonkanjanaram Meditation Center, 251
Borchert, William, 89
Boundary-disruption, 49–50
Bourdieu, Pierre, 134, 136, 138, 139–140, 144,
    150, 152
Bowen, Elenore, 83
Bowlby, John, 40, 87
Bowman, Glen, 80
Brady, M., 101
Bravo, M., 192
Breakdowns in fieldwork, 60
Breath, mindful awareness of: Buddhist
    monasticism, 250
Brecht, Bertolt, 63–64
Briggs, Jean L., 201
Bruyn, S. T., 4
Bryman, A., 30n9
Buddhaghosa, 265n8

Buddhist monasticism, 239–265

Candea, M., 264n5
Carrithers, Michael, 253
Casagrande, Joseph, 7, 29n2
Casey, Conerly, 126n3
Casey, Edward, 192
Causation, collective dogmas of, 49
Celebration of Discipline (Foster), 222
Certainty, conditional: divination, 49
Cesara, M., 11
Chants: Greenland, 208
Chinese medicine, traditional, 155
Choice: privilege of fieldworkers, 177
Christians, American, 221–228
Chronotopes, 199–204
Clifford, J., 172
Cliterodectomy: Kuranko, 44
Codification, 11–12, 26
Collier, J. F., 172
Collins, Steven, 252
Commitment to beliefs, 220
Community, sense of: Buddhist monasteries,
    240
"Complex" societies, 68
Comprehensiveness: anthropological object,
    198
Compression of experience, 201
CONADEP, 176
Conatus, 139–140, 152
Conflict, social ontology of, 58
Connolly, Bob, 97n4
Contingency: importance in fieldwork, 60
Conversion, Christian, 69–70, 225, 237n1
Cook, Joanna, 253, 264n3, 265nn7, 10
Coping mechanisms, 15–16, 37, 40, 48–49,
    50–51, 51–52
Coping strategies: disorientation, 81, 84–85
Copp, M. A., 12, 265n6
Costa, P., 230
Countertransference, 6, 17, 40, 54n1, 64,
    98–108, 221, 264n6
Crapanzano, Vincent, 9, 11, 16–17, 21, 50, 55, 59,
    67, 68, 69, 71, 73, 99–100, 200, 221, 237n4
Csordas, Thomas J., 30n8, 213
Cultural moorings: unanchored, 83
Cultural reductionism, 25
Culture shock, 55, 95, 112
Cunningham, L., 223

Danish Social Science Foundation, 98
Das, Veena, 184

Data and experience, 213–214
Davies, James, 245, 246
De Certeau, Michel, 192
De Laine, Marlene, 12
De Vaus, D., 12
Defamiliarization, 64, 72
Deleuze, Guy, 134, 199, 200–201, 204, 208
Demonstrations (China, 1989), 159–161
Denmark: cultural context, 108–109
Departure, anthropologist's, 61–62
Deportment: Buddhist monasticism, 252–257, 261, 265n8
Depression, 98–99, 105, 107, 110–123
Desjarlais, Robert R., 30n8, 105, 106, 213
DeSoto, H. G., 156
Detachment: Buddhist monasticism, 240; fieldwork, 11, 87, 93, 150
Devereux, George, 7, 8, 30n8, 35–40, 48, 57, 64, 99, 264n6
DeWalt, B. R., 12
DeWalt, K. M., 12
Dialogue with God (Virkler and Virkler), 223–224
Dilthey, Wilhelm, 4
Disappeared (Argentina), 174–180
Disbelief, suspension of, 49
Discipline: physical and mental: Buddhist monasticism, 241; spiritual, 218, 222–223
Discourse: in magic and religion, 217, 233
Disorientation, 17, 38, 81–83; coping strategies, 83–86, 93
Displacement, sense of, 88–89
Dissociative Experiences Scale, 230
Dissonance, 89–90, 93
Distance: Arctic landscapes, 195–196; critical, 199; geographical: validity of research and, 24–25; social: collapse, 202–203
Distinction (Bourdieu), 136
Distrust of fieldworker, 176
Diversity, respect of, 173
Divination, 44–49
Djinns: Kuranko, 46–47
Dogma, collective, 49
Dominguez, V. R., 30n8
Doubt, 22; Buddhist meditation, 239–240, 249–252, 258, 260; fieldworkers' experience, 86–87, 244–246, 258, 260, 261, 262
Dreams, 41–43, 46, 91–92, 117; interpretation, 42–43; magical symbolism, 219
Dudwick, N., 156
Dumont, Jean-Paul, 6, 9
Durkheim, Emile, 15

Economic and Social Research Council, 30n11
Edgerton, Robert, 126n3
Editorial vantage point, 72
Ego, temporal: impairment, 38
Einfühlung, 4
El-Zein, Abbas, 142
Embodiment, 213, 214
Emergence from language: poetic image, 194–195
Emotion: insight from, 10–11; pathology and: history, 30n10; thinking split from, 112
Emotions: interhuman quality, 173–174; shared, 172, 178, 180; social conceptions, 59
Empathy, 106, 122, 220; moral, 172, 173, 179, 184
Empiricism, radical, 3, 11, 22–25, 122; complementary to traditional empiricism, 23–24, 26, 31n14
Empiricism, traditional, 2–3, 8–9, 12, 13, 23–24, 26, 29n1, 31n141
Emplacement, 192, 197, 199, 203, 208
Empowerment: countertransference reaction, 113, 117, 119–120
Emptiness, sense of: depression, 105
Encounter as chronotope, 203
Enculturation: emotional, 52, 112
Engagement, anthropological: concept, 20; dangers of, 182; fieldwork encounters, 178; nature of, 171–174, 183, 184–186
Environment, immersion in, 195
Estrangement, sense of, 81
Estroff, Sue, 100, 105, 106, 114, 121
Ethical relationships in intellectual enquiry, 172
Ethics (Spinoza), 139, 148
Ethnographic vacillation, 18–19, 149–153
Ethnography: specific emotions, 151
Euphoria: countertransference reaction, 111, 113, 117, 120
Evans-Pritchard, Edward, 5, 6, 80, 82, 220, 245, 256
Ewing, K. P., 64, 99–100
Exercise, lack of: Buddhist monasticism, 259
Existentialism, 9
Exorcisms, 67
Exotic, the, 58
Experience, compression of, 201
Experience, lived: close to clichés, 159
Experience of the Inner Worlds (Knight), 214
Experiencing God (Blackaby and King), 223
Experiential responses (Tellegen Absorption Scale), 229–230

Experiential space, internalisation of, 91–92
Expertise: magical or religious, 228
Externalization, mastery of emotions through, 48–49

Faculty psychology, 8–9
Fairy tales: Jungian analysis, 105
Familiarisation: altered perception and, 90–92; impact of withdrawal strategies, 86
Familiarity: dangers, 72
Farmer, P., 185
Favret-Saada, Jeanne, 9
Fear, 178, 180; raw moments, 204–205; white South Africans, 74–75
Feelings: interhuman quality, 173–174; talking about, 134
Feinberg, M., 223
Feld, Steven, 191, 196, 204
Feminist research, 12
Ferme, M., 52
Fernandez, J., 247
Fiction: concept, 63
Field: geographical metaphor: weaknesses, 155; psychological concept, 25, 31n13, 90; spatial connotations: merits, 192, 208–209
Fieldwork: critical reflection on, 56–57; life experiences undermined by, 167–168
Firth, Rosemary, 84
Fischer, M. M. J., 172
Foreigners: scapegoating in crisis situations, 161–162
Forgetting, 19, 156, 164–165, 169
Fortes, Meyer, 29n5, 36
Foster, Richard, 222
Foucault, Michel, 63
Fragmentation, sense of, 138, 140–141
Frank, Thomas, 221
Frankfurt School, 9–10
Freeman, Derek, 36
Freilich, Morris, 7, 29n3
Freud, Sigmund, 6, 50, 87
Friedman, H. S., 40
From Anxiety to Method in the Behavioural Sciences (Devereux), 36
Functionalism, structural, British, 212

Gadamer, Hans Georg, 58, 71
Gatens, M., 139
Gaze of the other, 63
Geertz, Clifford, 55, 80, 85, 198, 207, 212, 234, 260
Genealogy: sense of self, 196
Gestimmtheit, 4

Gilsenan, M., 134
Girls: puberty: Kuranko, 43–44
Goal, anthropologist's: impact on fieldwork, 60–61
God, sensory experience of, 222–234
God Whispers (Feinberg), 223
Godelier, M., 172
Golde, Peggy, 7
Gombrich, R., 240
Good, Byron, 30n13, 106
Gordon, D. A., 172
Goulet, Jean-Guy, 13
Grandmothers of the Plaza de Mayo, 174–180
Green, Linda, 13, 30n8
Greenhouse, C. J., 156
Greenland chants, 208
Greimas, A. J., 147–148
Grief and a Headhunter's Rage (Rosaldo), 185
Grolnick, S., 99–100
Guattari, F., 134, 199, 200–201, 204, 208
Guggenbuhl-Craig, A., 126n3
Guilt (emotion), 178–179, 180, 184, 185

Habermas, Jürgen, 9–10
Habitus, 139–140
Haddon, A. C., 5
Hage, Ghassan, 96n1, 130, 132, 171
Hallucinations, 216, 231–232, 233–234
Hamadsha (Morocco), 66–67
Hammersley, M., 12
Handwerker, W. P., 12
Harding, C. M., 114
Hardon, S., 114
Harkis, 75
Harvard University Department of Social Relations, 212
Hastrup, Kirsten, 11, 80, 82, 90, 191, 192, 195, 196, 202, 203, 204, 208, 213, 247
Heald, S., 11
Health and safety: fieldwork in political crises, 170n2
Health-care: China, 180
Hearing God (Willard), 223
Heidegger, Martin, 4, 60
Heisenberg's uncertainty principle, 37
Helplessness: anthropologists, 75–76; guilt, 179; See also Powerlessness: anthropologists
Herder, Gottfried, 4
Herdt, G., 99–100
Hermes' dilemma, 50

Hervik, P., 247
Herzfeld, Michael, 170n1, 247
Hezbollah, responses to, 147, 148–149
Hidden people (Iceland), 204–205
Hill, Carole, 7
Hirsch, E., 192
Historical moment: anthropological research framed by, 76
History, Analytical, and subjectivity, 6
History of fieldwork and emotions, 4–14
Home, returning: psychological difficulties, 88–89, 93
Home, sense of, as centre, 201
Home: psychological concept, 25, 31n13, 90; criticism and repudiation, 86–87; inaccessibility in the field, 81, 82
Hospital culture: patient relationships, 107–108, 113–120
Houtman, G., 247
Hsu, Elisabeth, 157, 164, 166
Hu Yaobang, 156
Hume, Lynne, 12
Humiliation, 65, 133–134
Hunan Medical School, 181–183
Hunt, Jennifer C., 64
"Hurt", affection of, by powerful, 137
Hymes, Dell, 10
Hypnosis: susceptibility, 228–229, 230

Icelandic sagas, 196, 208
Ideas as schemas, 219
Identification with characters, 58
Identity, negotiation of, 72
Identity, sense of, 40; loss in the field, 82, 83, 89; nationalism and, 138, 139, 144
Ideological paradigms: dangers, 76–77
Ignatian Spiritual Exercises, 223, 237n1
Ignorance, affected, 179, 185
Illusio, 138, 140, 144, 152
Imagined communities, 138
Immersion: altered perception and, 90–92, 93; contents of, 80; difficulties of, 82, 94; regulation of, 90; responses to, 95; solitary experience, 205; withdrawal strategies and, 86, 93
Impartiality, guise of, 185
Imperialism, fieldwork viewed as, 2
Inadequacy, sense of, 88
Incorporation, 80
Infantilization: defense mechanism, 67
Ingold, Tim, 202, 207
Initiation, 43–44, 52, 65, 248

Institutional structures: impact on anthropological research, 76
Institute of Social and Cultural Anthropology (Oxford), 30n11
Institutionalization: sense of self and, 105
Intellectualist bias: debate on divination, 48
Intellectuals: identification with dominated peoples, 136; inability to act politically, 148
Intension, 200–201, 208
Interactions: knowledge of phenomena, 37
Inter-materiality, 23
Inter-methodology, 23
Interhuman order, 173
Interpretive drift, 218, 227, 233
Intersubjectivity, 104; nature of fieldwork, 9, 11, 12, 16–17, 23, 64, 171–172, 173; perpetuation of depression, 99; place and, 191, 203, 207
Intertextuality and sense of place, 191, 192
Interviews, semi-directed: value, 166
Intimacy, engagement and, 171, 173
Intimate and personal: distinction, 170n1
Intuition: dream analysis, 42–43
Irrational thought, study of, 214, 220
Is That Really You, God? (Cunningham), 223
Israeli-Palestinian conflict: responses to, 130, 135–138, 142–144

Jackson, Michael, 11, 22–23, 30n7, 48, 52, 86, 88, 97nn3, 4, 142, 201, 206
Jackson, P. A., 257
Jacoby, M., 120
James, Wendy, 191, 193–194
James, William, 3, 9, 22–23, 49, 79, 102
Jenkins, J. H., 104, 106, 107, 112, 123
Jet-lag: disorientation, 38
Jiménez, Corsín, 199, 207
Jnun, belief in, 66, 67
Jorgensen, D. L., 12
Joy, 138, 139
Jungian psychoanalytical techniques, 102–103, 105, 112

Kahneman, Daniel, 237n3
Kakar, Sudhir, 138, 145
Kargbo II, Fode, 42–43
Kendon, Adam, 36
Keyes, C., 257
Kimball, Solon, 7
King, C., 223
Kirmayer, L., 106
Kirsch, T., 257

Klandermans, B., 12
Kleinman, Arthur, 30n13, 105, 106, 109, 121–122,
    172, 184, 185
Kleinman, Joan, 182
Kleinman, Sherryl, 12, 265n6
Klima, A., 265n10
Kluckhohn, Clyde, 212
Knight, Gareth, 214
Knowing, premaure: as coping strategy, 84–85
Kohut, H., 120
Kondo, Dorinne, 82
Kosslyn, Stephen, 234
Kracke, W., 64, 89
Kristeva, Julia, 133
Kristjánsson, J., 196
Kroeber, Alfred, 6
Kuiken, D., 230
Kuku-Yalanji, 98, 105, 108–109
Kuranko, Sierra Leone, 41–52

La Barre, W., 40
Lacan, Jacques, 138, 141, 144, 173
Laidlaw, James, 261
Laity: Buddhist monasticism, 242, 254, 255
Lambek, Michael, 92
Lamphere, L., 172
Landscape: psychological significance, 20–21,
    191–211
Language: emotion and, 135–136; expression
    of pain, 184
Larsen, J. A., 106
Lave, J., 265n9
Lebanese Christians: views on Israel, 135
Lebanon: Israeli bombardment (2006), 131,
    142–147
LePlay, Frederic, 4
Levinas, Emmanuel, 172–173, 176, 179, 180
Levine, R., 230
Lévi-Strauss, Claude, 7, 86–87
Libido, social, 140
Lichterman, Paul, 12
Liminality: in fieldwork, 15–16, 41, 96n1
Lingis, Alphonso, 148
Linguistic assumptions, 62–63
Listening: psychotherapy, 221
Lived chronotopes, 199
Llamas: domestication, 151–152
Lloyd, G., 139
Loneliness: anthropological imperative, 63–64
Lorde, Audre, 179
Lorimer, F., 100, 101, 105, 109
Loss, fear of, 51; fieldworkers' experience,

    86–90, 97n4
Loyalty, 175, 177
Lucas, Rodney H., 125n2
Luhrmann, Tanya, 10, 23–24, 99–100, 106, 121,
    217, 248
Lutz, Catherine, 12, 30n8, 132, 192
Lynn, S., 230

MacIntyre, Alasdair, 233
Magic, 214–221
Malinowski, Bronislaw, 5, 6, 86, 132, 246
Marah, Noah, 41
Marcus, G. E., 172
Marginality, sense of, 39
Marx, Karl, 6
Marxist anthropology, 10
Materiality and meaning: inseparability, 91
Matter, unresponsiveness of, 37
McCargo, D., 257
McCrae, R., 230
Mead, Margaret, 65, 82, 84, 221
Meaning and materiality: inseperability, 91
Mechanic, David, 181
Medical anthropology, 172
Meditation, 215, 218, 219, 222, 237n1;
    Vipassanā, 240–265
Meggitt, Mervin, 55
Meintel, Deirdre, 7, 89
Mental illness: expression of suffering, 107
Mental images: clarity, 216
Merleau-Ponty, Maurice, 193, 205, 213
Methodology, concern with: American
    anthropology, 55–56
Methods: bias and, 7; intellect and emotion,
    8–9; personality and, 8; "reality" and,
    13–14; shared experiences and, 166–167;
    subjectivity and, 13–14, 23, 25
Migration, 197, 201
Milbank, John, 58–59
Miller, Bruce, 13
Miller, D., 221–222
Mills, C. W., 13
Milton, K., 132
Mind/body distinctions, 92, 121, 213
Mindfulness: Buddhist monasticism, 240,
    241, 249–260, 265n8
Minima Ethnographica (Jackson), 88
Mirror stage, 173
Mitchell, Jon, 206
Monasticism, Buddhist, 239–265
Moods and motivations: coincidentality, 198

Moody-Adams, M. M., 179
Moral ambivalence: South African
    Pentecostalists, 68–69
Moral experience: in fieldwork encounter,
    171–174, 184
Morganthaler, F., 64
Mortality, awareness of, 259
Motivations and moods: coincidentality, 198
Mourning, 163; fieldworkers' experience,
    86–90, 93; forgetting and, 164, 168–169;
    transnational: emotional participation,
    144–145, 150–151
Movement: Arctic, 195–196, 201–203
Mulcock, Jane, 12
Muslim immigrants: social integration,
    129–130
Mutual responsibility, 172, 173, 174, 176

Nadon, R., 230
Narcissistic wounding, 120
Nash, Dennison, 7
Nash, M., 230
National identification, 138, 139, 144
Natural environment: limited contact in
    modern life, 193
Natural sciences: methods and personality
    in, 8
Navajo, 65–66
Negative capability, 58
Nell, V., 230
Neophytes: Kuranko, 43–44
Nietzsche, Friedrich, 139, 148
Non-Self: Buddhist principle, 250–251, 252, 259
Nordstrom, C., 156
Note-taking: impact on field encounters, 61

Obeysekere, Gananath, 11, 240
Objectification, 10; mastery of emotions
    through, 48–49
Objectivism, 37
Objectivity, politicisation of, 9–10
Observation, participant. See Participant
    observation
Ogden, T., 19
O'Hanlon, M., 192
Oneiromancy, 42–43
O'Nell, T., 106
Ontological security, 40, 51
Opacity in field encounters, 63–64
Oppressed, solidarity with, 172
Order, illusion of: anthropological
    systemising, 37

Ordination: Buddhist monasticism, 241–261,
    264n1
Orientation: home as place of, 201; loss of
    horizon, 206
Other, the, recognition of, 173, 179
Othering, 59
Otherness: effaced or simplified, 132–133;
    experienced in self, 82; to oneself, 133
Overing, J., 100

Pain: Buddhist meditation and, 251;
    expressed through speaking, 184; source
    of fortitude, 52; source of understanding,
    43
Palestinian-Israeli conflict: responses to, 130,
    135–138, 142–144
Parin, P., 64
Parin-Matthèy, G., 64
Parsons, Talcott, 212
Participant observation: altered
    perception and, 90–92; conceptual
    detemporalization, 59; formalisation,
    11–12; nature of, 171; significance of, 56–57
Participation: disorientation through, 82;
    emotional: transnational mourning,
    144–145, 150–151; significance of, 5–6, 47
Particular, the: avoidance of, 59
A Passage to Anthropology (Hastrup), 90
Patients: subculture: psychiatric hospital,
    107–108
Patriarchal power, 136–137, 142
Pattana, K., 257
Pekala, R., 230
Perception, altered: and familiarisation,
    90–92, 97n5
Perception, challenged: Arctic, 193–196,
    203–204
Perfection, 139
Performance, mindful: Buddhist
    monasticism, 252–256, 261
Personal and intimate: distinction, 170n1
Personality, theories of, 92
Perspective, negotiation of, 62
Persuasions of the Witch's Craft (Luhrmann),
    217
Petrie, Flinders, Sir, 5
Pew Research Center, 174
Phaedrus (Plato), 61
Phenomena, conditioning of: Buddhist truth,
    248
Phylogenic reductionism, 25
Place: psychological significance, 21, 191–211

Place: social space and physical, 192–193
Plato, 5, 61
Poetic image, 194–195
Poetics of space, 193–199, 208
Point of view, 58
Political action, anthropologists and, 20
Political interests, personal: social science and, 136
Politics: emotions and, 129–190
Postmodernism, 2
Powdermaker, Hortense, 7, 82, 87
Power: patriarchal, 136–137, 142; political: anger and, 147–149; sense of: nationalism and, 139, 141
Prayer, 222–234
Prejudice: impact on field encounters, 58
Presences: raw moments, 205, 206
Preunderstanding: impact on field encounters, 58
Primitive, notion of the, 67–68
Private life: relationship to fieldwork, 168–169
Proclivity: influences on field responses, 21; spiritual disciplines, 227–234
Psychiatric hospital, fieldwork in, 101–113
Psychic unity of humankind, 37
Psychoanalysis and subjectivity, 6
Psychoanalytical techniques: Jungian, 102–103, 105, 112
Psychological adjustment, 30n8
Psychological concepts: applied to fieldwork, 94
Psychological proclivities: fieldworkers, 21
Psychological theory, 15

Qandish, 73
Qualitification of scale, 198
Quinn Patton, M., 12

Rabinow, Paul, 7, 9, 82, 84, 88, 89
Racialist assumptions, 58
Racism: self-constitution and, 141
Racism, perceived anti-Muslim, by the West, 130
Radcliffe-Brown, Arthur R., 6
Radical empiricism, 3, 11, 22–25, 122; complementary to traditional empiricism, 23–24, 26, 31n14
Rasmussen, Knud, 192, 197, 202
Raw moments, 204–208, 213, 214, 220, 228
Read, K. E., 6
Reciprocity, cycle of, 183
Recognition of the Other, 173, 179

Recording: impact on field encounters, 61
Reflexivity: difficulties, 132
Reflexivity, ethnographic method and, 49
Refrain, Deleuze and Guatari's, 208
Regionalism: material issue, 191
Reintegration, difficulties of, 88–89
Relations, negotiation of, 73–74
Relationship qualities, 59
Relationships, ethical, in intellectual enquiry, 172
Relationships, social: patients, 107–108, 113–120
Renunciation: Buddhism, 248, 252, 255–261
Repression, social: and forgetting, 164–165, United States, 175
Research funding, 13, 30n11
Resentment of sympathy, 76
Responsibility, mutual, 172, 173, 174, 176
Retreat: Buddhist monasticism, 240
Reynolds, Peter, 36
Rhodes, L., 105, 106
Rituals, 216–21, 248, 260
Rivers, W. H. R., 5
Road, the, as chronotope, 202–203
Robben, Antonius, 12–13, 30n9, 100, 156
Robbins, Joel, 58, 106
Roof, Wade Clark, 221
Rosaldo, Renato, 10, 172, 185
Rosenberg, D. V., 59
Rwanda: genocide (1994), 75
Rycroft, C., 19

Sacrifice, 45, 47, 49
Sadness, 139
Sagas, Icelandic, 196, 208
Saint-Hilaire, Isodore Geoffroy, 151–152
Sartre, Jean-Paul, 9
Scale, qualification of, 198
Scapegoating: foreigners in crisis situations, 161–162
Schizophrenia, 100, 107
Schneider, David, 212
Schopflocher, D., 230
Scientists: personal suitability, 9
Security, ontological, 40, 51
Self: Buddhist monasticism, 252–256; challenged, 82, 83, 89; conception of, 213; recognition of the other, 173, 179
Self, Non-: Buddhist principle, 250–251, 252, 259
Self-experience: patients, 103–104
Seligman, C. G., 5
Semi-directed interviews: value, 166

Separation: source of understanding, 43
Separation anxiety, 40, 48–50, 52, 87–88
Serendipity, value of, 167
Shaffir, W. B., 12
Shamanism, 99, 237n1
Shameful emotions, 133, 141
Sharing, precarious living and, 200
Shaw, R., 52
Sierra Leone, 41–52
Silver, R. C., 40
Singer, M., 19
Sise, Doron Mamburu, 44–47
Size: Arctic landscapes, 195–196, 200, 208
Sluka, J., 30n9
Smell: orientation: Arctic, 196
Smith Bowen, Elenore (pseud.), 6
Smith, Lindsay, 185
Snodgrass, M., 230
Social arrival, 80
Social contract, 173
Social domination, source of responses to,
      136–137
Social gravity, 150
Social integration: Muslim immigrants,
      129–130
Social pressure: and forgetting, 165
Social space: formatting, 191
Social space and physical place, 192–193
Socialisation: Buddhist monasticism, 249, 252
Solidarity with the oppressed, 172
Solitude and transcoding, 205
Sörlin, S., 192
Soundscape (Arctic), 194, 197, 208
South Africa: Pentecostalists, 67–70
Space, poetics of, 193–199, 208
Space, social: formatting, 191; physical place
      and, 192–193
Space-time fusion: travel, 203
Spaces, open and enclosed: Arctic, 200
Specificity of fieldwork conditions, 94
Spengler, Oswald, 6
Spiegel, D., 230
Spiegel, H., 230
Spinoza, B. de, 138–139, 140, 144, 148, 152
Spiritual disciplines, 218, 222–223
Spradley, J. P., 12
Staggenborg, S., 12
Stebbins, R. A., 12
Stein, H., 99–100
Stoller, Paul, 11, 213
Stories as tests, 65–66
Storr, A., 4

Strangeness, preservation of, 63–64
Structural functionalism, British, 212
Study, field of: delimitation of phenomena, 52
Subjective understanding: distortions, 64
Subjectivity: academic space and, 30n12;
      Arctic landscape, 195, 196; definition,
      30n13; as intersubjectivity, 104; negative
      interpretations, 2–6, 29n1
Suffering: Buddhist meditation and, 251;
      expression of, 184; mental illness, 107, 112;
      unintentional complicity, 179
Suffering, social, 172–173; solidarity, 178, 180
Suggestibility, 73
Suspicion, Kuranko: of America, 50–51
Sutton, Peter, 101
Svašek, M., 132
Swing: idea of participant observation, 153
Sympathy, resentment of, 76

Tambiah, S. J., 264n1
Taussig, Michael, 13
Taylor, Christopher, 75
Taylor, J. L., 257
Teaching: Buddhist monasticism, 240, 257
Tellegen, Auke, 228–229
Tellegen Absorption Scale, 228–232
Territorialisation, lack of: Arctic, 199–200
Testing: informants of anthropologists,
      65–66
Theoretical paradigms: dangers, 76–77
Theory: model building as defence
      mechanism, 37
Thinking: split from emotion, 112
Third, Crapanzano's, 16–17, 21, 73–74
Threshold as chronotope, 204
Thymos, 5
Tian'enmen protests (1989), 156–170
Tillich, Paul, 71
Time perception, altered, 38
Time, fieldwork's extension over, 59–60, 60–61
Time-space fusion: travel, 203
Tonalité, 4
Topography, emotional: "feel for place", 192,
      193; incorporation by ethnographer, 207
Topophilia, 195
Torture: Americans' views, 174
Tourist companies: managing dissonance,
      89–90
Toynbee, Arnold, 6
Tradition: abridgement, 197
Traditions, national: anthropology, 55–56
Traimond, Bernard, 61

Training: in magic, 215–220, 229; in religion, 221–225, 237n1
Trance states, 218
Transcoding, 204, 205, 206
Transference, 17, 64, 264n6; adjustment, 80
Transformation, processes of: emotional engagement, 173, 174
Transport, modes of: Arctic, 201–202, 208
Trauma: separation, 40
Travel: Arctic, 201–203
Tristes Tropique (Lévi-Strauss), 86–87
Tronick, E., 123
Truth: Buddhist understanding, 248, 252; concept of, 257
Tuan, Yi-Fu, 193, 195, 196, 200, 204
Tuhami (Crapanzano), 72, 237n4
Turnbull, C., 204
Tversky, Amos, 237n3

Ulysse, Gina, 13, 30n8
Uncertainty: fear of, 51; transformed by divination, 49
Uncertainty principle, Heisenberg's, 37
Understanding: sources, 43; subjective: distortions, 64
The Uses of Anger (Lorde), 179

Vacillation, ethnographic, 18–19, 149–153
Value and affect, confusion between, 184
Van der Geest, S., 114
Van Dongen, E., 105, 106
Vendler, H., 197
Veranda as coping strategy, 85, 96–97n2
Verstehen, 4
Vineyard Christian fellowship, 221–228, 238n6
Violation, fieldwork as, 57
Violence, 74–75, 76; social ontology of, 58
Vipassanā meditation, 240–265
Virkler, M. 223–224

Virkler, P., 223–224
Visual field: Arctic landscapes, 195–196
Visualization, 215–216, 218, 219, 237n1
Visuddhimagga, 265n8
Volkan, Vamik, 138
Vorhanden, 60
Vulnerability of ethnographers, 185

Walsh, D., 12
Watson, James, 7
Waud, K., 99–100
Wax, Rosalie, 84
Weber, Max, 4
Wenger, C., 230
Wenger, E., 265n9
Wengle, John, 11, 64, 84, 86
Westermarck, Edvard, 5
Whalen, J., 230
White, G., 132
Whyte, S., 114
Wikan, Unni, 11
Wild, T. C., 230
Willard, Dallas, 223
Wilson, Sheryl, 230
Winch, Peter, 233
Winthrop, Robert, 84
Wintrob, Ronald, 7
Withdrawal, strategies of, 83–86, 93, 246
Witnessing, evangelical, 69–70, 72–73, 73–74
Wittgenstein, Ludwig, 184
Wolff, Eric, 10
Worldviews, others': internalization, 173
Writing Culture, 10
Written word: impact on field encounters, 61
Wuthnow, Robert, 221

Yanagisako, S., 172
Young, Michael, 36, 106

Zuhanden, 60

Made in the USA
Las Vegas, NV
14 March 2022

45618177R00169